THE 1995
BETULA GUIDE
TO GOLF
AROUND LONDON

THE 1995 BETULA GUIDE TO GOLF AROUND LONDON

Edited by Peter Wren-Hilton

Deputy Editor Jacqueline Fox

BETULA PUBLISHING

This edition published 1994 by Betula Publishing
83 Mill Lane
West Hampstead
London NW6 1NB

ISBN O 9524168 0 8

Copyright © Betula Publishing 1994

British Library Cataloguing in Publication Data A CIP catalogue record for this book is available from the British Library

Disclaimer
Every effort has been taken to ensure that the information contained in this book is correct. The Publishers or Editors take no responsibility however for any errors or ommissions.

Cover Photograph: Hever Golf Club

Printed and Bound in Great Britain by
Ashford Press

INTRODUCTION

Welcome to the first edition of the Betula Guide to Golf Around London.

Never has the game of golf been so popular. According to recent research, there are over one and a half million adult golfers in the South-East of England. With over 400 golf courses and an ever growing number of driving ranges seeking to meet demand, it remains a sad fact that for the vast majority of these players, finding a course to play on, at a reasonable cost and within a reasonable distance from home, remains a daunting task.

In recent years, the growth in popularity of the game has been matched by a surge in new golfing developments. Where once the land was used for cattle and crops, today it is irrigated for a very different kind of use.

Yet as the range of facilities grows, so does the inexorable rise in the number of new players taking up the game. For many, finding a course to play on remains the most testing part of the day's round.

This Guide has been produced, in part, to address this problem. The Guide outlines the restrictions imposed on visiting players. By referring to the Guide in advance, readers around London will be able to better plan their day's golf. For unlike many sports, some advance planning is often necessary to ensure that the day is not spoilt by frustrations and delay.

To use this Guide to its best effect, the Publishers wish to point out the following:

- In the listing of all Clubs within each county, the name of the Secretary and the Club's main telephone number have been included. Please note that with effect from April 1st 1995, all telephone numbers will change. All the numbers listed will have a '1' added after the first digit of the STD code.

- In the sections on 'Course Details', the course length indicated is from the visitors' tees wherever possible.

- In the sections on 'Shop Facilities', the availability of clubs for hire and their cost have been included. Excluded are details of trolley hire and club repair services. These are common to most Clubs and the Professional will be pleased to advise on the extent of service available.

- In the sections on 'Tuition Details', coaching facilities and the cost of individual lessons have been given. Many professionals offer group classes for juniors, ladies, seniors and beginners. The Professionals will supply details of these classes on request.

- In the sections on 'Clubhouse Facilities' reference is made to 'normal dress code'. Unless otherwise indicated, assume that the Clubs listed do not allow jeans, T-shirts, singlets, non-tailored shorts, trainers or track-suits on either the course or in the Clubhouse.

- The sections on 'Visitor Restrictions and How to Book', include details of each Club's and course's restrictions on visitors. Societies will note that Society days have been identified, together with the name of the contact at the Club or course.

- The costs of playing are largely based on 1994 prices. As the Guide went to press, a number of Clubs had not set their prices for 1995.

- As a general comment, having decided on which Clubs or courses to approach, telephone the Pro shop for advice. Club competitions, Society days and Company days often see large numbers of tee-times being pre-booked. A single telephone call can prevent a wasted journey.

For many players, their first introduction to the game of golf is through driving ranges. With their rapid growth and the general improvement in the quality of their facilities, a separate section covering Driving Ranges has been included in the Guide.

The Publishers would like to hear the views of readers on their experience of golf around London. We would like your comments on the courses and ranges included in this edition. We would also like to hear your comments and observations on those courses and those ranges that do not appear on these pages.

Finally, the Publishers would like to acknowledge the support and the assistance of Club Secretaries and Club Professionals in the preparation of this Guide. Their contribution has been invaluable and without their support, this guide could not have been produced.

Peter Wren-Hilton
The Editor
September 1994

Chiltern Forest Golf Club, Buckinghamshire

Rusper Golf Club, Surrey

Tenterden Golf Club, Kent

READERS' COMMENTS

The publishers of this Guide are anxious that the information provided is as accurate as possible. We do however need to know what you think of the clubs, courses and driving ranges that have been included in the Guide.

Perhaps your favourite course, club or driving range has not been featured. If so, please send details for possible inclusion in the next edition. We will acknowledge your assistance in the next Guide, unless you request otherwise.

If you are opening a new golfing facility which you think will interest our readers, please let us know.

REMEMBER: Clubs, courses and driving ranges do not pay to enter this Guide. It is an independent publication which requires the support of its readers to ensure that the information supplied is as relevant and up-to-date as possible.

If you have any comments, criticisms, suggestions, then please write to us. We will attempt to acknowledge all individual letters. Your comments will be read and may be included in the next edition.

Please send your comments to our editorial address:

THE EDITOR
BETULA PUBLISHING
83 MILL LANE
WEST HAMPSTEAD
LONDON NW6 1NB

Editors Note: Your comments are important. Do let us know your views of the courses and driving ranges covered in this edition. We are also keen to hear your recommendations of courses and driving ranges NOT included in this Guide. Your comments will be considered for future editions.

"Golf Etiquette"

A Brief Guide to Dress Codes and On-Course Etiquette.

Whilst the Rules of Golf as approved by the Royal & Ancient Golf Club of St Andrews set out verbatim the detailed rules of Etiquette in Section 1 of the Rules, what follows is a brief layman's guide to the matter.

A large number of the Clubs which feature in this Guide apply these rules. Special notice should be given to what can and what cannot be worn on the course and in the Clubhouse. The following rules normally apply.

DRESS CODE:

Should:	Wear:	Proper Golf Shoes

Should Not:	Wear:	Trainers
		Jeans
		T-Shirts
		Singlets
		Shorts, unless tailored with knee-length socks
		Shell suits

Away from dress codes, most clubs which state that there are no visitor restrictions do expect players to have an understanding of the basic rules of the game.

Each player is expected to use their own set of clubs (no sharing). Slow play is not tolerated, and players are expected to wave through the players behind them if a ball is lost. Players must leave a green, once the putting has been completed. Players are expected to replace divots on the fairway and repair pitch marks on the green.

Normally a single player has no special standing and is expected to allow groups of any kind through. Players are expected to observe local rules where these are stated on the card or in the Clubhouse. Players are also expected to follow temporary rules.

Respect for other players on the course is essential to ensure that all players maximise the enjoyment of their game.

INDEX TO GOLF CLUB ENTRIES

Buckinghamshire

CONTENTS

Puttenham Golf Club, Surrey

Barnehurst Golf Club, Kent

GOLF IN LONDON AND MIDDLESEX

Combining London and Middlesex into a single category might at first glance appear a little strange. It is a fact however that there are only a limited number of courses in Central London and where courses do begin to appear in the more central suburbs, Middlesex grabs the lion's share.

To the north of the centre, **Hampstead Golf Club, Highgate Golf Club, Finchley Golf Club** and **Hendon Golf Club** all offer testing golf. Though without the large terrain of many county courses, these more centrally located courses remain competitive.

To the north west and west of the capital, there are a number of courses in relative close proximity. **Sudbury Golf Club** in Wembley, **Ealing Golf Club** in Greenford, **Haste Hill Golf Course** in Northwood, **Hounslow Heath Golf Club** in Hounslow, **The London Golf Centre** in Northolt, **Perivale Park Golf Club** in Greenford, **Ruislip Golf Club, Stanmore Golf Club** and **Uxbridge Golf Club** all provide a range of testing holes and challenges to the visiting player. For a geographical area so close, there is quite a contrast in the terrain of these courses. The second nine at

The 1st Tee at Springfield Golf Club

1

Haste Hill plays over a hill, whilst Hounslow Heath has a heathland feel. The majority of courses however are parkland with well designed holes making up for the lack of length that some courses may occasionally suffer.

Possibly the best views of the City come from south of the river. **Dulwich and Sydenham Hill Golf Club** offers not only fine views of the City, but also a testing eighteen hole, parkland course.

There is a cluster of good courses to the South-West of the capital. **Fulwell Golf Club** in Hampton Hill, **Strawberry Hill** in Twickenham, **Wimbledon Park Golf Club** and **Wimbledon Common Golf Club** (shared with London Scottish), both in Wimbledon.

Though based around the capital, there are plenty of opportunities to play on 'pay and play' courses that offer few restrictions. **Edgewarebury Golf Club** near Edgeware, **Haste Hill Golf Course** in Northwood, **Hazelwood Golf Centre** in Sunbury-on-Thames, **Hounslow Heath Golf Club** in Hounslow, the **London Golf Centre** in Northolt, **Perivale Park Golf Club** in Greenford, **Rectory Park Golf Course** in Northolt, the **Riverside Golf Club** in Thamesmead, **Springfield Park Golf Club** (special facilities for disabled players) in Wandsworth, **Trent Park Golf Club** in Southgate and **Twickenham Park Golf Club** in Twickenham are all courses that fall into this category.

There is an abundance of driving ranges based around London. Many of the newer 'pay and play' courses have built ranges to accompany the course. There are in addition a number of stand alone ranges. Details of these can be found in the section on Driving Ranges.

LONDON

Aquarius Golf Club
Marmora Road
Honor Oak
London
SE22 0RY

Mrs ML Moss
081-693 1626

Brent Valley Golf Club
Church Road
Hanwell
London
W7

Mr P Bryant
081-567 1287

Bush Hill Park Golf Club
Bush Hill
Winchmore Hill
London
N21 2BU

Mr Michael Burnend
081-360 5738

Dulwich and Sydenham Hill Golf Club
Grange Lane
College Road
Dulwich
London
SE21 7LH

Mrs Susan Alexander
081-693 3961

Eltham Warren Golf Club
Bexley Road
Eltham
London
SE9 2PE

Mr D.J. Clare
081-850 4477

Finchley Golf Club
Nether Court
Frith Lane
London
NW7 1PU

Mr Keith Monk
081-346 2436

Hampstead Golf Club
Winnington Road
London
N2 0TU

Mr K.F. Young
081-455 0203

Hendon Golf Club
Sanders Lane
Devonshire Road
Mill Hill
London
NW7 1DG

Mr David Cooper
081-346 6023

Highgate Golf Club
Denewood Road
Highgate
London
N6 4AH

Mr Gordon Wilson
081-340 3745

Lee Valley Golf Course
Lee Valley Leisure
Picketts Lock Lane
Edmonton
London
N9 0AS

Mr R Gerkin
081-345 6666

London Scottish Golf Club
Windmill Enclosure
Windmill Road
Wimbledon
London
SW19 5NQ

Mr Peter Dell
081-789 7517

Mill Hill Golf Club
100 Barnet Way
Mill Hill
London
NW7 3AL

Mr F.H. Scott
081-959 2339

Muswell Hill Golf Club
Rhodes Avenue
Wood Green
London
N22 4UT

Mr David Beer
081-888 1764

North Middlesex Golf Club
The Manor House
Friern Barnet Lane
Whetstone
London
N20 0NL

Malcom Reding
081-946 1250

Picketts Lock Golf Club
Picketts Lock Lane

Edmonton
London
N9 0AS

Mr Richard Gerken
081-803 3611

Richmond Park Golf Club
Roehampton Gate
Richmond Park
London
SW15 5JR

Mr P Ryan
081-876 3205/1795

Riverside Golf Club
Summerton Way
Thamesmead
London
SE28 8PP

E.J. Springham
081-310 7975

Roehampton Golf Club
Roehampton lane
London
SW15 5LR

Mr M Yates
081-876 5505

Royal Epping Forest Golf Club
Forest Approach
Station Road
Chingford
London
E4 7AZ

Mrs P Runciman
081-529 2195

Royal Wimbledon Golf Club
29 Camp Road

Wimbledon
London
SW19 4UW

Major G.E. Jones
081-946 2125

Royal Blackheath Golf Club
Court Road
Eltham
London
SE9 5AF

Wg Cdr R Barriball
081-850 1795

Shooters Hill Golf Club
Lowood
Eaglesfield Road
London
SE18 3DA

Mr B.R. Adams
081-854 6368

South Herts Golf Club
Links Drive
Totteridge
London
N20 8QU

Mr P.F. Wise
081-445 2035

Springfield Park Golf Club
Burntwood Lane
Wandsworth
London
SW17 0AT

Mr Bryan Davies
081-871 2221

Trent Park Golf Club
Bramley Road

Southgate
London
N14 4UW
Mr Jeremy Sturgess
081-366 7432

Wanstead Golf Club
Overton Drive
Wanstead
London
E11 2LW

Mr Keith Jones
081-989 3938

Wimbledon Common Golf Club
19 Camp Road
Wimbledon Common
London
SW19 4UW

Mr B.K. Cox
081-946 7571

Wimbledon Park Golf Club
Home Park Road
Wimbledon
London
SW19 7HR

Mr K. Hale
081-445 1604

MIDDLESEX

Airlinks Golf Club
Southall Lane
Hounslow
Middlesex TW5 9PE

Mr K Macarthy
081-561 1418

COURSES IN LONDON / MIDDLESEX

Ashford Manor Golf Club
Fordbridge Road
Ashford
Middlesex TW15 3RT

Mr B.J. Duffy
0784-257687

C & L Country Club
West End Road
Northolt
Middlesex UB5 6RD

Mr S Rudki
081-845 5662

Crews Hill Golf Club
Cattlegate Road
Crews Hill
Enfield
Middlesex EN2 8AZ

Mr E.J. Hunt
081-363 0787

Ealing Golf Club
Perivale Lane
Greenford
Middlesex UB6 8SS

Mr Michael Scargill
081-997 0937

Edgewarebury Golf Club
Edgeware Way
Edgeware
Middlesex HA8

081-905 3393

Enfield Golf Club
Old Park Road South
Enfield
Middlesex EN2 7DA

Mr NA Challis
081-342 0313

Fulwell Golf Club
Wellington Road
Hampton Hill
Middlesex TW12 1JY

Mr Peter Butcher
081-977 2733

Grim's Dyke Golf Club
Oxhey Lane
Hatch End
Pinner
Middlesex HA5 4AL

Mr P.H. Payne
081-428 4539

Harrow Hill Golf Club
Kenton Road
Harrow
Middlesex

081-864 3754

Harrow School Golf Club
Harrow-on-the-Hill
Middlesex

Mr D.A. Fothergill
081-869 1214

Haste Hill Golf Course
The Drive
Northwood
Middlesex HA6 1HN

Ms Clare Lloyd
0923-825224

Hazelwood Golf Centre
Croysdale Avenue
Sunbury - on - Thames

COURSES IN LONDON / MIDDLESEX

Middlesex TW16 6QU

Mark Jellicoe
0932-770932

Hillingdon Golf Club
18 Dorset Way
Hillingdon
Uxbridge
Middlesex UB10 0JR

Mrs AM Cooper
0895-233956

Holiday Inn Golf Club
Stockley Road
West Drayton
Middlesex

Mr P.A. Davis
0895-444232

Horsenden Hill Golf Club
55 Lowther Road
Queensbury
Stanmore
Middlesex HA7 1ER

Mr George Oakley
081-902 4555

Hounslow Heath Golf Course
Staines Road
Hounslow
Middlesex TW4 5DS

Mr Roy Loader
081-570 5271

The London Golf Centre
Lime Trees Park Public Golf Course
Ruislip Road
Northolt
Middlesex UB5 6QZ

Mr Nigel Sturgess
081-842 0442

Northwood Golf Club
Rickmansworth Road
Northwood
Middlesex HA6 2QW
Mr R.A. Bond
0923-821384

Perivale Park Golf Club
Stockdove Way
Argyle Road
Greenford
Middlesex UB6 8EN

Mr George Taylor
081-575 7116

Pinner Hill Golf Club
Southview Road
Pinner Hill
Middlesex HA5 3YA

Mr J.P. Devitt
081-866 0963

Rectory Park Golf Club
Huxley Close
Northolt
Middlesex UB5 5UL

Mr C White
081-841 5550

Ruislip Golf Club
Ickenham Road
Ruislip
Middlesex HA4 7DQ

Mr Jim Channing
0895-638081

COURSES IN LONDON / MIDDLESEX

Sandy Lodge Golf Club
Sandy Lodge Lane
Northwood
Middlesex HA6 2JD

Mr J.N. Blair
0923-825429

Stanmore Golf Club
29 Gordon Avenue
Stanmore
Middlesex HA7 2RL

Mr L.J. Pertwee
081-954 2599

Strawberry Hill Golf Club
Wellesley Road
Twickenham
Middlesex TW2 5SD

Mr G Hanbury
081-894 1246

Stockley Park Golf Club
The Clubhouse
Stockley Park
Uxbridge
Middlesex UB11 1AQ

Mrs S Hubbard
081-813 5700

Sudbury Golf Club
Bridgewater Road
Wembley
Middlesex HA0 1AL

Mr A.J. Poole
081-902 3713

Sunbury Golf Course
Charlton Lane
Shepperton
Middlesex TW17 8QA

Mr R Williams
0932-772898

Twickenham Park Golf Club
Staines Road
Twickenham
Middlesex TW2 5JD

Mr John Pascoe
081-783 1698

Uxbridge Golf Club
Harefield Place
The Drive
Uxbridge
Middlesex UB10 8PA

Mr Brian Russell
0895-237287

West Middlesex Golf Club
Greenford Road
Southall
Middlesex UB1 3EE

Mr PJ Furness
081-574 3450

Whitewebbs Golf Club
Beggars Hollow
Clay Hill
Enfield
Middlesex EN2 9JN

Mr Victor Van Graan
081-363 2951

Wyke Green Golf Club
Syon Lane
Isleworth
Middlesex TW7 5PT

Mr D Wentworth-Pollock
081-560 8777

Dulwich and Sydenham Hill Golf Club

Grange Lane
College Road
Dulwich
London SE21 7LH

Secretary:

Mrs. S. Alexander
081-693 3961

Professional:

David Baillie
081-693 8491

Directions:

By Car: The course is located off the A205 (South Circular) by Dulwich College.

By BR: Sydenham Hill Station.

Course Details:

This is a 6051 yard, eighteen hole parkland course.

The course provides superb views of the City of London. Perhaps the most difficult hole is the par 3, 14th hole which requires a drive to a three tier green surrounded by bunkers.

Shop Facilities:

The shop stocks a range of golf equipment and accessories. Club hire is available.

Tuition Details:

Lessons are available from David Baillie at £15.00 for 1/2 hour. Video analysis is also available. Contact David on 081-693 8491 to book a lesson.

Clubhouse Facilities:

The clubhouse provides a range of catering services.

Lunch is available daily. There is a dining room and bar on the first floor which require jacket and tie. Casual wear can be worn in the 19th bar on the ground floor.

Visitor Restrictions and How to Book:

A handicap certificate is required. Visitors are not permitted to play at weekends, unless accompanying a member or on club competition days. Visitors should book and pay at the Pro shop.

Societies are welcome by prior arrangement with the Secretary.

Visitor Playing Costs:

Weekday Only:

18 holes - £25.00

Day - £30.00

Ealing Golf Club

Perivale Lane
Greenford
Middlesex UB6 8SS

Secretary:

Michael Scargill
081-997 0937

Professional:

Arnold Stickley
081-997 3959

Directions:

By Car: Off the Western Avenue (A40) opposite the Hoover building.

By LUG: Perivale Station on the Central Line is 1/2 a mile away.

Course Details:

This is an eighteen hole, par 70, parkland course.

The principal feature of the course is the River Brent which comes into play on 9 holes. The Stroke Indices 1 & 2 (the 6th and 10th holes) both require long drives to carry the River Brent with the second shot. The course finishes with the two longest holes of the course at 508 and 481 yards respectively.

Shop Facilities:

The shop offers the full range of Hogan clubs and accessories, plus designer wear.

Tuition Details:

The practice area is limited, though lessons are available at £20 per 45 minutes. Book through the pro shop.

Clubhouse Facilities:

A full snack menu is available from 10.30am and the restaurant provides an a la carte luncheon. A jacket and tie are required. Smart casual dress is required in all other areas. Spikes can be worn in the mens Spike bar.

Visitors Restrictions and How to Book:

Bookings are made through the Pro shop and handicap certificates are required. No visitors are permitted on weekends or bank holidays. Tuesday am is Ladies Day.

Society days are on Monday, Wednesday and Thursday. A full day package, including 36 holes, snack lunch and evening meal costs £45, plus VAT. (min 24 players if evening meal required). In first instance, contact the Secretary.

Visitor Playing Costs:

Weekday only:

Daily or Round Rate is £30.

Edgewarebury Golf Club

*Edgeware Way
Edgeware
Middlesex HA8*

The Office:
081-905 3393

Directions:
By Car: Edgeware Way is on the left of the A41 between Edgeware and Elstree.

Course Details:
This is a nine hole, 1084 yard, par 3 course.

With the exception of the 8th and 9th, you rarely need anything more than an eight or nine iron to tackle the short holes.

Shop Facilities:
The shop supplies balls, tees and pencils. Clubs are available for hire at £1 per round.

Visitor Restrictions and How to Book:
This is a pay and play course and is open to the public.

On weekdays, it is open from 9.00 am - dusk and weekends from 8.00am - dusk. At weekends, it becomes very busy.

To book, turn up and play on a first come, first serve basis.

Visitor Playing Costs:
9 holes - £4.00

18 holes - £6.00

Eltham Warren Golf Club

Bexley Road
Eltham
London SE9 2PE

Secretary:
D. J. Clare
081-850 4477

Professional:
R.V. Taylor
081-859 7909

Directions:
By Car: Off the A210 at Eltham.

By BR: Eltham is the nearest Station.

Course Details:
This 9 hole parkland course offers a testing par of 69 for two rounds.

The course starts and finishes with par 3 holes. The 4th hole (Stroke Index 1) is a dog-leg right with out of bounds down the length of the fairway. The 8th hole, a 500 yard, par 5 offers out of bounds on the right together with a very narrow fairway. Narrow ditches feature on several of the holes.

Shop Facilities:
The shop stocks a wide range of golf equipment, accessories and designer wear. The shop also supplies light snacks.

Tuition Details:
The Club has both a practice ground and golf nets. Lessons from the Pro cost £12 for 30 minutes. A 9 hole playing lesson costs £20. Contact the Pro for details.

Clubhouse Facilities:
Food is available during the day until 2.00pm and in the evening on request. There are two bars, a lounge, a dining room and an annexe. Formal wear is required in both the club lounge and the dining room. No jeans are permitted either in the clubhouse or on the course.

Visitor Restrictions and How to Book:
Visitors are welcome on weekdays only.

Bookings are made through either the Secretary or the golf shop and a handicap certificate is required. Payment is made in the golf shop or at the bar if the shop is closed. Visitors must display a bag tag at all times.

Societies are welcome on Thursdays subject to each player having a bona fide handicap. Full catering arrangements are available.

Contact the Secretary for further details.

Visitor Playing Costs:
A Day Ticket is £25.

Fulwell Golf Club

Wellington Road
Hampton Hill
Middlesex TW12 1JY

Secretary:

Peter Butcher
081-977 2733

Professional:

David Haslam
081-977 3844

Directions:

By Car: The course is located opposite Fulwell Railway Station.

Course Details:

This is a 6544 yard, eighteen hole parkland course.

This is a challenging course with a number of well positioned fairway bunkers, particularly on the outward nine.

Ditches and water play a role on several holes, including a lake which requires driving on the 9th hole and a ditch in front of the green on the finishing hole.

Shop Facilities:

The shop stocks a range of golf equipment and accessories.

Tuition Details:

Lessons are available from the Pro staff at £25 for 45 minutes. Contact the Pro shop on 081-977 3844 for details.

Clubhouse Facilities:

The clubhouse has full changing facilities, including showers.

The clubhouse provides a range of catering facilities with a fully licensed bar, lounge and restaurant.

Visitor Restrictions and How to Book:

A handicap certificate is required. Visitors are welcome during the week, but must accompany a member at weekends. Visitors should book via the Pro shop on 081-977 3844.

Societies are welcome and should contact the Secretary's office on 081-977 2733 for details of packages available.

Visitor Playing Costs:

Weekdays Only:

£30.00 per round or day.

Hampstead Golf Club

£7.50 per round.

Winnington Road London N2 0TU

Secretary:

K.F. Young
081-455 0203

Professional:

P.J. Brown
081-455 7089

Directions:

By Car: The course is located 300 yards down Winnington Road from Hampstead Lane near the Spaniards Inn.

Course Details:

This 9 hole undulating parkland course provides a two round par of 68 for men and 71 for ladies.

The 2nd hole, a challenging par 4, and 467 yards in length, is included in the PGA Guide as one of the most testing 18 holes in the region. Together with the testing 6th and 7th holes at 463 and 421 yards respectively, these make up for the lack of any par 5 holes.

Shop Facilities:

The shop stocks a full range of golf equipment, accessories and designer wear. Clubs are available for hire at

Tuition Details:

Limited practice facilities mean that the coaching takes place at the side of and on the course. Lessons from the Pro cost £12 per 30 minutes.

Clubhouse Facilities:

The clubhouse has limited catering facilities. Lunch time bar snacks (not Sundays) and afternoon teas are available. Sunday lunch is available for members and guests. Jackets and ties are required when eating in the dining room.

Visitor Restrictions and How to Book:

Bookings and payment are made via the Pro shop. Availability for visitors is restricted at weekends and on Tuesdays. The Club do not book specific tee-off times. Tee-off is in the order of members and visitors making up their games and being present at the 1st tee.

Only small societies can be accommodated. Prior arrangement should be made with the Secretary.

Visitor Playing Costs:

Weekday: 9 holes / 18 holes:

£15.00 / £23.00

Weekend: 18 holes - £30.00

Haste Hill Golf Course

The Drive
Northwood
Middlesex HA6 1HN

Secretary:

Clare Lloyd
0923-825224

Directions:

By Car: The course is located off Rickmansworth Road (A404).

Course Details:

This is a 5290 yard, eighteen hole parkland course.

The first nine holes are relatively flat, whilst the inward nine are played over Haste Hill.

Shop Facilities:

The shop stcoks a range of golf equipment and accessories. Clubs are available for hire at £10 per set.

Tuition Details:

There are 2 practice areas, nets, driving area and chipping area. The training Pro travels from Ruislip golf course. Lessons will be organised however from the shop at Haste Hill.

Clubhouse Facilities:

There is a changing room and showers (No locker room).

A bar, function room and lounge provide daily catering. There is also a members' room.

Visitor Restrictions and How to Book:

There are no visitor restrictions.

Visitors are welcome and should book on 0923-822877.

Societies are welcome. Packages cost £12.75, but play cannot commence before 12.30pm. At weekends, the cost is £14.50.

Visitor Playing Costs:

Weekday / Weekend (before 12.00pm):

£10.00 / £15.00

(£12.50 after 12.00pm)

Hazelwood Golf Centre

Contact the Pro shop for details.

Croysdale Avenue Sunbury-on-Thames Middlesex TW16 6QU

Centre Manager:

Mark Jellicoe
0932 770932

Directions:

The course is located 1/2 a mile from Junction 1 (M3) and 5 miles from the M25.

Course Details:

This is a nine hole, 2830 yard parkland course.

Opened in May 1994, with USGA greens, a large lake comes into play at two holes.

Shop Facilities:

The shop stocks a full range of golf equipment and accessories. Clubs are available for hire at £5 for a 1/2 set.

Tuition Details:

There is a 36 bay driving range, together with a 1000 square foot floodlit putting green and bunker facility. Lessons are available from £9 for 30 minutes. Video analysis is available from £15 for 45 minutes.

Clubhouse Facilities:

Catering is provided by the 'Bunker's' theme bar and restaurant. There is a large terrace with a barbecue.

There is a fully-equipped seminar room available for hire.

Visitor Restrictions and How to Book:

There are no visitor restrictions.

Visitors should book and pay in the Pro shop. There is a computerised tee booking system. Visitors can book a tee up to 6 days in advance by telephone.

Societies should contact Mark Jellicoe for details of Society options.

Visitor Playing Costs:

Weekday / Weekend:

9 holes:

£7.00 / £8.50

18 holes:

£12.00 / £14.00

There are reduced rates for Seniors and Juniors.

Hendon Golf Club

Sanders Lane
Devonshire Road
Mill Hill
London NW7 1DG

Secretary:

David Cooper
081-346 6023

Professional:

Stuart Murray
081-346 8990

Directions:

By Car: Off Junction 2, (M1) Southbound. Turn left at lights.

By LUG: Mill Hill East Station on the Northern Line.

Course Details:

This is an eighteen hole, par 70, undulating parkland course.

The 2nd, 11th and 16th holes are all challenging par 4's. The 6th hole, is a difficult 175 yard uphill par 3. The course is generally well bunkered.

Shop Facilities:

The shop stocks the full range of golf equipment, accessories and designer wear. Club hire (inc. trolley) costs £20.

Tuition Details:

There is no practice ground. Lessons are available for £20/£25 for one hour from the Assistant/Head Professional in the Teaching Shed. Video analysis can be arranged.

Contact the Pro shop with requirements.

Clubhouse Facilities:

Changing facilities, including showers, are available to visitors.

Full bar and catering facilities are available throughout the day. Casual dress is permitted until 6.00pm, though this is extended in the 19th Bar. Players are expected to change out of golfing clothes.

Visitor Restrictions and How to Book:

Visitors are expected to be bona fide golfers. Handicap certificates are not required. Visitors should book through the Shop and pay before playing.

Societies are welcome on weekdays, except Monday. All day and half day packages are available. Enquiries and reservations should be made through the General Manager's office.

Visitor Playing Costs:

Weekday: 18 holes - £25

Day - £30

Weekend - £35

Hounslow Heath Golf Course

Staines Road
Hounslow
Middlesex TW4 5DS

Secretary:

Roy Loader
081-570 5271

Directions:

By Car: Situated along the Staines Road in Hounslow. The Staines Road is accessible from the M3 and M4.

Course Details:

This is a 5649 yard, eighteen hole heathland course.

Though not particularly long by some standards, this is a tight heathland course requiring accurate play. This is particularly so with the back nine. The 14th, 15th and 16th holes are the most scenic on the course. Water comes into play on a number of the holes.

Shop Facilities:

The shop stocks a range of golf equipment and accessories. Club hire is available at £5.00.

Tuition Details:

There is both a practice area and putting green. Lessons are available from £8.00 per half hour. Contact the Pro shop for details.

Clubhouse Facilities:

There are both male and female changing areas.

There is no bar in the clubhouse but catering is supplied by a cafe. Smart casual wear is required.

Visitor Restrictions and How to Book:

This is a public course and there are no visitor restrictions.

Weekday bookings are not taken. Bookings can be made up to 7 days in advance for weekends. Telephone bookings are taken, but a non-refundable green fee must be paid 48 hours prior to playing.

Societies are catered for with prices from £12.00.

Visitor Playing Costs:

Weekday / Weekend:

18 holes - £7.50 / £10.50

Day - £12.00 (weekday only)

There are junior reductions.

The London Golf Centre

Lime Trees Park
Ruislip Road
Northolt
Middlesex UB5 6QZ

Secretary:

Nigel Sturgess
081-842 0442

Professional:

Gary Newall
081-845 3180

Directions:

By Car: 12 miles west of London on the A40 about 3 miles inside the M25. Take exit signposted Yeading (A4180) at the Polish War Memorial. The course is 500 yards on the left.

Course Details:

This is a 9 hole, 18 tee, par 69 undulating parkland course.

The course has several water hazards and situated on a hill plays like a links course when the wind picks up. The par 5, 15th hole normally plays into the wind, fully justifying its Stroke Index 1 status.

Shop Facilities:

The shop stocks an extensive range of equipment and accessories. Clubs are available for hire at £5 per round.

Tuition Details:

A floodlit driving range is available. Lessons are available at £50 for ten, one hour lessons in a Group class or individually at £13 per half hour.

Clubhouse Facilities:

Changing facilities, including showers are available.

The clubhouse has a spike bar/ function room which provide daily catering.

Visitor Restrictions and How to Book:

As a public course, no restrictions apply. You can book via the shop up to seven days in advance and the course is open from dawn to dusk.

Golf societies can book by prior arrangement with the Secretary. Group packages for 18 holes including lunch start at £13 per person.

Visitor Playing Costs:

Weekdays/ Weekends per 9 holes:

(Juniors up to 16) - £2.30 / 5.00
(Seniors over 65) - £3.50 / £5.00
(Adults) - £5.00 / £6.50
per 18 holes:
(Juniors up to 16) - £5.00 / £10.00
(Seniors over 65) - £5.00 - £10.00
(Adults) - £6.75 / £12.75

London Scottish Golf Club

Windmill Enclosure
Windmill Road
Wimbledon
London SW19 5NQ

Secretary:

P. Dell
081-789 7517

Professional:

S. Barr
081-789 1207

Directions:

By Car: The course is located off Parkside. Parkside is the road from Tibbetts Corner to Wimbledon Village.

By BR / LUG: Wimbledon Station.

Course Details:

This is a 5400 yard, eighteen hole, common land course.

The course is heavily tree-lined with narrow fairways making accuracy unusually important. Though the course is not as long as some, it has 3 long par 3 holes.

Shop Facilities:

The shop stocks a range of golf equipment and accessories. Clubs are not available for hire.

Tuition Details:

There is a limited practice area. Lessons are available at £15 for 30 minutes. Contact the Pro shop for details and to book.

Clubhouse Facilities:

Changing facilities are available, including showers. The changing facilities for ladies are somewhat limited.

There is a Spike bar which allows casual wear. The lounge bar requires a jacket and tie.

Visitor Restrictions and How to Book:

There are no handicap restrictions, though visitors are only permitted to play on weekdays.

Visitors must wear a pillar box RED upper garment due to local regulations. It must include sleeves.

Telephone the Pro on 081-789 1207 for details of availability.

Societies are welcome with numbers of 15 to 40 players. Contact the Secretary for details of the packages available.

Visitor Playing Costs

Weekdays Only:

18 holes - £15.00

Day - £22.00

North Middlesex Golf Club

The Manor House
Frier Barnet Lane
Whetstone
London N20 0NL

Secretary:

Malcolm Reding
081-445 1604

Professional:

Steve Roberts
081-445 3060

Directions:

By Car: 5 miles north of Finchley off the A1000 and 5 miles south of Junction 23 (South Mimms) off M25 via the A1081 through Barnet.

By LUG: Totteridge and Whetstone on the Northern Line and Arnos Grove on the Piccadilly Line.

Course Details:

This 18 hole parkland course, designed by course architect Willie Park jnr, is a 69 par course for men and 70 par for ladies.

The course provides a range of testing shots. In particular, the 18th hole offers an interesting shot over a lake in the approach to the green in front of the Clubhouse.

Shop Facilities:

The shop stocks a full range of golf equipment, accessories and designer wear.

Tuition Details:

Coaching is available from the professional. Lessons cost £12 for 30 minutes, £16 for 45 minutes and £20 for one hour.

Clubhouse Facilities:

Changing facilities, including showers are available to visitors.

The Clubhouse provides comprehensive catering and bar facilities.

Visitor Restrictions and How to Book:

Visitors are welcome and there is no handicap certificate restriction. Visitors should however be bona fide players. Visitors should book via the shop.

Societies are welcome and should make prior arrangements through the General Manager.

Visitor Playing Costs:

Weekday:

18 holes - £22.00

Day - £27.50

Perivale Park Golf Club

Stockdove Way
Argyle Road
Greenford
Middlesex UB6 8EN

Secretary:

G. Taylor
081-575 7116

Professional:

P. Bryant
081-575 7116

Directions:

By Car: Off the A40 to Argyle Road to Stockdove Way.

By BR: South Greenford Station.

Course Details:

This is a 9 hole, par 34, parkland course.

The River Brent is adjacent to the 1st, 4th and 6th greens. The ditch along the 9th fairway poses a hazard to those playing from the 3rd and 4th holes. Apart from the par 5, 9th hole, this course ideally suits those who want to improve their short game.

Shop Facilities:

The shop stocks a wide range of golfing equipment, accessories and designer wear.

Tuition Details:

Coaching is available from the resident professional on the practice area. Lessons cost £15 for 45 minutes.

Contact the Pro shop on 081-575 7116 to book.

Clubhouse Facilities:

Changing rooms, including showers are available.

A cafeteria, providing a range of refreshments is open during the day.

Visitor Restrictions and How to Book:

Handicap certificates are not required. Times are bookable on weekend mornings. During the week, book and pay at the pro shop.

Visitor Playing Costs:

Pay and Play:

Weekday - £4.20

Weekend/Public Holiday - £6.20

Rectory Park Golf Course

Huxley Close
Northolt
Middlesex UB5 5UL

Secretary:

Chris White
081-841 5550

Directions:

By Car: The course is located close to the main Northolt roundabout on the A40 near the MacDonalds Restaurant.

Course Details:

This is a short, 1270 yard, parkland, nine hole course.

Shop Facilities:

The shop stocks a range of golf equipment and accessories.

Tuition Details:

There is both an indoor net and an outdoor practice area. Lessons are available from the established teaching academy at £10 per 30 minutes.

Video analysis is available at £25 for one hour.

Clubhouse Facilities:

There are no changing facilities at the course.

Limited catering comes in the form of tea, coffee and soft drinks.

Visitor Restrictions and How to Book:

There are no visitor restrictions.

To book, contact the Club on 081-841 5550.

Societies should also contact the Club for details.

Visitor Playing Costs:

Weekdays / Weekends: (9 holes)

£3.95 / £4.95

18 holes:

£6.50 / £8.00

Riverside Golf Club

Summerton Way
Thamesmead
London SE28 8PP

Secretary:

E.J Springham
081-310 7975

Professional:

Mark Parker
081-310 7975

Directions:

By Car: Exit at the Bexleyheath turn-off on the A2. Follow the signs towards Abbeywood and Thamesmead.

Course Details:

This is an eighteen hole course, playing nine holes from two sets of tee positions.

This is a public course where water comes into play on several holes. At 5,272 yards, this is a course which will suit players of all abilities.

Shop Facilities:

The shop stocks a range of golf equipment and accessories.

Tuition Details:

There is a 31 bay driving range within the course enclosure.

Lessons are available with group junior tuition starting at £3 per hour. Adult lessons cost £8 for 30 minutes. Video analysis is available. Contact Mark Parker for more details.

Clubhouse Facilities:

Changing facilities are available.

All day catering is provided. There is a restaurant and two bars (one for members only).

Visitor Restrictions and How to Book:

There are no visitor restrictions.

Visitors can book either in person (by signing in) at the Pro shop or by telephoning 081-310 7975 for a reservation.

Visitor Playing Costs:

Weekdays / Weekends:(Adults):

9 holes: £6.50 / £7.50

18 holes: £10.50 / £12.00

(Juniors) 9 holes: £4.00 / £4.00

18 holes: £7.00 / £7.00

Ruislip Golf Club

Ickenham Road
Ruislip
Middlesex HA4 7DQ

Secretary:
Jim Channing
0895-638081

Professional:
Paul Glozier
0895-623980

Directions:
By Car: The entrance is directly off the B466 opposite West Ruislip Underground station.

By LUG / BR: West Ruislip Station.

Course Details:
This is an eighteen hole, 5702 yard parkland course.

The first seven holes are all testing and there are a good group of finishing holes, including 3, par 3's in the last five home.

Shop Facilities:
The shop stocks a range of golf equipment and accessories. Open from 6.00am, club hire is available at £10 per round.

Tuition Details:
There is a 40 bay undercover floodlit driving range attached to the course. PGA qualified professionals are available to give lessons. Lessons cost £12 for 30 minutes.

Clubhouse Facilities:
There are full changing facilities, including showers.

The clubhouse has a bar and restaurant on the ground floor, together with a conservatory area. There is a members bar, restaurant and Club room upstairs. All day catering is provided.

Visitor Restrictions and How to Book:
There are no restrictions on visitors. This is a pay and play public course. There is however a private members club attached to the course.

Book in person or for advance bookings, by telephone. Registration booking cards are available from the Pro shop.

Societies are welcome on weekdays and packages start at £12.75. Society booking forms are available from the Pro shop.

Visitor Playing Costs:
Weekday / Weekend: (18 holes):

£10.00 / £15.00

There are Junior / OAP discounts.

South Herts Golf Club

Links Drive
Totteridge
London N20 8QU

Secretary:

P.F. Wise

081-445 2035

Professional:

R.Y. Mitchell

081-445 4633

Directions:

By Car: Totteridge Lane (A5109) is half a mile west of the junction with the High Road in Whetstone (A1000).

By LUG: Whetstone Station.

Course Details:

This is a 6093 yard, eighteen hole parkland course.

Set in 125 acres of established parkland, the 7th hole is a long par 4 with a sloping difficult green.

There is also a short 1582 yard, nine hole course which is good for beginners.

Shop Facilities:

The shop stocks a range of golf equipment and accessories. Golf clubs are available for hire at £5 a set.

Tuition Details:

Lessons are provided by the PGA qualified professional staff. Lessons cost £20 per hour. (£25 with the Head Pro). Contact the Pro shop for details.

Clubhouse Facilities:

Bar snacks are available from the fully licensed bar and the dining room can be used by visitors who are playing on the main course on Wednesdays, Thursdays and Fridays.

Visitor Restrictions and How to Book:

Visitors are welcome on weekdays and weekends if playing with a member. Visitors must be a member of a recognised golf club and have a handicap of 24 or better.

Tuesday is Ladies day.

Visitors may use the short course seven days a week, but are not permitted to use the clubhouse. Book through the Pro shop by telephoning 081-445 4633.

Societies are welcome on Wednesdays, Thursdays and Fridays on application to the Secretary's office.

Visitor Playing Costs:

Weekdays Only:

£30.00 per round / day

£10.00 Short Course

Springfield Park Golf Club

Burntwood Lane
Wandsworth
London SW17 0AT

Secretary:

Bryan Davies
081-871 2221

Professionals:

Patrick Tallack /Gratton Smallwood
081-871 2468

Directions:

By car: Burnt Wood Lane is between Garrett Lane and Trinity Road. Situated in the former grounds of the Springfield Hospital.

By BR: 1 mile from Earlsfield and 1.5 miles from Clapham Common.

Course Details:

This, par 62, 4,658 yard parkland course is both flat and tree-lined.

It is ideal for new golfers and those who do not seek a long testing track. Like many flat courses, club selection can be tricky. Springfield Park is the London section HQ of the English Blind Golf Movement.

Shop Facilities:

The shop stocks a wide range of equip-ment and accessories. Golf clubs can be hired for £5 per round.

Tuition Details:

A pitching area with bunkers and nets is available. Lessons cost £10 for 30/40 minutes.

Clubhouse Facilities:

Changing facilities, including showers are available.

The clubhouse has a spacious lounge bar and separate function room with its own bar.

Visitor Restrictions and How to Book:

Bookings are made through the Pro shop. You do not need a handicap cer-tificate or be a member of another club. No visitors can play before 12.00pm on Saturdays and Sundays.

Societies can be catered for by prior arrangement with the General Manager.

Visitor Playing Costs:

Weekdays:

18 holes (before 9.00am) - £5.00

18 holes (between 9.00 - 6pm) - £6.50

Weekends:

18 holes (after 6.00pm) -£5.00

18 holes (12.00pm - 6.00pm) - £8.50

Stanmore Golf Club

29 Gordon Avenue Stanmore Middlesex HA7 2RL

Secretary:
L.J Pertwee
0181-954 2599

Professional:
Viv Law
0181-954 2646

Directions:
By Car: Gordon Avenue is located off Old Church Lane on the Stanmore - Belmont Road which in turn, is off the Uxbridge Road.

By LUG: Stanmore Station on the Jubilee Line.

Course Details:
This is a 5656 yard, par 68 wooded parkland course.

Shop Facilities:
The shop stocks a full range of golfing equipment, accessories and designer wear.

Tuition Details:
There is a practice area and coaching is available through the two coaching staff. Lessons cost £20 for 60 minutes.

Contact Viv Law in the Pro shop on 0181-954 2646 to book.

Clubhouse Facilities:
The clubhouse has changing facilities, including showers.

Full catering facilities are available with both a bar and restaurant.

Visitor Restrictions and How to Book:
Visitors are welcome during the week, but may not play at weekends, unless accompanying a member.

No prior bookings are taken except for Societies who should contact the Secretary by prior arrangement.

Mondays and Fridays are public days, whilst Tuesdays, Wednesdays and Thursdays are normal days.

Visitor Playing Costs:
Weekdays Only:

Public Days (Monday and Friday) - £8.10

Normal Days (Tuesday - Thursday) - £25

Trent Park Golf Club

Bramley Road
Southgate
London N14 4UW

Secretary:

Jeremy Sturgess
081-366 7432

Professional:

Tony Sheaff
081-366 7432

Directions:

By LUG: Situated opposite Oakwood Station on the Piccadilly Line.

Course Details:

This is an undulating 18 hole, 6008 yard parkland course with several water features.

The 1st, a demanding par 5, includes a dog-leg over 2 lakes onto a recessed green. The downhill par 3, 5th hole, has water behind the green to catch the unwary. The course finishes with an uphill par 4 where the drive is all important.

Shop Facilities:

A large golf superstore stocks an extensive range of golf equipment, accessories and designer wear. Clubs can be hired for £5.

Tuition Details:

The course has its own newly built floodlit driving range with Japanese style bay dividers, carpeted walkways and outdoor heaters.

Lessons are available at £14 for 30 minutes. A session of beginner group classes costs £50.

Clubhouse Facilities:

Changing facilities, including showers are available.

Catering facilities include a function suite and two bars.

Visitor Restrictions and How to Book:

This a public facility. A handicap certificate is not required. Jeans are not allowed. Book through the Shop.

Societies should contact William O'Brien (Societies Co-ordinator) for information. Packages including 18 holes and lunch start at £15 and 36 holes, including dinner at £36.

Visitor Playing Costs:

Weekdays / Weekends:

18 holes - £10 / £12

Concessionary Rates available for juniors and senior citizens.

Twickenham Park Golf Club

*Staines Road
Twickenham
Middlesex TW2 5JD*

Secretary:

John Pascoe
081-783 1748

Professional:

Steve Lloyd
081-783 1698

Directions:

By Car: From A316, exit at signpost to Twickenham and take the A305 from roundabout. The course is 300 yards on the right.

Course Details:

This is a flat nine hole parkland course, playing as a par 72 when played as an eighteen hole course.

Heavily tree-lined, the course features an interesting par 3, 3rd hole, which in addition to being protected by a bunker on the front right, has water to the left and right joined by a ditch with a bridge.

Shop Facilities:

The shop stocks a range of golf equipment and accessories.

Club hire is available at £5 (£50

deposit).

Tuition Details:

There is a 27 bay floodlit driving range attached to the course with a practice bunker and putting green.

Lessons are available from the Steve Lloyd Golf academy at £13/£15 for 30 minutes with the Assistant/Head Professional.

4 x 2 hour sessions for beginners are available for £50 (Group session).

Clubhouse Facilities:

The Clubhouse provides food all day and the large bar overlooks the 9th green.

Visitor Restrictions and How to Book:

There are no visitor restrictions, though there are club competitions approximately every other week on Saturdays and Sundays.

Book via the Pro shop and from Tuesdays for the following weekend.

Societies are welcome. They should contact the Secretary for details.

Visitor Playing Costs:

9 holes:

Weekdays - £5.00

Weekends - £6.00

Uxbridge Golf Club

Harefield Place
The Drive
Uxbridge
Middlesex UB10 8PA

Secretary:

Brian Russell
0895-237287

Professional:

Phil Howard
0895-237287

Directions:

By Car: Off the M40 and A40. Located close to the Swalklys Junction (B467). Follow the signs to Ruislip.

Course Details:

This is an 18 hole, par 68, undulating parkland course.

The course offers a good test of golf and includes one of the toughest par 4 holes in Middlesex.

Shop Facilities:

The shop stocks an extensive range of discount golf equipment, accessories and designer wear.

Sets of golf clubs are available for hire at £5 per set.

Tuition Details:

There is a practice ground and lessons are available at £10 per 30 minutes.

Contact Phil Howard on 0895-237287 to book.

Clubhouse Facilities:

The Clubhouse has full changing facilities, including showers.

The Clubhouse provides extensive bar and restaurant facilities. A function room, seating up to 150, is available.

Visitor Restrictions and How to Book:

There are no restrictions on visitors. Bookings are made via the Shop for both casual and Society bookings.

Contact the professional for details of the variety of Society packages available.

Visitor Playing Costs:

Weekday: £10 per round

Weekend:

£15 - (before12.00pm)

£12.50 - (after 12.00pm)

Wanstead Golf Club

Overton Drive
Wanstead
London E11 2LW

Secretary:

Keith Jones
081-989 3938

Professional:

David Hawkins
081-989 9876

Directions:

By Car: The course is 1 mile from the junction of the A406 and A12. From the junction, take the A12 towards London. Turn left at first set of lights, then second left at St. Marys Church.

By LUG: Wanstead Station is 400 yards away.

Course Details:

This is a 6004 yard, eighteen hole parkland course.

Bordering Epping Forest, its principal landmark is a featured lake. This comes into play on both the 16th and 17th holes.

Shop Facilities:

The shop stocks a range of golf equipment and accessories. Clubs are not

Tuition Details:

Tuition is available from the resident PGA qualified professional for between £12 and £15 per half hour.

Advance booking is essential. Contact David Hawkins in the Pro shop.

Clubhouse Facilities:

The Clubhouse has a fully licensed bar and a full restaurant and snack service is available throughout the day. A stud bar service is also available.

Dress regulations apply to the bars and restaurant.

Visitor Restrictions and How to Book:

A handicap certificate is required. Visitors are welcome on Mondays, Tuesdays and Fridays by prior arrangement with the Secretary. Visitors should pay in the Pro shop.

Societies are also welcome with a range of packages available on Mondays, Tuesdays and Fridays. Enquiries should be addressed to the Secretary.

Visitor Playing Costs:

Monday, Tuesday and Friday only:

£25.00 per day.

Wimbledon Common Golf Club

19 Camp Road
Wimbledon Common
London SW19 4UW

Secretary:

B. K Cox
081-946 7571

Professional:

J. S. Jukes
081-946 0294

Directions:

By Car: Located on the South East side of Wimbledon Common off Parkside by the Wimbledon War Memorial.

By BR and LUG: Wimbledon Station is on both Network SE and on the District Line.

Course Details:

This is an eighteen hole, par 68, heathland course. The course is shared with London Scottish.

It is well wooded and has no bunkers. Driving accuracy is necessary since the fairways tend to be fairly narrow.

Shop Facilities:

The shop stocks a range of golf equipment, accessories and designer wear.

Tuition Details:

Lessons cost £8 for 30 minutes and £13 for an hour. The practice area is available to members only. Contact the Pro shop for details.

Clubhouse Facilities:

Changing facilities are available in the Locker Room.

Full catering facilities are available in the main bar.

Visitor Restrictions and How to Book:

Visitors are welcome during the week and a handicap certificate is not required.

Visitors may not play at weekends, unless as guests of a member.

All players must wear a plain pillar-box RED upper garment, due to local regulations.

Societies are welcomed. Societies should contact the Secretary's office for details.

Visitor Playing Costs:

Weekdays only:

Per round - £15

By Day - £22

Wimbledon Park Golf Club

Home Park Road
Wimbledon
London SW19 7HR

Secretary:

M. K Hale
081-946 1250

Professional:

D. Wingrove
081-946 4053

Directions:

By Car: The course is approximately 600 yards from Wimbledon Park Underground Station.

Course Details:

This is an eighteen hole parkland course.

Its principal feature is a large lake in the centre of the course.

Shop Facilities:

The shop stocks a range of golf equipment, accessories and designer wear.

Tuition Details:

There is a limited practice area. Tuition is available from the two resident professionals.

Lessons cost £15/£20 for 40 minutes

with the Assistant/ Head Pro.

Contact the Pro shop for details.

Clubhouse Facilities:

There are full mens and ladies changing facilities.

The Clubhouse provides a range of catering facilities through its restaurant and bars.

Visitor Restrictions and How to Book:

A handicap certificate is required. Visitors are not permitted to play before 3.30pm at weekends. Otherwise they are welcome to play at any time. Book through the Pro shop.

Societies are welcome on Tuesdays and Thursdays. Contact the Secretary for details.

Visitor Playing Costs:

Weekday:

18 Holes - £25.00

Day - £30.00

Weekend:

(18 holes) - £25.00

GOLF IN KENT

Kent offers a range of different golfing terrains from the undulating parkland courses of the north and central parts of the county to the great links courses on its southern coast. Though perhaps it stretches the definition of 'Around London', what better than a day tackling the elements at **Royal St. Georges, Princes and Royal Cinque Ports.** Nowhere in England, except perhaps on the Lancashire coast does one find such a collection of challenging links.

Yet inland, Kent offers many fine courses. **Hever Golf Club** is an eighteen hole parkland course whose careful design has incorporated both the natural surroundings of Hever Castle with the requirements of a modern course. **Knole Park Golf Club** at Sevenoaks is set in established parkland enjoying views of Knole House. Like Hever, **Chart Hills Golf Club** at Biddenden, only open since 1993, is one of several courses which offer design incorporating both environmental concern with up-to-date facilities. Kent has perhaps benefited more than most from the recent development of well-designed courses. **The London Golf Club** at Ash, opened within the last year, epitomises this trend.

However, golfers do not require debentures or large cheque books to find challeng-

Edenbridge Golf and Country Club

35

ing courses in the county, for Kent is blessed with many fine public and private courses that have few visitor restrictions.

Barnehurst Golf Club at Bexleyheath, **Beckenham Place Park** at Beckenham, **Leeds Castle Golf Club** at Maidstone, **Oastpark Golf Club** at Snodland, **Poult Wood Public Golf Centre** at Tonbridge, **Ruxley Park Golf Centre** at Orpington and **Upchurch River Valley Golf Courses** at Sittingbourne are amongst those that fall into this category. The range of courses available in Kent today mean that there will be a course or driving range to cater for the needs of most of the county's golfers.

Birchwood Park Golf Club

Darenth Valley Golf Club

Beckenham Place Park Golf Club

36

COURSES IN KENT

Ashford Golf Club
Sandyhurst Lane
Ashford
Kent TN25 4NT

Mr AH Story
0233-622655

Austin Lodge Golf Club
Eynsford
Kent DA4 0HU

Mr Steve Bevan
0322-868944

Barnehurst Golf Club
Mayplace Road East
Bexleyheath
Kent DA7 6JU

Mr Paul Casey
0322-552952

Bearsted Golf Club
Ware Street
Bearsted
Kent ME14 4PQ

Mrs L Siems
0622-738198

Beckenham Place Park Golf Course
The Mansion
Beckenham Place Park
Beckenham
Kent BR3 2BP

Mr HUW Davies-Thomas
081-650 2292

Bexleyheath Golf Club
Mount Road
Bexleyheath
Kent DA6 8JS

Mr SE Squires
081-303 6951

Birchwood Park Golf Club Ltd
Birchwood Road
Wilmington
Dartford
Kent DA2 7HJ

Julie Smith
0322-662038

Boughton Golf Club
Brickfield Lane
Boughton
Nr Faversham
Kent ME13 9AJ

Mr Philip Sparks
0227-752277

Broke Hill Golf Club
Sevenoaks Road
Halstead
Kent TN14 7HR

Mr T Collingwood
0959-533225

Bromley Golf Club
Magpie Hall Lane
Bromley
Kent BR2 8HF

081-462 7014

Broome Park Golf & CC
Broome Park Estate
Barham
Canterbury
Kent CT4 6QX

Mr J.W. Cowling
0227-831701 x263

Canterbury Golf Club
Scotland Hills
Canterbury
Kent CT1 1TW

Mr Lucas
0227-453532

Chart Hills Golf Club
Weeks Lane
Biddenden
Kent TN27 8JX

Mr Roger Hyder
0580-292222

Chelsfield Lakes Golf Centre
Court Road
Orpington
Kent BR6 9BX

Derek Howe
0689-896266

Chestfield Golf Club
103 Chestfield Road
Whitstable
Kent CT5 3LU

Mr MA Sutcliffe
0227-794411

Cherry Lodge Golf Club
Jail Lane
Biggin Hill
Kent TN16 3AX

Chislehurst Golf Club
Camden Park Road
Chislehurst
Kent BR7 5HJ

Mr N.E. Pearson
081-467 2782

Cobtree Manor Park Golf Club
Chatham Road
Boxley
Maidstone
Kent ME14 3AZ

Mr Tony Ferras
0622-753276

Corinthian Golf Club
Gay Dawn Farm
Fawkham Valley Road
Fawkham
Kent DA3 8LY

Ms Lisa Rycraft
0474-707559

Cranbrook Golf Club
Benenden Road
Cranbrook
Kent TN17 4AL

Mr Alan Gillard
0580-712833

Cray Valley Golf Club
Sandy Lane
St. Paul's Cray
Orpington
Kent BR5 3HY

Mr E.R. Hill
0689-839677

Darenth Valley Golf Club
Station Road
Shoreham
Nr Sevenoaks
Kent TN14 7SA

Mr Neil Morgan
0959-522944

COURSES IN KENT

Dartford Golf Club
Dartford Heath
Dartford
Kent

Mrs Margaret Gronow
0322-226455

Edenbridge Golf and Country Club
Crouch House Road
Edenbridge
Kent TN8 5LQ

Mrs J Scully
0732-867381

Faversham Golf Club
Belmont Park
Faversham
Kent ME13 0HB

Mr David Christie
0795-890561

Deangate Ridge Golf Club
24 Trubridge Road
Hoo
Nr Rochester
Kent ME3 9EW

Mr John Orr
0634-255111

Gillingham Golf Club
Woodlands Road
Gillingham ME7 2AP
Kent

Mr Liam O'Grady
0634-853017

Hawkhurst Golf Club
High Street
Hawkhurst
Kent TN18 4JS

Mr Richard Fowles
0580-752396

Herne Bay Golf Club
Eddington
Herne Bay
Kent CT6 7PG

Mr B Warren
0227-373964

Hever Golf Club
Hever
Kent TN8 7NP

Mr Tim Ewer
0732-700771

High Elms Golf Club
High Elms Road
Downe
Orpington
Kent

Mr Pat O'Keefe
0689-858175

Holtye Golf Club
Holtye
Cowden
Nr. Edenbridge
Kent TN8 7ED

Mr J.P. Holmes
0342-850576

Hythe Imperial Golf Club
Prince's Parade
Hythe
Kent CT21 6AE

Mr R Barrett
0303-267554

Knole Park Golf Club
Seal Hollow Road
Sevenoaks
Kent TN15 0HJ

Mr D.J.L. Hoppe
0732-452150

Lamberhurst Golf Club
Church Road
Lamberhurst
Kent TN3 8DT

Mrs P Gleeson
0892-890591

Langley Park Golf Club
Barnfield Wood Road
Beckenham
Kent BR3 2SZ

Mr John Smart
081-658 6849

Leeds Castle Golf Club
Leeds Castle
Hollingbourne
Maidstone
Kent ME17 1PL

Miss Jill Skinner
0622-880467

Littlestone Golf Club
St Andrews Road
Littlestone
New Romney
Kent TH28 8RB

Mr J.D. Lewis
0797-362310

The London Golf Club
South Ash Manor Estate

Stansted Lane
Ash, Sevenoaks
Kent TN15 7EN

Mr Christopher May
0474-879899

Lullingstone Park Golf Club
Parkgate Road
Chelsfield
Kent BR6 7PX

Mr Brian Vallance
0959-533793

Moatlands Golf Club
Watermans Lane
Brenchley
Kent TN12 6ND

Miss S Worster
0892-724400

Mid Kent Golf Club
Shinglewell Road
Gravesend
Kent DA11 7RB

Mr P Quadling
0474-568035

Nevill Golf Club
Benhall Mill Road
Tunbridge Wells
Kent TN2 5JW

Miss Cathleen Pudner
0892-525818

Nizels Golf Club
Nizels Lane
Hildenborough
Tonbridge
Kent TN11 8NX

COURSES IN KENT

Mr Dyke
0732-833138

North Foreland Golf Club
Convent Road
Kingsgate
Broadstairs
Kent CT10 3PU

Mr B.J. Preston
0843-862140

Oastpark Golf Club
Malling Road
Snodland
Kent ME6 5LG

Mrs Valerie Hagger
0634-242818

Poult Wood Public Golf Centre
Higham Lane
Tonbridge
Kent TN11 9QR

Mr A Hope
0732-366180

Prince's Golf Club
Prince's Drive
Sandwich Bay
Sandwich
Kent CT13 9QB

Mr Bill Howie
0304-611118

Redlibbets Golf Club
The Corinthian Sports Club
Fawkham
Lonfield
Kent

Richard Fletton
0474-707559

The Ridge Golf Club
Chartway Street
East Sutton
Maidstone
Kent ME17 3DL

Mr G Sones
0622-844382

The Rochester & Cobham Park Golf Club
Park Pale By Rochester
Kent   ME2 3UL

Mr J.W. Irvine
0474-823411

Romney Warren Golf Club
St Andrews Road
Littlestone
New Romney
Kent TN28 8RB

Mr J.D. Lewis
0797-363355

Ruxley Park Golf Club
Sandy Lane
St. Paul's Cray
Orpington
Kent BR5 3HY

Mr Paul Davis
0689-871490

Royal Cinque Ports Golf Club
Golf Road
Deal
Kent CT14 6RF

Mr C.C. Hammond
0304-367856

Royal St George's Golf Club
Sandwich
Kent CT13 9PB

Mr G.E. Watts
0304-613090

St Augustines Golf Club
Cottington Road
Cliffsend
Ramsgate
Kent CT12 5JN

Mr R.G. Worthington
0843-590333

Sene Valley Golf Club
Blackhouse Hill
Sene
Folkestone
Kent CT18 8BL

Mr R.W. Leaver
0303-268513

Sheerness Golf Club
Power Station Road
Sheerness
Kent ME12 3AE

Mr J.W. Gavins
0795-662585

Shortlands Golf Club
Meadow Road
Shortlands
Bromley
Kent BR2 0PB

Mr Gordon Harrison
081-460 2471

Sidcup Golf Club (1926) Ltd.
7 Hurst Road

Sidcup
Kent DA15 9AE

Mr S Watt
081-300 2150

Sittingbourne & Milton Regis Golf Club
Wormdale
Newington
Sittingbourne
Kent ME9 7PX

Mr H.D.G. Wylie
0795-842261

Sundridge Park Golf Club
Garden Road
Bromley
Kent BR1 3NE

Mr D Lowton
081-460 0278

Sweetwoods Park Golf Club
Cowden
Edenbridge
Kent TN8 7JN

Mr P Strand
0342-850729

Tenterden Golf Club
Woodchurch Road
Tenterden
Kent TN30 7DR

Mr J.B Shaw
0580-763987

Tudor Park Golf Club
Ashford Road
Bearsted
Maidstone
Kent ME14 4NQ

COURSES IN KENT

Mr G Oliver
0622-734334

Tunbridge Wells Golf Club
Langton Road
Tunbridge Wells
Kent TN4 8XH

Mr PF Janes
0892-536918

Upchurch River Valley Golf Courses
Oak Lane
Upchurch
Sittingbourne
Kent ME9 7AY

0634-379592

Walmer & Kingsdown Golf Club
The Leas
Kingsdown
Deal
Kent CT14 8ER

Mr BW Cockerill
0304-373256

Weald of Kent Golf Club
Maidstone Road
Headcorn
Kent TN27 9PT

Mr J Millen
0622-890866

West Kent Golf Club
West Hill
Downe
Orpington
Kent BR6 7JJ

West Malling Golf Club
London Road
Addington

West Malling
Kent ME19 5AR

Mr M.R. Ellis
0732-844785

Westgate & Birchington Golf Club
176 Canterbury Road
Westgate-on-Sea
Kent CT8 8LT

Mr J.M. Wood
0843-831115

Whitstable & Seasalter Golf Club
Collingwood Road
Whitstable
Kent CT5 1EB

Mr G.A. Hodson
0227-272020

Wildernesse Golf Club
Seal
Sevenoaks
Kent TN15 0JE

Mr R Foster
0732-761199

Woodlands Manor Golf Club
Woodlands
Sevenoaks TN15 6AB
Kent

Wrotham Heath Golf Club
7 Mile Lane
Borough Green
Sevenoaks
Kent TN15 6AB

Mr L.J Bryne
0732-884800

Ashford Golf Club

Sandyhurst Lane
Ashford
Kent TN25 4NT

Secretary:

A.H.Story
0233-622655

Professional:

H.Sherman
0233-629644

Directions:

By Car: Off the A20, the course is located 1.5 mile west of Ashford town centre.

By BR: Ashford Station.

Course Details:

This is an eighteen hole parkland course.

A dominant feature is the stream that runs through the course and features on several holes.

Shop Facilities:

The shop is well stocked and offers a wide range of golf equipment and accessories.

Tuition Details:

There are practice facilities and lessons are available from £10 for 1/2 hour.

Contact the Pro shop for details.

Clubhouse Facilities:

Changing facilities are available.

Food is available in the clubhouse from 11.30am. Smart casual dress may be worn, though jeans, track suits, trainers and collarless T-shirts are not permitted in the Clubhouse.

Visitor Restrictions and How to Book:

A handicap certificate is required. Bookings are taken in the Pro shop. Visitors are welcome on weekdays, but must accompany a member at weekends and bank holidays.

Society days are on Tuesdays and Thursdays. Bookings are made through the Secretary.

Visitor Playing Costs:

Weekday:

Day rate - £27.00

Barnehurst Golf Club

Mayplace Road East
Bexleyheath
Kent DA7 6JU

General Manager:
Paul Casey
0322-552952

Professional:
Patrick Tallack
0322-551205

Directions:
By Car: 1.5 miles from Crayford Greyhound Stadium. Take Mayplace Road East from the Town Centre.

By BR: Barnehurst Station (1 mile).

Course Details:
This is a nine hole parkland course with an eighteen hole par of 72.

The 505 yard, par 5, 2nd hole requires two accurate shots to set up a possible birdie. The 17th hole at 415 yards has a slightly uphill second shot to make a tough par. Watch out for the cross bunkers on the last hole known as the 'Spectacles'.

Shop Facilities:
The shop stocks a range of golf equipment, accessories and designer wear.

Sets of clubs can be hired for £5.00.

Tuition Details:
A practice area adjacent to the final hole is used to coach both individuals and classes. Lessons are available from the Head Pro at £12 per 1/2 hour.

Clubhouse Facilities:
Changing facilities including showers are available.

The recently refurbished lounge bar provides a full catering service from 11.00am. Coffee and tea is available from 8.00am.

Visitor Restrictions and How to Book:
A handicap certificate is not required and visitors can play at any time. Book through the Pro shop. Telephone for reservations on 0322-551205

Societies should contact the General Manager for details.

Visitor Playing Costs:
Weekdays / Weekends (18 holes)

£5.70 / £9.20

Bearsted Golf Club

Ware Street
Bearsted
Kent ME14 4PQ

Secretary:

Mrs L. Siems
01622-738198

Professional:

Tim Simpson
01622-738024

Directions:

By Car: Leave the M20 at Junction 7
(A249). Follow the signs to Bearsted
Green. The course is by Bearsted
Railway station.
By BR: Bearsted Station.

Course Details:

This is an eighteen hole, par 72, parkland course.

It features both opening and closing par
3 holes. The short par 4, 11th hole
requires a solid teeshot between two
ponds and over a ditch to a dog-leg second shot to the green. The 17th hole also
requires an accurate drive to avoid the
trees on the left and a pond on the right.

Shop Facilities:

The shop stocks a full range of golf
equipment, accessories and designer
wear.

Tuition Details:

Practice facilities are available. Lessons
cost £15 for 40 minutes and £18 for one
hour. Six lessons can be booked for the
price of five.

Clubhouse Facilities:

A bar and dining room provide daily
catering. A jacket and tie must be worn
in the dining room after 7.00pm. Where
possible, catering should be booked in
advance.

Visitor Restrictions and How to Book:

A handicap certificate is required.
Visitors can play on weekdays and after
4.00pm on weekends.

Book and pay at the Pro shop.

Societies are welcome and should contact the Administration Secretary for
dates and prices.

Visitor Playing Costs:

Weekday:

18 holes - £24.00

Day - £32.00

Weekends:

18 holes - £30.00

Beckenham Place Park Golf Course

The Mansion
Beckenham Place Park
Beckenham
Kent BR3 2BP

Professional:

Huw Davies-Thomas
081-650 2292

Directions:

By Car: Just off the A21 from Bromley to Catford on the A222 to Beckenham. By BR: Beckenham Junction. The station is 300 yards from the Clubhouse.

Course Details:

This is an eighteen hole, 5722 yard, parkland course.

Managed by David Lloyd Leisure plc and set in established woodlands, it is not the most demanding course but offers a pleasant challenge to most levels of player. The inward nine possess the holes to turn a match.

Shop Facilities:

The shop stocks a comprehensive range of golf equipment and accessories. Sets of clubs can be hired for £10 for 18 holes and £5 for 9 holes.

Tuition Details:

A short practice ground of 120 yards in length is available, but for coaching, a larger area is available. Lessons cost £12.50 for 1/2 hour.

Clubhouse Facilities:

There are no showers and changing facilities are restricted.

The clubhouse is open from daylight till dark providing a range of catering facilities from its bar and restaurant. There are no dress restrictions in the Clubhouse.

Visitor Restrictions and How to Book:

As a public course there are no visitor restrictions. Jeans and T-Shirts are not permitted on the course.

It is necessary to book at weekends and bookings can be taken up to one week in advance and in person. There is a booking fee of £3.00.

Societies should contact the Pro shop for details of the times and the packages available.

Visitor Playing Costs:

Weekday / Weekend (18 holes)

Adult (over 18) - £9.15 / £14.70

Winter £8.00 / £13.00

Junior (Mon/Wed/Fri) - £4.80

OAP - £4.80

Bexleyheath Golf Club

Mount Road
Bexleyheath
Kent DA6 8JS

Secretary:

Mr. S.E Squires
081-303 6951

Directions:

By Car: From the A2, exit at the Bexleyheath turn-off. The entrance to the course is in Mount Road.

By BR: Bexleyheath Station.

Course Details:

This is a nine hole parkland course with an eighteen hole length of 4773 yards.

Though short by some standards, it offers a good challenge to a range of players' standards including those looking to improve their short game.

Shop and Tuition Facilities:

There is no shop and there are currently no practice facilities.

Clubhouse Facilities:

The clubhouse has a fully licensed bar which provides a range of snacks and full meals. Catering is limited on Mondays.

Visitor Restrictions and How to Book:

Visitors are welcome on weekdays, but are not permitted at weekends.

A handicap certificate is required.

Casual visitors do not have to book in advance.

Societies are welcome and should contact the Secretary for details of the packages available.

Visitor Playing Costs:

Weekdays Only:

£20.00 per round.

Birchwood Park Golf Club Ltd

Birchwood Road
Wilmington
Dartford
Kent DA2 7HJ

Administration Manager:

Julie Smith

0322-662038

Professional:

Martyn Hirst

0322-660554

Directions:

The course is located just 15 miles from Central London, using either the A2 or A20 and is 5 minutes from Junctions 2 and 3 (M25).

Course Details:

There are two course at Birchwood Park. There is an eighteen hole, 6364 yard parkland course and a nine hole, par 3 course.

The eighteen hole course has a strong finish. The 15th hole is a demanding dog-leg, whilst the 17th and 18th holes both have significant water hazards.

Shop Facilities:

There are two shops on the course stocking a wide range of golf equipment and accessories. Club hire costs £5.

Tuition Details:

There is a 38-bay covered, floodlit driving range and indoor teaching centre.

Lessons are available from £10 per 30 minutes. Video analysis is available at no extra cost.

Clubhouse Facilities:

There are full changing facilities, including showers. Bar snacks and meals are available all day, Monday - Saturday, from 8.00am - 9.30pm.

Visitor Restrictions and How to Book:

Visitors are welcome at any time. No handicap certificate is required (except by juniors on the 18 hole course, unless accompanied by an adult).

Book and pay at the Reception in the clubhouse. Telephone bookings are taken up to 6 days in advance for the 18 hole course on 0322-660554.

A range of Society options are available from £20 per person. Telephone 0322-660554 for a Group Booking form.

Visitor Playing Costs:

Weekday / Weekend: 18 hole course

18 holes - £18.00 / £23.00

Day - £32.00 / £42.00

9 hole course - £4.00 / £5.00

Boughton Golf Club

Brickfield Lane
Boughton
Nr Faversham
Kent ME13 9AJ

Secretary / Professional:

Philip Sparks
0227-752277

Directions:

By Car: Exit Junction 7 (M2) and take the A2 to Dover. 20 yards from round-about, take left turn to Boughton. Drive 1/4 mile to 'T' junction. Turn right and first left into Brickfield Lane.

Course Details:

This is a 6452 yard, eighteen hole, downland course.

Opened in 1993, the course is set in a typical Kent rural setting. The 14th hole has an interesting second shot over water, whilst the 15th hole has a ditch running across the slightly doglegging fairway. The par 5, 4th hole at 621 yards is one of the longest in the country.

Shop Facilities:

The shop stocks a wide range of golf equipment, accessories and designer wear. Half sets of clubs are available for hire at £7.50.

Tuition Details:

There is a practice area adjacent to the clubhouse. Lessons are available from the four P.G.A professionals. Video analysis is available. Contact the Pro shop for details.

Clubhouse Facilities:

Changing facilities, including showers are available.

The Clubhouse has a main bar and lounge providing a range of catering together with a restaurant. There is a galleried snooker room.

Visitor Restrictions and How to Book:

There are no visitor restrictions.

It is possible to book groups of up to 7 players, three days in advance. Contact the Reception from 8.00am - 5.00pm on 0227-752277.

Society packages are available for groups of 8 players and over. Contact the Reception for details.

Visitor Playing Costs:

Weekday / Weekend:

18 holes: £16.00 / £21.00

Day: £24.00 / £32.00

Chart Hills Golf Club

Weeks Lane
Biddenden
Kent TN27 8JX

Director of Golf:

Roger Hyder
0580-292222

Professional:

Roger Hyder
0580-292148

Directions:

By Car: Exit Junction 8 (M20), follow signs to Lenham and Leeds Castle. Pass Leeds Castle and turn left at 'T' junction to Tenterden (A274). After the Heartsay Garage on your right, take first left into Weeks Lane.

Course Details:

This is an eighteen hole, 7,086 yard parkland course.

Opened in 1993 and set in 200 acres, the course provides a range of challenging holes. The 17th hole offers a 'do-or-die' island hole. Water plays a major role on the course. The left hand side of the 13th fairway is bordered all the way by water.

Shop Facilities:

The shop stocks a range of golf equipment, accessories and designer wear.

Tuition Details:

Facilities include a practice range, practice holes and putting greens.

There is an Academy offering a range of coaching options. Lessons are available at £15 for 45 minutes.

Clubhouse Facilities:

The modern clubhouse built to a high specification provides a range of catering facilities. In addition to bars and a restaurant, there are spa's, saunas, a gymnasium, snooker room and other leisure facilities.

Visitor Restrictions and How to Book:

Weekday and weekend slots are available on a limited basis. Members have priority and it is advisable that visitors contact the Pro shop to check availability.

Societies are welcome and a variety of packages are available. Contact Roger Hyder for details.

Visitor Playing Costs:

Limited Availability:

Weekday / Weekend:

18 holes - £45.00 / £48.00

Day - £60.00 / £65.00

Twilight rates are available at £25.00.

Chelsfield Lakes Golf Centre

Court Road
Orpington
Kent BR6 9BX

General Manager:

Derek Howe
0689-896266

Professionals:

Nigel Lee / Bill Hodkin
0689-896266

Directions:

By Car: Court Road (A224) is off Junction 4 (M25).

By BR: Orpington Station.

Course Details:

There are two courses at the Chelsfield Lakes Golf Centre.

There is the 6077 yard eighteen hole, Chelsfield Downs course.

The Warren course is a nine hole, par 3 course.

The front nine of the Chelsfield Downs course offer a downland playing environment in open Kent countryside. The second nine are played back through orchards.

Shop Facilities:

The shop stocks a range of golf equipment and accessories.

Tuition Details:

There is a 40 bay floodlit driving range attached to the course.

Tuition is available for individuals, juniors and groups. Lessons for adults start at £11 for 1/2 hour with an assistant to £13 for 1/2 hour with the Head Pro.

Clubhouse Facilities:

There are full changing facilities, including showers.

The clubhouse provides catering with a bar, restaurant and a private function room. There are special facilities for the handicapped, including ramps and lifts.

Visitor Restrictions and How to Book:

There are no restrictions.

There is a computerised booking system on 0689-896266. Visitors can book up to one week in advance.

Visitor Playing Costs:

Weekdays / Weekends:

£13.00 / £16.00

from 1/4/95: £14.00 / £18.00

There are twilight golf reductions.

Chestfield Golf Club

103 Chestfield Road
Whitstable
Kent CT5 3LU

Secretary:

M.A. Sutcliffe
0227-794411

Professional:

J.J. Brotherton
0227-793563

Directions:

By Car: Off the M2 follow the A299 to Margate / Ramsgate. In Chestfield, the Club is half a mile from Chestfield Station.

By BR: Chestfield Station.

Course Details:

This is an eighteen hole, 6009 yard, parkland course with sea views.

In windy conditions, the 3rd hole, a 225 yard par 3, can play long when into the wind. The 4th hole offers a similar challenge at 434 yards.

Shop Facilities:

The shop is stocked with a wide range of golf equipment and accessories.

Tuition Details:

A full practice area is adjacent to the 13th hole, whilst a practice net, bunker and pitching area is adjacent to the 1st hole. Lessons cost £12 for 45 minutes. Video analysis is available at £15.

Clubhouse Facilities:

Full changing facilities are available.

A wide range of catering facilities are available, together with a licensed bar from 11.00am - 11.00pm.

Visitor Restrictions and How to Book:

A handicap certificate is required. Visitors are welcome during the week but are not permitted on weekends, unless accompanying a member. Thursday is Ladies Day.

For booking enquiries, contact the Secretary's office on 0227-794411.

Societies are welcome with a minimum of 12 members. Contact the Secretary's office for details.

Visitor Playing Costs:

Weekday Only:

18 holes - £18.00

Day - £28.00

Chislehurst Golf Club

Camden Park Road
Chislehurst
Kent BR7 5HJ

Secretary:

N.E. Pearson
081-467 2782

Professional:

M. Lawrence
081-467 6798

Directions:

By Car: Drive down Prince Imperial Road from Chislehurst High Street. Camden Park Road is on the right.

By BR: Chislehurst Station.

Course Details:

This is an eighteen hole, par 66, parkland course. At just 4809 yards, this is a fairly short course featuring 8 par 3 holes and can lead to some over-use. The course itself is situated in 68 acres of pleasant parkland setting.

Shop Facilities:

The shop stocks a range of golf equipment and accessories.

Tuition Details:

There is no practice area but tuition is available. Lessons cost £15/£10 for 30 minutes with the Head Pro/Assistant. Video analysis is available. A 9 hole playing lesson with the Head Pro costs £35. Contact the Pro shop to book.

Clubhouse Facilities:

The clubhouse provides lunchtime food and bar facilities. Societies can book evening meals through the Secretary's office. The Clubhouse is only available to members and guests at weekends.

Visitor Restrictions and How to Book:

Visitors are welcome on weekdays but must accompany a member at the weekend. Bookings are taken through the Professional shop.

Societies are welcome and should contact the Secretary for details of the Society options available.

Visitor Playing Costs:

Weekdays Only:

Day - £25.00

Society - (36 holes - £33)

(Thursday only for 36 holes)

Catering (by prior arrangement) - The Club Caterer: 081-467 2888

Cranbrook Golf Club

Benenden Road
Cranbrook
Kent TN17 4AL

Secretary / Professional:

Alan Gillard
0580-712833

Directions:

By Car: Turn off the M25 Junction 5 (south) onto the A21 Hastings Road. Follow the A262 for Ashford into Sissinghurst village. Turn right at the Bull. The course lies approximately 1.5 miles south of Sissinghurst.

Course Details:

This is an eighteen hole, par 70, parkland course.

The course is heavily wooded and gently undulating with natural ponds coming into play on 5 holes. The par 4,14th hole plays downhill between an avenue of trees leaving a 2nd shot over a pond to a well-bunkered green backed by forest.

Shop Facilities:

The shop doubles as Reception and stocks a full range of golf equipment and accessories. Club hire is available at £7.50 per round (bookable in advance).

Tuition Details:

There is a practice ground and warm up area with nets close to the 1st hole. Coaching is available from the Professional at £15 for 40 minutes.

Clubhouse Facilities:

The clubhouse, a converted oast, provides changing facilities, including showers. Smart casual wear can be worn in all parts of the Clubhouse.

Visitor Restrictions and How to Book:

Handicap certificates are not required. Visitors can play on all days though the following time restrictions apply. Tuesday (after 9.30am): Thursday (after 10.30am): Weekends (between 12.00 - 12.30 or after 3.30pm).

Book through the Reception on 0580-712833.

Societies should contact the Reception for details.

Visitor Playing Costs:

Weekday:

18 holes -£19.00

Day - £30.00

Weekend:

18 holes only - £27.00

Cray Valley Golf Club

Sandy Lane
St. Pauls Cray
Orpington
Kent BR5 3HY

Secretary:

Mr E.R Hill
0689-839677

Professional:

John Gregory
0689-837909

Directions:

By Car: Off the Ruxley roundabout, turn into Sandy Lane. The course is 3/4 of a mile on the left.

Course Details:

This is an eighteen hole, par 70, parkland course.

The course is reasonably flat and well-wooded. It is fairly short and offers a testing and enjoyable round of golf.

Shop Facilities:

The shop stocks the leading brands of golf equipment and accessories.

Club hire is available on weekdays at £7.50 for 18 holes and all week at £3.80 for 9 holes.

Tuition Details:

There is a practice area and lessons are available. Prices for group classes start at £25 for 5 one hour sessions. Contact John Gregory for full details.

Clubhouse Facilities:

The clubhouse provides changing facilities, including showers.

Snacks are available all day. There is a fully licensed bar and restaurant. Smart casual wear is required.

Visitor Restrictions:

No handicap certificate is required.

It is necessary to book at weekends. Call the shop on 0689-837909 to book. Weekday bookings can be made at the Pro shop.

Tuesday am is Ladies Day between 10.00am - 11.00am.

Societies are welcome and should contact the Secretary's office on 0689-839677.

Visitor Playing Costs:

Weekday:

£11.00 (after 2.00pm - £8.00)

Weekend:

£16.00

(after 3.00pm - £8.00)

Darenth Valley Golf Club

Station Road
Shoreham
Nr Sevenoaks
Kent TN14 7SA

Secretary:
Neil Morgan
0959-522944

Professional:
Scott Fotheringham
0959-522922

Directions:
By Car: East of Shoreham village off the A225.

By BR: Next to Shoreham Station.

Course Details:
This is an eighteen hole, 6195 yard, par 72, parkland course.

Relatively flat, the course features a number of tight entrances to small greens. The 4th and 12th holes, both par 4's, are probably the most challenging holes on the course at 455 and 442 yards respectively. The 8th and 17th holes are certainly the most picturesque.

Shop Facilities:
The shop stocks a wide range of golf equipment and accessories. Club hire is available at £7.50 per round.

Tuition Details:
The course has two grass teaching grounds and driving nets. Lessons are available at £15 for 40 minutes. Contact the Pro shop to book.

Clubhouse Facilities:
Changing facilities, including showers are available.

The bar and dining room can cater for up to 150 covers. Food is available until 8.00pm. Denims are not allowed.

Visitor Restrictions and How to Book:
Tee times must be booked through the professional shop. These can be booked up to a week in advance. A booking fee of £1 is charged on weekdays and £2 on weekends and bank holidays.

Society bookings should be made via the Secretary and a range of packages are available, including coffee on arrival, 18 holes, buffet lunch, 18 holes and 5-course evening meal at £45.

Visitor Playing Costs:
Weekday / Weekend:

18 holes - £12.00 / £16.00

Twilight - £8.00 / £12.00

OAP / Juniors 18 holes - £7.00

9 holes - £5.00

Edenbridge Golf and Country Club

Crouch House Road
Edenbridge
Kent TN8 5LQ

Secretary:

Mrs. Judith Scully
0732-867381

Professional:

Mr. Keith Burkin
0732-865097

Directions:

By Car: Exit Junction 6 (M25), take the A22 to Godstone, then turn left onto the A25 to Sevenoaks. After 3 miles, take the B2026 to Edenbridge.

Course Details:

There are two courses at Edenbridge. The Old Course is an eighteen hole, gently undulating parkland course. The 9th hole is a 385 yard, par 4 with water hazards off the tee and in front of the green. The 191 yard, 15th hole is surrounded by water. The Skeynes course is slightly more undulating than the Old course with some very testing par 3's. There is a 9 hole, par 3 course, together with a 9 hole pitch and putt.

Shop Facilities:

The shop stocks a wide range of golf equipment, accessories and designer wear. Clubs can be hired for £5.00.

Tuition Details:

A 16-bay floodlit driving range is attached to the course. There is also a pitching area and two putting greens. Coaching is available from £12.00 per 1/2 hour. Video training is available at £20 for 45 minutes.

Clubhouse Facilities:

Full changing facilities, including showers are available. The clubhouse provides extensive catering facilities with three bars and a restaurant. A jacket and tie is required in the dining room.

There is a fully equipped gym, sunbed and toning rooms. There are also five tennis courts.

Visitor Restrictions and How to Book:

Visitors are welcome on the Old course, though prior bookings are required. The Skeynes course is available at all times. Book (up to 6 days in advance) and pay through the Pro shop.

Societies are welcome. Contact the Secretary for details.

Visitor Playing Costs:

(Weekday / Weekend)

Old Course - £15.00 / £18.00

Skeynes - £10.00 / £12.00

Faversham Golf Club

Belmont Park
Faversham
Kent ME13 0HB

Secretary:
David Christie
0795-890561

Professional:
Stuart Rokes
0795-890275

Directions:
By Car: Exit A251 off the M2 towards Faversham. Turn left at the A2 junction towards Sittingbourne. Turn left into Brogdale Road and follow the road for 3 miles bearing left at any junction.

Course Details:
This is an eighteen hole parkland course.

The first 6 holes are tree-lined and tight, providing a testing start to the round. The course has good quality greens and provides a pleasant round of golf.

Shop Facilities:
The shop is well stocked with a range of leading golf brands and accessories.

Tuition Details:
There are two practice areas and coaching is available from the two teaching professionals. Lessons cost £12.50 for 30-40 minutes. Contact Stuart Rokes in the Pro shop for details.

Clubhouse Facilities:
Changing facilities are available, including showers.

The clubhouse provides full catering and bar facilities. No jeans, sweat shirts, trainers, T-shirts or shorts are allowed in the clubhouse.

Visitor Restrictions and How to Book:
A handicap certificate is required. Visitors are welcome on weekdays but are not permitted at weekends, unless accompanying a member. Telephone bookings are accepted.

Society days are available on Tuesday (max. 16) and Wednesday and Friday (max. 44). Enquire initially through the Secretary's office.

Visitor Playing Costs:
Weekday:

18 holes - £25.00

Day - £30.00

Hawkhurst Golf Club

High Street
Hawkhurst
Kent TN18 4JS

Secretary:

Richard C. Fowles
0580-752396

Professional:

Tony Collins
0580-753600

Directions:

By Car: From the A21, the course is located on the A268 Rye road from Tunbridge Wells.

Course Details:

This is a nine hole, parkland course. From different tees, this plays as a 6,000 yard eighteen hole course.

This is a tight course with out of bounds dangers on the left hand side of 14 holes. The course has some lovely views. Two of the par 3 holes play over a pond and a river.

Shop Facilities:

The shop stocks a range of golf equipment and accessories. Club hire is available.

Tuition Details:

There is a practice net, together with a practice hole, bunker and green. Video analysis is available. Lessons cost £15 for 30 minutes.

Contact Tony Collins on 0580-753600 to book.

Clubhouse Facilities:

Changing facilities are available with Gents and Ladies locker rooms.

There is a large bar/restaurant and a function room is available.

A security card system is in operation in the Clubhouse.

Visitor Restrictions and How to Book:

Visitors are welcome on weekdays, but must accompany a member at weekends.

Advance booking is not necessary for casual visitors. Pay at the Pro shop.

Societies are welcome. Contact Tony Collins in the Pro shop for details of the packages available.

Visitor Playing Costs:

Weekdays Only:

9 holes - £9.00

18 holes/day - £15.00

Hever Golf Club

Hever
Kent TN8 7NP

Secretary:

Tim Ewer
0732-700771

Professional:

John Powell
0732-700785

Directions:

By Car: From the M25 follow the A21 to Hastings. Follow signs to Hever Castle. The club is 1/2 a mile before the Castle entrance.

Course Details:

This is a 6502 yard (from the yellow tees), 6761 (from the white tees) and 7002 yard (from the blue tees), eighteen hole parkland course.

Water comes into play on 10 of the eighteen holes. The feature holes are the par 3, 12th hole which resembles the 12th at Augusta and the par 5, 17th hole at 644 yards. (one of the longest in Europe).

Shop Facilities:

The shop stocks a range of golf equipment and accessories. Sets of clubs are available for hire at £10 per round.

Tuition Details:

There are two practice areas. One is full length and adjacent to the 1st tee. The other is 150 yards long with a bunker. Nets are also available.

Lessons starts at £15.00 for 30 minutes. Contact the Pro shop on 0732-700785 for details.

Clubhouse Facilities:

Full changing facilities, including showers are available.

A bar and restaurant provide daily catering. (Members only in first floor lounge). There is an all day spike bar.

A jacket and tie must be worn after 7.30pm.

Visitor Restrictions and How to Book:

A handicap certificate is required. Visitors are welcome on weekdays and after 11.00am at weekends in maximum groups of 4.

Tuesday is Ladies Day.

Societies are welcome on weekdays. All bookings and enquiries should be made through Tim Ewer on 0732-700711.

Visitor Playing Costs:

Weekday / Weekend

18 holes - £26.00 / £39.00

Day - £39.00 / £55.00 (after 11.00am)

Holtye Golf Club

Holtye
Cowden
Nr. Edenbridge
Kent TN8 7ED

Secretary:

Mr. J.P. Holmes
0342-850576

Professional:

Mr. K. Hinton
0342-850635

Directions:

By Car: The course is located mid-way between East Grinstead and Tunbridge Wells on the A264.

Course Details:

This is a nine hole, heathland course with alternative tees on the back nine.

The course is 101 years old and its feature hole is the 4th/13th: a par 3 that plays to a small island green.

Shop Facilities:

The shop stocks a range of golf equipment and accessories.

Tuition Details:

There is a large practice ground and coaching is available. Lessons with the Pro cost £10 for 30 minutes. Contact the Pro shop for details.

Clubhouse Facilities:

Full changing facilities, including showers are available.

Food is available in the bar from 11.30am - 2.30pm daily. Evening food is available on Wednesdays and Fridays.

Visitor Restrictions and How to Book:

A handicap certificate is not required. Visitors are not allowed to play on Wednesday, Thursday, Saturday or Sunday mornings.

Societies are welcomed on Tuesdays and Fridays.

All bookings are taken through the Secretary.

Visitor Playing Costs:

Weekday:

18 holes / Day - £15.00

Weekend:

£18.00 (pm only)

9 holes:

£10.00

Knole Park Golf Club

Seal Hollow Road
Sevenoaks
Kent TN15 0HJ

Secretary:

D. J. L Hoppe
0732-452150

Professional:

P. E. Gill
0732-451740

Directions:

By Car: 1/2 mile from the centre of Sevenoaks on Seal Hollow Road.

Course Details:

This is an eighteen hole, 6249 yards (from the medal tees), par 70, parkland course.

The course enjoys views of Knole House and is set in one of the oldest deer parks in the UK. Many of the holes feature well established trees and they form an important role on this attractive undulating course.

Shop Facilities:

The shop stocks a wide range of golfing equipment and accessories.

Tuition Details:

Coaching is available, though the practice ground facilities are limited. Lessons cost £10 for 30 minutes. Contact the Pro shop to book.

Clubhouse Facilities:

Changing facilities are available for visiting players.

The traditional clubhouse offers a range of catering and bar facilities.

Visitor Restrictions and How to Book:

Whilst a handicap certificate is preferred, visitors must be bona fide players and understand the etiquette of golf. Visitors should book through the Secretary's office.

Society days are normally Tuesday, Thursday and Friday. Small groups of 12 or under can often be accommodated on any weekday, provided the course is free.

Contact the Secretary to enquire.

Visitor Playing Costs:

18 holes - £26.00

Day - £37.00

Langley Park Golf Club

Barnfield Wood Road
Beckenham
Kent BR3 2SZ

Secretary:

John Lyall Smart
081-658 6849

Professional:

Colin Staff
081-650 1663

Directions:

By Car: 1 mile from Bromley South Station via Westmoreland Road off Bromley High Street at the Mason's Hill road junction. (A21)

Course Details:

This is an eighteen hole 6,488 yard parkland course.

The course has 8 par 4's over 400 yards and plays alongside tree-lined fairways. The round finishes with a short par 3 over a lake to the green.

Shop Facilities:

The shop stocks a wide range of golf equipment, accessories and designer wear. Sets of clubs are available for hire by prior arrangement.

Tuition Details:

Coaching is provided by the PGA qualified staff on the practice areas. Lessons cost £10/£12 for 30 minutes from the Assistant/Head Pro. Six lessons can be booked for the price of five.

Clubhouse Facilities:

There are full changing facilities, including showers.

Catering is provided in the bar, lounge and restaurant. Golfing attire is allowed in the lounge and bar until 11.30am after which collar, jacket and tie are required.

Visitor Restrictions and How to Book:

A handicap certificate is required.

Visitors are welcome during the week but are not permitted to play at weekends unless accompanying a member. Book and pay through the Pro shop.

Societies are welcome to play on Wednesdays, though groups of up to 24 players can play on Thursdays. For full details of available packages and prices, contact the Secretary's office.

Visitor Playing Costs:

Weekdays Only:

18 holes or day: £35.00

Leeds Castle Golf Club

Leeds Castle
Hollingbourne
Maidstone
Kent ME17 1PL

Secretary:

Jill Skinner
0622-880467

Professional:

Chris Miller
0622-880467

Directions:

By Car: Off Junction 8, M2. Follow the signs to Leeds Castle. Situated off the A20 in the car park of the Park Gate Inn.

Course Details:

This is a 9 hole, 2880 yard, par 34, parkland course.

Dominated by Leeds Castle, the course has some fine holes. The 5th hole requires a second shot to be lined up on one of the towers. To overshoot means you make contact with the moat. The 7th hole also offers a death or glory water hazard.

Shop Facilities:

The shop stocks a full range of golf equipment, accessories and designer wear. Golf sets are available for hire at £10 for a full set and £5 for a half set.

Tuition Details:

An extensive practice area includes driving areas, bunkers and greens. Lessons are available at £12.50 for a 1/2 hour session or £45.00 for 5 sessions. Tuition is available for both the blind and disabled.

Clubhouse Facilities:

Changing facilities and showers are available.

Refreshments are on sale in the professional shop, whilst more extensive catering facilities are provided in the Park Gate Inn, situated in the car park of the course.

Visitor Restrictions and How to Book:

No handicap certificate is required, though visitors should be bona fide players. Bookings can be taken over the telephone. 4 ball booking times are at 10 minute intervals.

Bookings for societies and companies (over 16 in number) can be taken up to 2 years in advance. Weekend Society bookings require a deposit. Telephone 0622-880467 for reservations.

Visitor Playing Costs:

9 holes - £9.00

18 holes (weekday) - £15.50

Juniors (9 holes) - weekdays - £6.50

Moatlands Golf Club

Watermans Lane
Brenchley
Kent TN12 6ND

Secretary:

Miss S. Worster

0892-724400

Professional:

Mr. Tom Murphy

0892-724252

Directions:

By Car: From the A21 (Sevenoaks to Hastings) take the B2160 to Matfield / Paddock Wood. Drive through Matfield and continue downhill through double bends, turn right at post box into Chantlers Hill and then right again into Watermans Lane.

Course Details:

This is a 6230 yard, eighteen hole parkland course.

The par 4, 8th hole is probably the hardest on the course at 452 yards with an uphill tee shot into the prevailing wind. One of the largest bunkers in the region, the 'Gobi', protects the double 9th and 18th green.

Shop Facilities:

The shop stocks a range of golf equip-ment, accessories and designer wear. Sets of Pings are available for hire at £15.00 per set.

Tuition Details:

There are practice areas and lessons are available from £12.50 per 1/2 hour with an Assistant Pro to £15.00 with the Head Pro.

Clubhouse Facilities:

Full changing facilities, including show-ers are available. A fully licensed bar and restaurant provide food all day.

There are currently outdoor tennis courts, and a health club and swimming pool are to be opened shortly.

Visitor Restrictions and How to Book:

A handicap certificate is preferred and visitors are not permitted to play before 11.30am at weekends. Visitors should book through the Pro Shop on 0892-724252.

Societies are welcome on Mondays and Thursdays. A range of society packages are available from £40.00 - £54.00. Contact the Secretary for further details.

Visitor Playing Costs:

Weekday / Weekend:

18 holes: £25.00 / £35.00

Day: £40.00 / £50.00

Oastpark Golf Club

Malling Road
Snodland
Kent ME6 5LG

Secretary:

Mrs. Valerie Hagger
0634-242818

Professional:

Terry Cullen
0634-242661

Directions:

By Car: Exit Junction 2 (M2) onto the A228 to Snodland. The course is located behind the Sandhole Farm shop on Malling Road.

Course Details:

This is an eighteen hole parkland course.

Several holes play through orchards and there are also some interesting water holes. It is a course that will appeal to all levels of golfer.

Shop Facilities:

The shop stocks a good range of golf equipment and accessories.

Tuition Details:

There is a large practice area, with facilities for both chipping and putting. Lessons cost £10/£12.50 for 30 minutes with the Assistant/Head Pro. A course of 5 lessons costs £45/£55.

Contact Terry Cullen in the Pro shop to book.

Clubhouse Facilities:

The clubhouse which is open during all playing hours provides a varied menu in its licensed bar and restaurant.

Visitor Restrictions and How to Book:

There are no restrictions for visitors. Tee-times can be booked up to 3 days in advance by telephoning the Pro shop on 0634-242661.

Societies are welcome on weekdays. There are several packages on offer and these can be booked through the Secretary's office which is open from 8.30am- 4.30pm.

Visitor Playing Costs:

Weekday / Weekend:

Adults: £10.00 / £13.00

Juniors: £5.00 / £6.50

Poult Wood Public Golf Centre

Higham Lane
Tonbridge
Kent TN11 9QR

Secretary:

Mr. A. Hope
0732-366180

Directions:

By Car: Just off the A227 Gravesend Road and 3 miles north of Tonbridge Town Centre.

By BR: Tonbridge Station.

Course Details:

There are two course at Poult Wood. There is a 5569 yard, eighteen hole woodland course. Set in 92 acres of former woodland, many of the oaks, birch and ash have been retained to give a rural setting.

There is a new short 9 hole course set in ancient woodland now open.

Shop Facilities:

The shop stocks a good range of golf equipment and accessories. Club hire is available at £6.50 a set.

Tuition Details:

The practice ground, nets and putting green are available free to the general public when not in use by the visiting Pro. (Ken Adwick on 0622-812719 will give individual tuition. Contact Ken for details.)

Clubhouse Facilities:

Changing facilities, including showers are available.

The bar and restaurant on the first floor have recently been refurbished and provide a full range of all day catering. There is a spike snack bar opposite the Pro shop. In addition, there are 4 squash courts on the ground floor.

Visitor Restrictions and How to Book:

There are no restrictions for visitors. A Registered Golfer scheme exists to enable golfers to book for weekends in advance. (Residents £7.00pa / Non-Residents £14.00pa). Weekdays can either be booked in advance by Registered golfers or on a first come, first served basis.

Societies are welcome. Contact the Clubhouse Manager on 0732-366180 for details of packages on offer.

Visitor Playing Costs:

18 hole course: Adult / Junior and OAP:

Weekday: £8.40 / £4.90

Weekend: £12.60

Prince's Golf Club

Prince's Drive
Sandwich Bay
Sandwich
Kent CT13 9QB

Secretary:

Bill Howie
0304-611118

Professional:

Chris Evans
0304-613797

Directions:

By Car: Follow the M2/A2 to Dover.
Take the A256 to Sandwich and follow
signs.

By BR: Sandwich Station.

Course Details:

This is a 27 hole traditional links championship course.

Initially constructed in 1904 and
redesigned in 1952 to facilitate 3 loops
of 9 holes: 'Dunes', 'Himalayas' and
'Shore' from a central clubhouse, this
course has hosted most major competitions including the Open.

Shop Facilities:

The shop stocks a range of golf equipment and accessories. Club hire is available on request.

Tuition Details:

There is a driving range, chipping area,
pitching area and practice bunkers and
green. Lessons cost £13 per 1/2 hour
with the Head Pro. Video analysis is
available at £25 per hour.

Clubhouse Facilities:

A purpose built modern clubhouse was
opened by Peter Allis in 1985. It provides extensive catering from 7.30am
till dusk, 7 days a week. The upstairs
lounge and restaurant cater for up to
200. There is a separate members bar.
Jacket and tie is not mandatory for dinner.

Visitor Restrictions and How to Book:

Visitors are welcome 7 days a week and
are expected to have a handicap. There
are no restrictions on lady visitors.
Casual bookings should contact the Pro
shop.

Societies are welcome (up to 160) and
should contact the Society Secretary,
Mike Stone, on 0304-611118, for details
of the Society packages available.

Visitor Playing Costs:

Weekday / Saturday / Sunday:

18 holes - £31.00 / £35.50 / £35.50

Day - £36.00 / £41.00 / £46.50

Royal Cinque Ports

Golf Road
Deal
Kent CT14 6RF

Secretary:

CC Hammond
0304-374007

Professional:

A. Reynolds
0304-374170

Directions:

By Car: Take the A258 from Dover to Deal. The course is approximately 1 mile north of the town.

Course Details:

This is a 6406 yard, eighteen hole links course.

As with many links courses, the wind and the weather can pose the greatest challenge. The fairways are narrow, well-bunkered with an undulating surface falling into fairly thick rough. Accuracy is very important. The finishing holes provide a serious test to a good card.

Shop Facilities:

The shop stocks a good range of golf equipment and accessories.

Tuition Details:

Lessons are available. Contact the Pro shop on 0304-374170 for details.

Clubhouse Facilities:

Full changing facilities are available.

Hot and cold snacks are provided all day by the bar, lounge and dining room. More extensive meals are available in the evening by arrangement.

A jacket and tie is required.

Visitor Restrictions and How to Book:

Visitors are permitted on weekdays, but must accompany a member at weekends.

Visitors must have a current handicap certificate (maximum 20) and be a member of a recognised golf club. Visitors should book by prior arrangement with the Office.

Societies are welcome on weekdays. Contact the Secretary on 0304-374007 for details.

Visitor Playing Costs:

Weekdays Only: 2 ball play only.

£45.00 per day / round (before 1.00pm)

£35.00 (after 1.00pm)

Royal St George's Golf Club

Sandwich
Kent CT13 9PB

Secretary:

Mr. G.E Watts
0304-613090

Professional:

Mr. Niall Cameron
0304-615236

Directions:

By Car: Take the A257 from Canterbury to Sandwich. Then follow the signs. The course is 1.5 miles on the seaward side of the town.

Course Details:

This is an eighteen hole championship links course. At 6,903 yards, the course offers the strictest test of golf with the dunes, the undulations and the weather all posing the visitor with difficult club positions and decisions. Who can forget Greg Norman's sensational final round 64 to take the 1993 Open Championship on this course.

Shop Facilities:

The shop stocks a wide range of golf equipment, accessories and designer wear.

Tuition Details:

There is an extensive practice ground. Lessons are available from the resident Pro staff at £20/£25 per hour with the Assistant/Head Professional. Contact the Pro shop to book.

Clubhouse Facilities:

There is a visitors locker room with full facilities.

A wide range of catering is provided by the snack bar, dining room and smoking room. Breakfast and dinner can be arranged by prior arrangement. Jacket and tie are required in the public rooms at all times.

Visitor Restrictions and How to Book:

Visitors are not permitted to play at weekends or on public holidays. Men must have a minimum handicap of 18 and Ladies of 15. There are no Ladies tees on the course. All tee-times must be pre-booked via the Secretary.

Societies are welcome. Full details of arrangements can be obtained from the Secretary's office.

Visitor Playing Costs:

Weekdays Only:

18 holes - £50.00

Day - £70.00

Ruxley Park Golf Centre

Sandy Lane
St. Paul's Cray
Orpington
Kent BR5 3HY

Secretary:

Paul Davis
0689-871490

Professional:

Richard Pilbury
0689-871490

Directions:

By Car: Exit Junction 3 (M25). The course is off the Ruxley roundabout on the A20.

Course Details:

There are two courses at Ruxley Park.

There is an eighteen hole, 5,800 yard parkland course. Set in rolling Kent countryside, the course provides some scenic views. The course offers a testing game that will suit most levels of golfer.

There is also a short, par 3, 9 hole course, ideal for beginners and those seeking to improve their short game, at £2.50 per round.

Shop Facilities:

The shop stocks a range of golf equipment and accessories. Club hire is available at £1 per 9 holes.

Tuition Details:

There is a 28 bay floodlit driving range attached to the course, together with practice bunker and chipping green. 7 PGA professional staff provide coaching at all levels.

Lessons are available at £10/£12.50 for 30 mins with the Assistant/Head Pro. 5 lessons are available at £45/£55 with the Assistant/Head Pro.

Contact the Pro shop for details.

Clubhouse Facilities:

Changing facilities are available. The clubhouse provides catering facilities in its bar and lounge from 8.00am - 11.00pm.

Visitor Restrictions and How to Book:

There are no visitor restrictions. Bookings are taken up to 6 days in advance on a computerised booking system. Telephone 0689-871490 to book.

Societies are welcome. Contact the Secretary's office for details.

Visitor Playing Costs:

Weekdays / Weekends:

from £7.00 / £10.00

Sene Valley Golf Club

Blackhouse Hill
Sene
Folkstone
Kent CT18 8BL

Secretary:

R. Leaver
0303-268513

Professional:

P. Moger
0303-268514

Directions:

By Car: The Club is situated on the B2065 just outside Hythe on Blackhouse Hill. From London, exit Junction 12 (M20) and take the A20 to the Etchinghill roundabout. Turn left towards Hythe.

Course Details:

This is a 5,944 yard, eighteen hole downland course.

This Henry Cotton designed course has views across the English channel. Accuracy is perhaps more important than length, since the rough can punish the wayward shot.

Shop Facilities:

The shop stocks a good range of golf equipment and accessories.

Tuition Details:

Coaching is available on the practice ground. Lessons cost £10 for 30 minutes. Contact the Pro shop for details.

Clubhouse Facilities:

Changing facilities are available.

The clubhouse provides a range of catering facilities with a bar, dining room and lounge which enjoy views of the coastline. Catering is limited on Mondays. Snooker is also available.

Visitor Restrictions and How to Book:

A handicap certificate is required. From 1st April - 31st October, it is necessary to pre-book a starting time through the Pro shop.

Societies are welcomed on Wednesdays, Thursdays and Fridays. There should be a minimum of 12 players. Contact the Secretary for details and booking.

Visitor Playing Costs:

Weekday / Weekend:

£20.00 / £30.00

There is a 50% discount for members of the Kent or Sussex Golf Unions.

Sidcup Golf Club (1926) Ltd.

7 Hurst Road
Sidcup
Kent DA15 9AE

Secretary:

Sandy Watt
081-300 2150

Professional:

John Murray
081-309 0679

Directions:

By Car: 2 miles from the A2/A20, the course is located on the A222.

By BR: Sidcup Station.

Course Details:

This is a nine hole parkland course which is 5722 yards in length over eighteen holes.

Founded 104 years ago, the major feature of the course is a large lake which comes into play on four holes with particular impact on the 3rd and 4th holes.

Shop Facilities:

The shop stocks a range of golf equipment and accessories.

Tuition Details:

There is a small practice ground and tuition is available from the resident PGA qualified professional. Lessons cost £12 for 1/2 hour and £20 for 1 hour. Contact John Murray on 081-309 0679 to book.

Clubhouse Facilities:

There is a fully licensed bar providing a full range of refreshments. Sandwiches, tea and coffee are available in addition to full meals.

Smart casual dress is required in the bar.

Visitor Restrictions and How to Book:

Visitors are welcome on weekdays, but at weekends must accompany a member.

Book through the Pro shop. Visitors are advised to check by telephone with regards to availability.

Societies (max. 30) are welcome. Contact the Secretary for details. Meals and their cost need to be agreed with the franchised caterer.

Visitor Playing Costs:

Weekdays Only:

£18.00 per round / day.

St Augustines Golf Club

Cottington Road
Cliffsend
Ramsgate
Kent CT12 5JN

Secretary:

R.G Worthington
0843-590333

Professional:

D. Scott
0843-590222

Directions:

By Car: Exit M2 at Canterbury onto the A299 to Ramsgate. At Margate, take the A253 to Manston Airport. Turn right into Thorn Hill, then left at crossroads. The club entrance is on right under the railway bridge.

Course Details:

This is a 5,138 yard, eighteen hole links course.

Not the longest course, but still challenging for the experienced golfer. Those with a tendency to slice will suffer: nowhere more than with the opening shot on the 1st tee. Like many links courses, variable wind conditions can make club selection difficult.

Shop Facilities:

The shop stocks a wide range of golf equipment, accessories and designer wear.

Tuition Details:

There is a practice ground, together with facilities for chipping and putting. Lessons from the resident Professional are £9.50 per half hour.

Clubhouse Facilities:

The clubhouse has full changing facilities.

A range of catering is provided during the day in the licensed bar and dining room. A jacket and tie should be worn in the dining room after 6.00pm. Summer Dress for gents.

Visitor Restrictions and How to Book:

Visitors must be members of a recognised golf club and must hold a handicap certificate. Visitors are welcome from Mondays to Saturdays. Green fees must be booked through the Pro shop.

Society packages are available. Discounts are available at off peak rates. Contact the Pro shop on 0843-590222 for details.

Visitor Playing Costs:

Weekday: £20.00

Weekend: £22.00

Off-Peak: £10.00

Sundridge Park Golf Club

Garden Road
Bromley
Kent BR1 3NE

Secretary:

D. Lowton
081-460 0278

Professional:

B. Cameron
081-460 5540

Directions:

By Car: Exit Junction 3/4 (M25). The course is located one mile north of Bromley, off Plaistow Lane opposite Sundridge Park Station.

Course Details:

There are two courses at Sundridge Park.

The East course is a 6,201 yard eighteen hole, parkland course. Chin Brook comes into play on the 4th and 5th holes.

The West course is a 5,716 yard eighteen hole course, with more water hazards, including a pond on the 12th hole. Both courses play around Sundridge Mansion.

Shop Facilities:

The shop stocks a good range of golfing equipment, accessories and designer wear.

Tuition Details:

Coaching is available. Lessons cost £15/£25 for 45 minutes with the Assistant/Head Professional. Contact the Pro shop on 081-460 5540 for further details.

Clubhouse Facilities:

There is a Clubhouse and Ladies clubhouse. Full changing and locker room facilities are available. The clubhouse has bars and restaurants which provide catering throughout the day.

Visitor Restrictions and How to Book:

A handicap certificate is required. Alternatively a letter of introduction from a current club secretary. Visitors are not permitted to play at weekends or bank holidays, unless as a guest of a member. Bookings are taken in the Pro shop.

Societies are welcome up to a maximum of 80. Contact the Secretary for details of the packages available.

Visitor Playing Costs:

Weekday:

18 holes / Day - £36.00

Tenterden Golf Club

Woodchurch Road
Tenterden
Kent TN30 7DR

Secretary:

J.B Shaw
01580-763987

Professional:

Darren Lewis
01580-762409

Directions:

By Car: 1 mile south east of Tenterden on the B2067 (Woodchurch Road)

Course Details:

Founded in 1905, this is an eighteen hole, par 70, 6050 yard parkland course.

A number of holes pose particular challenges. Both the par 4, 12th hole, and the par 4, 17th hole become difficult in east and south westerly winds respectively. The 17th's elevated green is guarded by two streams across the fairway.

Shop Facilities:

The shop stocks a full range of golf equipment, accessories and designer clothing. Golf cars can be hired at £15 per round and £25 per day.

Tuition Details:

There is a practice ground and coaching facilities are available. Lessons cost £10 per 1/2 hour or £18 for 1 hour. Societies can be videoed on request as the Club has full video recording facilities. Video analysis costs £15 for 40 minutes.

Clubhouse Facilities:

Changing facilities are available.

Bar food snacks are available from 11.00am - dusk. Full restaurant facilities are available at peak times.

Visitor Restrictions and How to Book:

A handicap certificate is not required though an understanding of golf etiquette is essential. Visitors are welcome on weekdays, but must accompany a member at weekends.

Green fees can be booked through the Pro shop. Tees are not reserved, but with two starting points (1st & 10th) near the Clubhouse, visitors will be informed of availability.

Societies are welcomed. Please contact the Secretary for information.

Visitor Playing Costs:

Weekday only:

18 holes - £20.00

The Rochester & Cobham Park Golf Club

Park Pale By Rochester Kent ME2 3UL

Secretary:

Mr. J.W Irvine
0474-823411

Professional:

J. Blair
0474-823658

Directions:

By Car: The course is 3 miles east of the Gravesend East exit on the A2.

Course Details:

This is a 6440 yard, eighteen hole parkland course.

The wind direction tends to vary daily creating problems for club selection. 'Great Expectations' is the aptly named 1st hole. By the 18th, you meet 'Round the Bend'.

Shop Facilities:

The shop stocks a range of golf equipment and accessories.

Tuition Details:

There is a large practice area adjacent to the 18th fairway. Lessons cost £15 for 45 minutes.

Contact the Pro shop for further coaching details.

Clubhouse Facilities:

Changing facilities are available with both a Mens and Ladies locker room.

There is a lounge area with balcony, a dining room and stud bar. A collar and tie are required after 7.00pm.

Visitor Restrictions and How to Book:

A handicap certificate is required. Visitors are welcome during the week, but must accompany a member at weekends. Bookings should be made through the Pro shop.

Bookings are not accepted for single green fees.

Societies are welcome on Tuesdays and Thursdays. Letters of confirmation are required. Societies packages cost approximately £55.00.

Visitor Playing Costs:

Weekdays Only:

18 holes: £26.00

Day: £36.00

Tunbridge Wells Golf Club

Langton Road
Tunbridge Wells
Kent TN4 8XH

Clubhouse:

0892-523034

Secretary:

P.F. Janes
0892-536918

Professional:

K. Smithson
0892-541386

Directions:

By Car: 1 mile from the town centre, the course adjoins the Spa Hotel on the A264.

Course Details:

This is a par 32, nine hole parkland course.

This is a hilly course where a good short game is essential. Lakes come in to play on the 2nd and 5th holes.

Shop Facilities:

The shop stocks a range of golf equipment, accessories and designer wear. A golf club repair service is available.

Tuition Details:

There is no practice ground, though lessons are available from the professional. Contact the Pro shop for details.

Clubhouse Facilities:

Changing facilities, including showers are available.

Snacks are available and lunches can be prepared by arrangement in advance.

Visitor Restrictions and How to Book:

A handicap certificate is required. Visitors are not permitted at weekends, unless accompanying a member.

Tuesday is Ladies day. Bookings should be made through the Pro shop.

Societies can be catered for 1/2 days only. Numbers should not exceed 20 visitors. Contact the Secretary for details.

Visitor Playing Costs:

Weekday Only:

18 holes - £22.00

Day - £29.50

Juniors

18 holes - £11.00

Day - £14.25

Upchurch River Valley Golf Courses

Oak Lane
Upchurch
Sittingbourne
Kent ME9 7AY

General Office:

0634-379592 / 0634-360626

Directions:

By Car: Leave the M2 at Junction 4 and drive towards the Gillingham Link Road. Follow directions to Rainham-Sittingbourne at the large roundabout. Take the A2 through Rainham and find the course 2 miles on the left down Oak Lane opposite the Little Chef.

Course Details:

There is an eighteen hole, par 69, course, together with a short nine hole course.

The course, built three years ago, is built on rolling countryside. The most scenic hole is probably the 6th which takes in both the high and the low points of the course. The short par nine course is excellent for beginners and is quiet at certain times.

Shop Facilities:

The shop stocks a full range of golf equipment, accessories and designer wear.

Tuition Details:

Coaching is available at the 16-bay driving range attached to the course. Lessons cost £9 for 30 minutes. Seven sessions can be booked for the price of six. Contact the Professional to book.

Clubhouse Facilities:

The large modern clubhouse has extensive catering facilities which are open from 10.00am - 11.00pm. In summer a heated swimming pool in a large courtyard is available to players.

Visitor Restrictions and How to Book:

A handicap certificate is not required. Jeans are not allowed on the course. Book at any time after 9.00am on a Monday for the weekend ahead via the Pro shop. Times are usually available.

There are a range of society packages. Details are available from the Company.

Visitor Playing Costs:

Weekday / Weekend:

(18 holes)

Adults - £9.95 / £12.95

Veterans - £6.20

Juniors - £4.10

Fees are also available for the 9 hole course.

Weald of Kent Golf Club

Maidstone Road
Headcorn
Kent TN27 9PT

Golf Manager:

John Millen
0622-890866

Directions:

The course is located between Sutton Valence and Headcorn on the A274.

Course Details:

This is an eighteen hole, 6169 yard parkland course.

The course features a range of natural hazards, including waterways, lakes, trees and undulating fairways. The course enjoys good views over the Weald of Kent.

Shop Facilities:

The shop is fully stocked with golf equipment and accessories. Club hire is available.

Tuition Details:

There are 4 practice nets by the 1st tee, together with a practice putting green. There is no resident Pro, but lessons are given by local professionals. Contact the Club on 0622-890866 for details.

Clubhouse Facilities:

The modern clubhouse provides restaurant meals and bar snacks throughout the day between 8.00am - 9.30pm. As well as the bar, silver service restaurant and lounge, there are three separate function suites available for hire.

Visitor Restrictions and How to Book:

A handicap certificate is not required. Visitors may book up to 3 days in advance. Telephone the shop on 0622-890866 to book.

Societies are welcome (minimum 12) and may book at any time. A summer 1995 package of 36 holes, coffee, ploughmans lunch and 2 course evening meal costs £38.50. Winter and Christmas packages are also on offer.

Visitor Playing Costs:

Weekdays / Weekends:

£14.50 / £18.50

Seniors and Juniors (after 11.00am)

£9.00 / £10.00

West Malling Golf Club

London Road
Addington
West Malling
Kent ME19 5AR

Secretary:

M.R. Ellis
0732-844785

Professional:

Jonathan Foss
0732-844022

Directions:

By Car: Leave M20 at Junction 4 (A228). Follow signs to West Malling along the old A20.

Course Details:

There are two parkland courses at West Malling called 'Spitfire' and 'Hurricane'.

The par 5, 610 yard hole which often plays into the wind is testing together with the 14th hole that plays up hill. The courses are fairly hilly and have a heathland feel to them.

Shop Facilities:

The shop stocks a full range of golf equipment and accessories.

Tuition Details:

Coaching is available either indoors or outdoors. Lessons are available at £20 per hour. Video facilities are available. Contact the Pro shop for details.

Clubhouse Facilities:

A full range of catering facilities are available with two restaurants and two bars.

For the energetic, there are squash courts. Snooker and table tennis tables are also available.

Visitor Restrictions and How to Book:

A handicap certificate is not required. Visitors are not permitted before 8.00am on weekdays or 11.30am at weekends. Bookings should be made via the Reception.

Societies are welcome on weekdays. Details are available from the Secretary.

Visitor Playing Costs:

Weekday:

18 holes -£20.00

Day - £28.00

Weekend:

18 holes - £30.00

Westgate & Birchington Golf Club

176 Canterbury Road Westgate-on-Sea Kent CT8 8LT

Secretary:

John M. Wood
0843-831115

Professional:

Roger Game
0843-831115

Directions:

By Car: The course is located on the A28 between Birchington and Margate.

Course Details:

This is an eighteen hole course which provides a blend of inland and seaside terrains.

The inland element occurs at the start and the finish of the round, whilst the seaside element provides the challenge in the centre of the circuit.

Shop Facilities:

The shop stocks a range of golf equipment and accessories.

Tuition Details:

Lessons are available from Roger Game. Lessons cost £9 for 30 minutes

and £18 for one hour. Contact Roger in the Pro shop for details.

Clubhouse Facilities:

Changing facilities are available.

A bar service is available daily and catering can be arranged subject to prior arrangement with the Steward. This service is not however available on Mondays or Fridays.

Visitor Restrictions and How to Book:

Visitors are welcome provided they are bona fide players.

Visitors can play after 10.00am on weekdays and after 11.00am at weekends. Book through either the Pro shop or the Secretary.

Societies are welcome on Thursdays. Contact John Wood for details on 0843-831115.

Visitor Playing Costs:

Weekdays / Weekend:

(before 2.00pm)

£12.00 / £15.00

(after 2.00pm)

£10.00 / £10.00

Wrotham Heath Golf Club

7 Mile Lane
Borough Green
Sevenoaks
Kent TN15 8QZ

Secretary:

L.J Byrne
0732-884800

Professional:

H. Dearden
0732-883854

Directions:

By Car: Located on the B2016, half a mile south of junction with the A20. It can be reached via the M20 Junction 2 and the M26 Junction 2A.

Course Details:

This is an eighteen hole, par 70, heathland and woodland course.

At the time of writing, new holes, designed by Donald Steele, are being introduced to the course. The present par 3, 7th hole, offers a severe test of golf whilst the par 5, 3rd offers spectacular views of the North Downs.

Shop Facilities:

The shop stocks a range of golf equipment, accessories and designer wear.

Tuition Details:

There is a practice ground attached to the course. Lessons are available for £12 for 30 minutes. Contact the Pro shop for details.

Clubhouse Facilities:

Breakfast, lunch and dinner are available by arrangement from Tuesday to Sunday. On Mondays, only light snacks are available.

Jacket, collar and tie is required in the clubhouse after 6.00pm.

Visitor Restrictions and How to Book:

A current handicap certificate is required. Visitors are permitted during weekdays, but must be guests of a member at weekends.

Advance bookings are not essential, but checking availability with the Pro shop by phone is recommended.

Societies are welcomed. Societies should contact the Secretary for details.

Visitor Playing Costs:

Weekdays Only:

18 holes - £22.00

Day - £32.00

GOLF IN SURREY

When it comes to inland golf, few counties can match Surrey for the quality and majesty of its golfing heritage.

This is golfing terrain dominated by heathland, heather, pine and silver birch. Famous names such as **Wentworth, West Hill, Walton Heath and Sunningdale** evoke memories of outstanding challenges and wonderfully testing golf.

With such a richness of famous courses, players might be forgiven for thinking that low handicaps and deep pockets are the norm. Fortunately, Surrey offers a wide range of golfing facilities to meet the requirements of players of all standards.

For the more experienced low handicapper, the choice is truly mouthwatering. **Wentworth**, famous for its West course, is in fact the home to three outstanding eighteen hole courses. With clubhouse facilities to match, Wentworth perhaps sets the standard by which Surrey's courses are judged. And the visitor is not let down.

West Hill at Brookwood offers a number of challenging holes on its wooded heathland terrain. **Foxhills** at Ottershaw, the home of two courses including 'Chertsey', has hosted numerous PGA and Pro-Am tournaments. **Walton Heath** at Tadworth, with its excellent Old and New courses offers a classic heathland terrain, including a particularly challenging group of finishing holes on the Old course.

Whilst these courses and others, including **Effingham, Royal Mid-Surrey, Addington** and **Coombe Hill** offer the sort of challenge that experienced golfers look for, Surrey also offers a range of courses to appeal to more recent entrants to the game.

For visitors looking for a pleasantly challenging round with few visitor restrictions, **Horton Park Country Club** at Epsom and **Hurtmore Golf Club** at Godalming both offer eighteen hole courses with interesting and testing holes. Water comes into play on both courses. **Effingham Golf Club** at Effingham and **Banstead Downs Golf Club** at Sutton both offer testing downland challenges in areas of outstanding natural beauty. Rich flora on Banstead Down's chalk grassland course and in season, the collection of wild orchids at Effingham, both add to the enjoyment of the round.

For the absolute beginner and those wishing to improve their short game, Surrey is not short of pay and play, par 3 and par 4 courses. Amongst others, **Broadwater Park Golf Club** at Farncombe, the **Pachesham Golf Centre** at Leatherhead and **Farnham Park Par 3 Golf Course** at Farnham all cater for those new to the game.

Puttenham Golf Club from the back of the 14th green

Like many pay and play courses built over the past five to six years, **Broadwater Park** and the **Pachesham Golf Centre** are both courses attached to floodlit driving ranges. The **Farnham Park Par 3** course has the distinction of being designed by Henry Cotton.

For both new and experienced players, driving ranges often offer the only opportunity to develop and improve golfing skills. Surrey is not short of good range facilities.

Perhaps, the largest existing driving range facility is found at **Beverley Park Golf Club** at New Malden with 60 floodlit bays. Other ranges can be found at **Croydon Golf Driving Range, Fairmile Golf Range** at Cobham, **Hoebridge Golf Centre** at Old Woking, **Lingfield Park Golf Range, the Oaks Sports Centre** at Carshalton, **Pine Ridge Golf Range** at Frimley, **Richmond Driving Range** and the **Sandown Golf Centre.** Other range facilities are detailed in the section on Driving Ranges.

Among new developments to follow in 1995 are **Clandon Regis Golf Club** and **Sutton Green Golf Club** near Guildford and **Chiddingfold Golf Club.**

The Clubhouse at Epsom Golf Club

Broadwater Park Golf Club

Putting Green at Leatherhead Golf Club

87

Addington Court Golf Club
Featherbed Lane
Addington
Croydon
Surrey CR0 9AA

Mr G Cotton
081-657 0281/2/3

Addington Golf Club
Shirley Church Road
Croydon
Surrey CR50 5AB

Mr JW Beale
081-777 1055

Addington Palace Golf Club
Addington Park
Gravel Hill
Croydon
Surrey CR0 5BB

Mr L Dennis-Smither
081 654 3061

Banstead Downs Golf Club
Burdon Lane
Belmont
Sutton
Surrey SM2 7DD

Mr Roger Steel
081-642 2284

Barrow Hills Golf Club
Barrow Hills
Longcross
Chertsey
Surrey KT16 0DS

Mr RW Routley
0932-848117

Betchworth Park Golf Club
Reigate Road
Dorking

Surrey RH4 1NZ

Mr DAS Bradney
0306-882052

Bletchingley Golf Club
Church Lane
Bletchingley
Surrey RH1 4LP

Mr CT Manktelow
0883-744666

Bramley Golf Club
Bramley
Nr Guildford
Surrey GU5 0AL

Ms M Lambert
0483-892696

Broadwater Park Golf Club
Guildford Road
Farncombe
Nr Godalming
Surrey GU7 3BB

R.J Ashby
0483-429955

Burhill Golf Club
Walton-on-Thames
Surrey KT12 4BL

Mr MB Richards
0932-227345

Camberley Heath Golf Club
Golf Drive
Camberley
Surrey GU15 1JG

Mr John Greenwod
0276-23258

Chessington Golf Centre
Garrison Lane

COURSES IN SURREY

Chessington
Surrey KT9 2LW

Mr A Maxtead
081-391 0948

Chipstead Golf Club Ltd.
How Lane
Coulsdon
Surrey CR5 3PR

Mr SLD Spencer-Skeen
0737-555781

Chiddingfold Golf Club
Petworth Road
Chiddingfold
Surrey GU8 4SL

Mr Mike Hills
0428 685888

Chobham Golf Club
Chobham Road
Knaphill
Woking
Surrey GU21 2TU

Ms Sue Gear
0276-855584

Clandon Regis Golf Club
Epsom Road
West Clandon
Guildford
Surrey

Mr Peter Digby
0483 224888

Coombe Hill Golf Club
Coombe Lane West
Kingston
Surrey

Mr Craig Defoy
081-942 2284

Coombe Wood Golf Club
George Road
Kingston Hill
Kingston-upon-Thames
Surrey KT2 7NS

Mr Peter Urwin
081-942 0388

Coulsdon Court Golf Centre
Coulsdon Road
Coulsdon
Surrey CR3 2LL

Mr Mike Homeward
081-660 6083

Croham Hurst Golf Club
Croham Road
South Croydon
Surrey CR2 7HJ

Mr R Passingham
081-657 5581

Cuddington Golf Club
Banstead Road
Banstead
Surrey SM7 1RD

Mr DM Scott
081-393 0952

Dorking Golf Club
Chart Park
Dorking
Surrey

Mr JB Hawkins
0306-886917

Drift Golf Club
The Drift
East Horsley
Surrey KT24 5HD

Mr C Rose
0483-284641

Dunsfold Aerodrome Golf Club
Dunsfold Aerodrome
Godalming
Surrey GU8 4BS

Mr RG Grout
0483-265472

Effingham Golf Club
Guildford Road
Effingham
Surrey KT24 5PZ

Lt Col Steve Manning OBE
0372-452203

Epsom Golf Club
Longdown Lane South
Epsom
Surrey KT17 4JR

Mr JH Carter FCA
0372-721666

Farnham Golf Club
The Sands
Farnham
Surrey GU10 1PX

Mr James Pevalin
0252-782109

Farnham Park Par 3 Golf Course
Folly Hill
Farnham
Surrey GU9 0AU

Mr Peter Chapman
0252-715216

Fernfell Golf & CC
Barhatch Lane
Cranleigh
Surrey GU6 7NG

Mr B Abdul
0483-268855

Foxhills
Stonehill Road
Ottershaw
Surrey KT16 0EL

Mr A Laking
0932-872050

Gatton Manor Hotel Golf & Country Club
Standon Lane
Ockley
nr Dorking
Surrey RH5 5PQ

Mr David Heath
0306-627555

Goal Farm Golf Club
Goal Road
Pirbright
Surrey GU24 0PZ

Mr R Church
0483-473183/473205

Guildford Golf Club
High Path Road
Merrow
Guildford
Surrey GU1 2HL

Mr Thomas
0483-63941

Hankley Common Golf Club
Tilford Road
Tilford
Farnham

Surrey GU10 2DD

Mr JKA O'Brien
0252-792493

Hindhead Golf Club
Churt Road
Hindhead
Surrey GU26 6HX

Miss A McMenemy
0428-604614

Hoebridge Golf Centre
The Club House
Old Woking Road
Old Woking
Surrey GU22 8JH

Mr TD Powell
0483-722611

Home Park Golf Club
Hampton Wick
Richmond-upon-Thames
Surrey KT1 4AD

Mr BW O'Farrell
081-977 2423

Horton Park Country Club
Hook Road
Ewell
Epsom
Surrey KT19 8QG

Mr P Hart
081-393 8400

Hurtmore Golf Club
Hurtmore Road
Hurtmore
Godalming
Surrey GU7 2RN

Mr Tony White
0483-426492

Kingswood Golf Club
Sandy Lane
Kingswood
Tadworth
Surrey KT20 6NE

Miss Lynn Thompson
0737-832188

Laleham Golf Club
Laleham Reach
Mixnams Lane
Chertsey
Surrey KT16 8RP

Mr R Fry
0932-564211

The Leatherhead Golf Club
Kingston Road
Leatherhead
Surrey KT22 0EE

Ms Louise Laithwaite
0372-843966

Limpsfield Chart Golf Club
Limpsfield
Oxted
Surrey RH8 0SL

Mr DS Adams
0883-723405

Lingfield Park Golf Club
Racecourse Road
Lingfield
Surrey RH7 6PQ

Ms Greer Milne
0342-834602

Malden Golf Club
Traps Lane
New Malden
Surrey KT3 4RS

Mr P Fletcher
081-942 0654

Milford Golf Club
Milford
Nr Guildford
Surrey GU8 5HS

Mr Ian Waitht
0483-419200

Mitcham Golf Club
Carshalton Road
Mitcham Junction
Surrey CR4 4HN

Mr CA McGahan
081-648 4197

Moore Place Golf Club
Portsmouth Road
Esher
Surrey KT10 9LN

Mr D Allen
0372-463533

New Zealand Golf Club
Woodham Lane
Woodham
Addlestone
Surrey KT15 3QD

Mr J Manley
0932-345049

North Downs Golf Club
Northdown Road
Woldingham
Surrey

Mr JAL Smith
0883-652057

Oak Park Golf Club
Heath Lane
Crondall
Nr Farnham
Surrey GU10 5PB

Mrs R Smythe
0252-850880

Oaks Sports Centre
Woodmansterne Road
Carshalton SM5 4AN
Surrey

Mr D McNab
081-643 8363

Pachesham Golf Centre
Oaklawn Road
Leatherhead
Surrey KT22 0BT

Mr Phil Taylor
0372-843453

Pine Ridge Golf Club
Old Bisley Road
Frimley
Camberley
Surrey GU16 5NX

Mr S Hodsdon
0276-20770

Purley Downs Golf Club
106 Purley Downs Road
South Croydon
Surrey CR2 0RB

Mr Peter Gallienne
081-657 8347

COURSES IN SURREY

Puttenham Golf Club
Puttenham Heath Road
Puttenham
Nr Guildford
Surrey GU3 1AL

Mr Gary Simmons
0483-810498

Pyrford Golf Club
Warren Lane
Pyrford
Surrey GU22 8XR

Mr David Renton
0483-723555

RAC Country Club
Woodcote Park
Epsom
Surrey KT18 7EW

Mr K Symons
0372-276311

Redhill & Reigate Golf Club
Clarence Lodge
Pendleton Road
Redhill
Surrey RH1 6LB

Mr FR Cole
0737-240777

Reigate Heath Golf Club
Flanchford Road
Reigate
Surrey RH2 8QR

Mr RJ Perkins
0737-226793

Richmond Golf Club
Sudbrook Park
Richmond
Surrey TW10 7AS

Mr RL Wilkins
081-940 4351

Roker Park Golf Club
Holly Lane
Guildford
Surrey GU3 3PB

Mr M Bedlow
0483-236677

Royal Mid-Surrey Golf Club
Old Deer Park
Richmond
Surrey TW9 2SB

Mr MSR Lunt
081-940 1894

Rusper Golf Club
Rusper Road
Newdigate
Surrey RH5 5BX

Mr G Hems
0293-871456

Sandown Park Golf Club
More Lane
Esher
Surrey KT10 8AN

Mr P Barriball
0372-465921

Selsdon Park Golf & CC
Addington Road
Sanderstead
South Croydon
Surrey CR2 8YA

Mrs Felicia Heaton-Armstrong
081-657 8811

Shillinglee Park Golf Club
Chiddingfold

Godalming
Surrey GU8 4TA

Mr R Mace
0428-653237

Shirley Park Golf Club
Addiscombe Road
Croydon
Surrey CR0 7LB

Mr A Baird
081-654 1143

Silvermere Golf Club
Redhill Road
Cobham
Surrey KT11 1EF

Mrs Pauline Devereux
0932-866007

St George's Hill Golf Club
St George's Hill
Weybridge
Surrey KT13 0NL

Mr J Robinson
0932-847758

Sunningdale Ladies Golf Club
Cross Road
Sunningdale
Surrey SL5 9RX

Mr JF Darroch
0344-20507

Sunningdale Golf Club
Sunningdale
Surrey SL5 9RW

Mr S Zuill
0344-21681

Surbiton Golf Club
Woodstock Lane

Chessington
Surrey KT9 1UG

Mr GA Keith
081-398 3101

Sutton Green Golf Club
New Lane
Sutton Green
Nr Guildford
Surrey

John Buchanan
0482 766849

Tandridge Golf Club
Oxted
Surrey RH8 9NQ

Mr AS Furnival
0883-712274

Thames Ditton & Esher Golf Club
Portsmouth Road
Esher
Surrey KT10 9AL

Mr DI Kaye
081-398 1551

Tyrells Wood Golf Club
Tyrells Wood
Leatherhead
Surrey KT22 8QP

Mr CGR Kydd
0372-376025

Walton Heath Golf Club
Tadworth
Surrey KT20 7TP

Gp Capt GR James
0737-812380

Wentworth Club Limited.
Wentworth Drive

COURSES IN SURREY

Virginia Water
Surrey GU25 4LS

Mr Keith Williams
0344-842201

West Byfleet Golf Club
Sheerwater Road
West Byfleet
Surrey KT14 6AA

Mrs J Pearce
0932-343433

West Hill Golf Club (1959) Ltd.
Bagshot Road
Brookwood
Surrey GU24 0BH

Mr MC Swatton
0483-474365

West Surrey Golf Club
Enton Green
Nr Godalming
Surrey GU8 5AF

Mr RS Fanshawe
0483-421275

Wildwood Golf Club
Horsham Road
Afold
Surrey GU6 8JE

Miss A Hill
0403-753255

Windlemere Golf Club
Windlesham Road
West End
Woking
Surrey GU24 9QL

Mr CD Smith
0276-858727

Windlesham Golf Club
Grove End
Bagshot
Surrey GU19 5HY

Mr Phillip Watts
0276-452220

Wisley Golf Club
Mill Lane
Ripley
Nr Woking
Surrey GU23 6QU

Mr J Arthur
0483-211022

Woking Golf Club
Pond Road
Hook Heath
Woking
Surrey GU22 0JZ

Col. I Holmes
0483-760053

Woodcote Park Golf Club
Meadow Hill
Bridle Way
Coulsdon
Surrey CR3 2QQ

Mr TJ Fenson
081-668 2788

Worplesdon Golf Club
Heath House Road
Woking
Surrey GU22 0RA

Major REE Jones
0483-472277

Addington Palace Golf Club

Addington Park
Gravel Hill
Croydon
Surrey CR0 5BB

Secretary:

Lawrence Dennis-Smither
081-654 3061

Professional:

Roger Williams
081-654 1786

Directions:

By Car: The club is situated 2 miles south east of Croydon, close to the junction of the A212 and A2022.

By BR: East Croydon Station.

Course Details:

This is a 6027 yard, eighteen hole, hilly, parkland course.

Notable holes are the 2nd and 10th, both long par 4's. The tight 3rd hole, a par 4, requires a well placed tee shot, whilst the 12th hole, a par 3, requires a shot over a fountain.

Shop Facilities:

The shop stocks a wide range of golf equipment, accessories and designer wear. Sets of clubs are available for hire.

Tuition Details:

There are three separate practice areas, including a new short game training facility. Video analysis is available.

Lessons cost £15 for 1/2 hour. A course of lessons costs £75. Contact Roger Williams on 081-654 1786 for details of coaching.

Clubhouse Facilities:

The Clubhouse is laid out as a quadrangle, surrounding a large putting green. There is a 19th hole bar, lounge bar and restaurant. A jacket and tie is required in the lounge bar after 6.30pm and on Sundays. The restaurant is closed on Mondays.

Visitor Restrictions and How to Book:

Visitors are welcome on weekdays. At weekends, visitors must accompany a member. Thursday am is Ladies Day. Contact the Secretary's office on 081-654 3061 to check availability.

Societies are welcome on Tuesdays, Wednesdays and Fridays. A minimum of 20 players are required to organise a dinner in the evening. Society packages range in price from £32.00 to £55.00.

Visitor Playing Costs:

Weekday Only:

£25.00

Banstead Downs Golf Club

Burdon Lane
Belmont
Sutton
Surrey SM2 7DD

Secretary:

Roger Steele
081-642 2284

Professional:

Robert Dickman
081-642 6884

Directions:

By Car: Exit Junction 8 (M25).   The course is located on the A217, between Cheam and Sutton.

By BR: Sutton Station (10 minutes.)

Course Details:

This is a 6168 yard, eighteen hole natural downland course.

The course is set on a Site of Special Scientific Interest for its chalk grassland and rich flora.

Shop Facilities:

The shop stocks a wide range of golf equipment and accessories.

Tuition Details:

Lessons are available from the Pro at £17.50 for 45 minutes. Contact Robert Dickman or his assistant in the Pro shop. There are covered practice nets available, and a practice area 10 minutes walk from the clubhouse.

Clubhouse Facilities:

Changing facilities, including showers are available.

A range of catering services are provided. There is a main lounge, ladies lounge, dining room and Spike bar. A jacket and tie must be worn in the main lounge and dining room in the evening.

Visitor Restrictions and How to Book:

Visitors are welcome on weekdays. They must have either a letter of introduction or a current handicap certificate. At weekends, visitors can only play as the guest of a member and only after 9.30am.

Book in advance through the Pro shop to confirm tee-time availability.

Societies are welcome on Thursdays. Contact the Secretary for details of Society packages available.

Visitor Playing Costs:

Weekday Only:

Before 12.00pm - £30.00
After 12.00pm   - £20.00

Bramley Golf Club

Secretary:

Margaret Lambert
0483-892696

Professional:

Gary Peddie
0483-893685

Directions:

By Car: 2 miles south of Guildford on the Horsham Road (A281) between the villages of Shalford and Bramley.

Course Details:

This is a 5990 yard, par 69, eighteen hole, hilly, parkland course.

Established in 1913, the course offers a considerable challenge with numerous 'out of bounds' and a large number of bunkers.

Shop Facilities:

The shop stocks a wide range of golf equipment and accessories. Clubs are available for hire at £7.50.

Tuition Details:

The practice ground facilities are only available to members and guests. There is a 7 bay undercover, 230 yard, driving range and a 100 yard pitching area.

Coaching is available from the Head Professional at £15.00 for 1/2 hour for members (£20 for non-members) and for £10.00 from the senior assistant.

Clubhouse Facilities:

Full changing facilities are available. The bar and restaurant serve food all day from 8.00am. Smart casual wear is the form, though players are asked to change out of golfing attire. A jacket and tie must be worn in the restaurant after 6.00pm.

Visitor Restrictions and How to Book:

Visitors are not permitted to play at weekends or on bank holidays, unless as the guest of a member. Individual tee reservations are not made. Contact the Pro shop to check availability.

Societies are welcome (min.12 players). Societies can book from March onwards for the following year. Telephone the Secretary for details of the two principal packages available.

Visitor Playing Costs:

Weekdays:

18 holes - £25.00
Day - £30.00

Broadwater Park Golf Club

Guildford Road
Farncombe
Nr Godalming
Surrey

Secretary:

R.J Ashby
0483-429955

Professional:

Kevin Milton
0483-429955

Directions:

The course is situated on the A3100 between Godalming and Guildford.

Course Details:

This is a nine hole pay and play, par 3 course.

The holes vary in length from 86 yards to 205 yards.

Shop Facilities:

The discount golf shop stocks a range of golf equipment and accessories.

Club hire is available at £2.50 for 9 holes and £3.75 for 18 holes. Club hire to juniors and seniors costs £1.75 for 9 holes and £2.25 for 18 holes.

Tuition Details:

There is a 16-bay floodlit covered driving range attached to the course.

Lessons are available from the Pro at £14 for 30 minutes. A playing lesson of 1 hour costs £18.

Clubhouse Facilities:

There is a licensed bar and pool table. Bar food is provided. There is however no restaurant.

Visitor Restrictions and How to Book:

There are no restrictions, though suitable footwear must be worn.

This is a pay and play course. Bookings are only accepted at weekends. Telephone 0483-429955 to book.

Societies are welcome. Contact the Secretary for details.

Visitor Playing Costs:

Weekday / Weekends:

9 holes:

Adults: £3.75 / £4.25

Juniors & OAPs: £2.95 / £3.25

18 holes:

Adults: £6.25 / £7.75

Juniors & OAPs: £4.95 / £5.75

Chipstead Golf Club Ltd.

How Lane
Coulsdon
Surrey CR5 3PR

Secretary:

S.L.D Spencer-Skeen
0737-555781

Professional:

G. Torbett
0737-554939

Directions:

By Car: Exit Junction 8 (M25). Take the A217 to Sutton. At the second roundabout, follow the signs to Chipstead.

By BR: Chipstead Station.

Course Details:

This is a 5,454 yard, eighteen hole parkland course.

With a first hole called 'Hopeful' and a final hole called 'Stumbleholm', it becomes clear that accuracy is more important than length. As with many courses perhaps shorter than average, Chipstead makes up for its apparent lack of length with enough challenges to task the club player.

Shop Facilities:

The shop stocks a range of golf equipment and accessories. Club hire is available at £10.

Tuition Details:

Coaching is available from the resident Pro. Lessons cost £15 for 40 minutes. Contact the Pro shop on 0737-554939 to book.

Clubhouse Facilities:

Full changing facilities are available. Catering is available seven days a week. There is a main bar and Spike bar together with dining room.

Visitor Restrictions and How to Book:

Visitors are welcome on weekdays, but must accompany a member at weeends.

Book through either the Pro shop or the Club Secretary.

Societies are welcome for 1/2 a day on Tuesday or all day Thursday. Societies should contact the Secretary for details.

Visitor Playing Costs:

Weekdays Only:

Day - £25.00

After 2.00pm - £20.00

Coombe Wood Golf Club

George Road
Kingston Hill
Kingston-upon-Thames
Surrey KT2 7NS

Secretary:

Peter M. Urwin
081-942 0388

Professional:

David Butler
081-942 6764

Directions:

Car: From the A3 Kingston By-Pass take Coombe Lane West into Warren Road (private estate) and then on to George Road.

By BR: Norbiton Station.

Course Details:

This is a 5,129 yard, eighteen hole parkland course.

Constructed in 1904, this is a short but challenging course with seven par 3 holes, ranging in length from the 135 yard, 17th hole to the 207 yard, 8th.

Shop Facilities:

The shop is fully stocked with a range of golf equipment and accessories.

Tuition Details:

Coaching is available from the professional staff. Lessons cost £15 for 1/2 hour. Contact the Pro shop on 081-9426764 for details.

Clubhouse Facilities:

Full changing facilities are available. The Clubhouse provides a range of catering facilities through its mixed lounge, mens bar and dining room.

Visitor Restrictions and How to Book:

Visitors are welcome on weekdays, but must accompany a member at the weekend. Visitors are advised to contact the Pro shop in advance to check for possible mid-week Club competitions. Visitors should book via the Pro shop, preferably in advance, by phone.

Societies are welcomed and should contact either the Secretary or Manager.

Trade vehicles are not permitted on the Estate Grounds.

Visitor Playing Costs:

Day - £26.00

Summer after 6.00pm - £13.00

Juniors - £10.00

After 6.00pm - £7.50

Dorking Golf Club

Chart Hill
Dorking
Surrey RH5 4BX

Secretary:

J.B. Hawkins
0306-886917

Professional:

Paul Napier
0306-886917

Directions:

By Car: Take the A24 Horsham Road from the roundabout on the A25 east of Dorking. After approximately 1/2 mile, the course car park is on the left just over the crest of a hill.

By BR: Dorking North or Deepdene Stations.

Course Details:

This is a 5,120 hilly, parkland, eighteen hole course, based on two rounds of nine holes.

Different tees create different challenges. The 3rd hole 'Pulpit' is played from a high tee, whilst the 17th, 'The Road Hole', is a 230 yard, par 3, played over a valley to a tightly bunkered green.

Shop Facilities:

The shop stocks a range of golf equipment and accessories. Club hire is available for £5.

Tuition Details:

Lessons are available from £10 for 1/2 hour. A 9-hole playing lesson (or up to 2 hours) costs £20. A course of 7 lessons costs £55.

Clubhouse Facilities:

There is a licensed bar and catering is available every day. On Mondays however, catering is limited to sandwiches. Basket meals are normally available from 12.00noon - 6.00pm and a full menu is available by arrangement.

Visitor Restrictions and How to Book:

Visitors are permitted to play on weekdays only, with the exception of Monday and Wednesday am. Book via the Pro shop, preferably in advance by telephone.

Societies are catered for and discounts are available for groups exceeding 16 players.

Visitor Playing Costs:

Weekdays Only:

18 holes - £16.00

Day - £20.00

Effingham Golf Club

Guildford Road
Effingham
Surrey KT24 5PZ

Secretary:

Lt. Col. Steve Manning OBE
0372-452203

Professional:

Steven Hoatson
0372-452606

Directions:

By Car: The course is located on the A246 Guildford to Leatherhead Road. From the M25, join the A3 towards Guildford. On the sliproad, signposted for Effingham, follow the road to the lights and turn right.

Course Details:

This is a 6,201 yard, eighteen hole downland course.

The long par 4, 5th is a testing hole. The short holes tend to be well protected by bunkers.

There is an abundance of wildlife on the course and in season, a fine collection of wild orchids can be found.

Shop Facilities:

The shop is well stocked with golf equipment and accessories. Club hire is available at £5 per round.

Tuition Details:

There is a large practice area, together with chipping and putting areas. Lessons are available at £12 for 30 minutes. Book through the Pro shop.

Clubhouse Facilities:

The clubhouse is a Grade 2 listed building. There are three dining areas and the main restaurant can seat 100. Other facilities include 4 tennis courts and 2 squash courts.

Visitor Restrictions and How to Book:

A handicap certificate is required, unless playing with a member.

Visitors are welcome on weekdays only, bar Monday and Tuesday am. There are no reserved tee times for casual visitors. Green fees are payable in the Pro shop. No play is allowed on the course before 8.00am.

Societies are welcome on Wednesdays, Thursdays and Fridays. Book through the Secretary.

Visitor Playing Costs:

Weekday Only:

Day: £35.00

1/2 Day (pm): £27.50

Epsom Golf Club

Longdown Lane South
Epsom
Surrey KT17 4JR

Secretary:

J. H Carter FCA
0372-721666

Professional:

Ron Goudie
0372-741867

Directions:

By Car: From the A240, take the B288. The course is 200 yards south of Epsom Downs Station.

By BR: Epsom Downs Station.

Course Details:

This is a 5,236 yard, eighteen hole downland links-style course.

Though not the longest course, its fast undulating greens require accurate play. The Club celebrated its centenary in 1989 and has seen some course changes over the past ten years. The course has unrivalled views across the Downs to London.

Shop Facilities:

The shop stocks a range of golf equipment, accessories and designer wear.

Clubs can be hired for £10 per round.

Tuition Details:

Coaching is available at £15 per 1/2 hour. Six lessons for the price of five. Putting lessons are a speciality!

Book via Ron Goudie in the Pro shop on 0372-741867.

Clubhouse Facilities:

There are full changing facilities, including showers.

There is a 19th Hole bar, together with lounge which offers a bar snack menu. The dining room provides a full menu service. There is also a billiard room.

Visitor Restrictions and How to Book:

Visitors are welcome on weekdays, except Tuesday am which is Ladies Day. At weekends, visitors are welcome after 12.00pm.

Societies are welcome and should contact the Secretary for details of several packages on offer (from £17.00).

Casual visitors should book via the Pro shop on 0372-741867.

Visitor Playing Costs:

Weekday /Weekend: (after 12.00pm)

18 holes - £16.00 /£18.00

Day - £24.00

Farnham Golf Club

The Sands
Farnham
Surrey GU10 1PX

Secretary:

Mr. James Pevalin
0252-782109

Professional:

Mr. Grahame Cowlishaw
0252-782198

Directions:

By Car: The course is situated at the Sands which is east of Farnham town centre. From the A31 eastbound, take the exit to Seale. From the A31 westbound, take the exit to Runfold.

Course Details:

This is an eighteen hole wooded, parkland course.

Founded in 1896, the course combines parkland and woodland. Holes 6 - 11 are played through woods whilst the first five and last seven are played in a parkland setting.

The par 4, 8th hole is probably the most challenging hole with an accurate tee-shot for position being followed by a second to a sunken green protected by a bunker on the right.

Shop Facilities:

The shop stocks a wide range of golf equipment, accessories and designer wear.

Tuition Details:

There is a large practice area, including a net. There is a practice green for chipping and bunker play. Lessons are available at £14.25 from the Pro and £11.50 from the Assistant Pro.

Clubhouse Facilities:

Full changing facilities, including showers are available. Full bar and catering services are provided from 11.00am daily (12.00pm on Sundays). A jacket and tie must be worn in the dining room.

Visitor Restrictions and How to Book:

Visitors are welcome on weekdays with a handicap certificate. At weekends they must accompany a member. Tuesday is Ladies day.

Societies are welcome on Wednesdays, Thursdays and Fridays, and can book up to 12 months in advance via the Secretary. (maximum 50 players).

Visitor Playing Costs:

Weekdays:

18 holes - £25.00

Day - £30.00

Farnham Park Par 3 Golf Course

Folly Hill
Farnham
Surrey GU9 0AU

Secretary:

Peter Chapman
0252-715216

Directions:

By Car: The course is located on the A287 outside Farnham next to Farnham Castle.

Course Details:

This is a par 3 nine hole course with an eighteen hole length of 2326 yards.

Originally designed by Henry Cotton, this course offers a challenge to all standards: both beginners and those more experienced seeking to improve their short game.

Shop Facilities:

The shop stocks a range of golf equipment and accessories.

Clubs are available for hire at £1.30 for nine holes.

Tuition Details:

Tuition is available either for individuals or as part of a group. Lessons cost £12 per 1/2 hour for adults and £8 per

1/2 hour for juniors/seniors.

Contact Peter Chapman on 0252-715216 to book and for further details.

Clubhouse Facilities:

The clubhouse provides daily catering through the licensed bar and lounge.

Bar snacks are available.

Visitor Restrictions and How to Book:

This is a pay and play course open to the public 7 days a week. There are no visitor restrictions.

Book at the shop. Discounts may be available to parties of 16 players or more. The shop will confirm any discount available.

Visitor Playing Costs:

Weekday / Weekend (9 holes):

Adults: £3.50 / £4.00

Junior/Seniors: £2.50 / £3.00

Foxhills

Stonehill Road
Ottershaw
Surrey KT16 0EL

Secretary:
Ashley Laking
0932-872050

Professional:
Alisdair Goode
0932-873961

Directions:
By Car: Exit Junction 11 (M25) following the signs to Woking. Turn off the 3rd exit on the 2nd roundabout into Foxhills Road. At the 'T' junction, turn left. The Club is 100 yards on the right.

Course Details:
Foxhills has two eighteen hole courses.

'Longcross' meanders through a forest demanding accuracy through tree-lined fairways. The picturesque par 3, 16th hole requires a long tee shot over a pond protecting the green. 'Chertsey' has hosted many PGA and Pro-Am events. It has a strong finishing three holes and many new bunkers and tee positions.

Shop Facilities:
There is a new shop which stocks a range of golf equipment, accessories and designer wear. Clubs are available for hire at £15 per set.

Tuition Details:
Coaching is available from the resident PGA pros headed by Bernard Hunt MBE and Alisdair Goode. Lessons cost £15/£25 for 30 minutes / 60 minutes from the Head Pro and £10/£20 from the Assistant Pro.

Members and guests have use of a 12 bay driving range. Tokens from the Pro shop cost £2.50 for 80 balls.

Clubhouse Facilities:
Full changing facilities are available.

There are extensive catering facilities on the complex which provide 24 hour coverage. Restaurants and bars are open all day.

Visitor Restrictions and How to Book:
Visitors are welcome to play, but not before noon on a Saturday or Sunday. Visitors should book via the Pro shop.

Societies are welcome. Contact Ms Karen John in the Sales office for details of the packages and options available.

Visitor Playing Costs:
Weekday / Weekend

18 holes: £45.00 / £55.00

36 holes: £65.00

Gatton Manor Hotel Golf & Country Club

Standon Lane
Ockley
Nr Dorking
Surrey RH5 5PQ

Secretary:

Mr. David G Heath
0306-627555

Professional:

Mr. Rae Sargent
0306-627557

Directions:

By Car: Exit Junction 9 (M25) and take the A24 towards Dorking. Continue south on the A24 to the end of the dual carriageway. Take the right turning onto A29 Ockley / Bognor Regis. Turn right in Ockley onto Cat Hill Lane. Follow signs to Gatton Manor (2 miles).

Course Details:

This is a 6,145 yard, eighteen hole parkland course.

Set in the grounds of Gatton Manor, natural water hazards come in to play on fourteen holes. Both the 3rd and the 6th holes require a tee shot through woods with water posing problems for the second shot. The 18th hole requires a tee shot over a river and a second shot that has a stream 50 yards from the green to contend with.

Shop Facilities:

The shop stocks a range of golf equipment and accessories. Club hire costs £5.

Tuition Details:

There is a practice range with balls available at £2 per basket. Lessons cost £12 per 1/2 hour. Contact the Pro shop for details of special offers.

Clubhouse Facilities:

Full changing facilities are available.

Catering is provided by a number of facilities. There is a large bar and an a la carte restaurant. Bar meals are available from 11.00am-3.30pm.

There is a residents private lounge, bar and restaurant. A jacket and tie must be worn in the evening in the restaurant.

Visitor Restrictions and How to Book:

Visitors are welcome, but are not permitted to play before 1.00pm on Sundays. Tee times can be booked up to two weeks in advance via the Pro shop.

Society days can be booked well in advance via the Hotel on 0306-627555.

Visitor Playing Costs:

Weekday / Weekend:

18 holes: £18.00 / £25.00 (Summer)
18 holes: £15.00 / £20.00 (Winter)

Hankley Common Golf Club

Tilford Road
Tilford
Farnham
Surrey GU10 2DD

Secretary:

J.K.A.O'Brien
0252-792493

Professional:

P. Stow
0252-793761

Directions:

By Car: From Farnham, turn left off the A31 at the first set of lights and keep to right fork after the level crossing gates. Through Tilford village, turn left after 3/4 miles, at the Duke of Cambridge Pub, for the Club.

Course Details:

This is a 6,438 yard eighteen hole heathland course. The par 3, 7th hole is one of the most challenging in the region. The tee shot requires a carry over heather to the two-tier green. Missing the green can be costly. The finishing hole with a fairway gathering towards the heather on the right requires a courageous tee shot down the left to get up in two.

Shop Facilities:

The shop stocks a wide range of golf equipment and accessories.

Tuition Details:

There is a large practice area with targets together with a net and chipping/putting facilities. Lessons cost from £15 for 45 mins. A course of 6 lessons cost from £80.

Clubhouse Facilities:

There are Ladies and Gents changing facilities.

The bar and restaurant provide a range of catering from snack meals to a full menu. A jacket and tie are required in the restaurant.

Visitor Restrictions and How to Book:

A handicap certificate is required. Visitors are welcome all week, but are not permitted to play before 2.00pm on weekends. To book, contact the Secretary on 0252-792493.

Societies are welcome on Tuesdays and Wednesdays. Contact the Secretary for details of packages on offer.

Visitor Playing Costs:

Weekdays / Weekends: (after 2.00pm)

18 holes: £28.00 / £35.00

Day: £35.00

Hindhead Golf Club

Churt Road
Hindhead
Surrey GU26 6HX

Secretary:

Miss A McMenemy
0428-604614

Professional:

N Ogilvy
0428-604458

Directions:

By Car: Junction 10 (M25/A3). The course is located 1.5 miles off the A3 on the A287 to Farnham.

Course Details:

This is a 6373 yard, eighteen hole heathland course.

The course is played through wooded valleys for the first nine holes and flatter heathland on the back nine, and offers glorious views of the surrounding countryside. A very challenging heathland course.

Shop Facilities:

The shop stocks a range of golf equipment, accessories and designer wear. Club hire is available at £5 per round.

Tuition Details:

There is a large practice area. Lessons are available from £12.50 per hour. Contact the Pro shop for details and booking on 0428-604458.

Clubhouse Facilities:

Catering is provided by a fully licensed bar, restaurant and snack service. Breakfasts are available by prior arrangement. Dinner is only available on Wednesday, Thursday and Friday.

Visitor Restrictions and How to Book:

There is a handicap limit of 20 at weekends. Starting times can be limited, particularly at weekends, because of Club competitions. Bookings are not taken for individuals or small groups. It is recommended that visitors should contact the Pro shop to check availability .

No 3 or 4 ball matches are allowed before 11.30am on Tuesdays.

Societies are welcome and should contact the Clubhouse office. Winter rates and a range of packages are available.

Visitor Playing Costs:

Weekdays / Weekends:

£35.00 / £42.00

(after 2.00pm) £27.00 / £32.00

Horton Park Country Club

Hook Road
Ewell
Epsom
Surrey KT19 8QG

General Manager:

Paul Hart
081-393 8400

Professional:

Gary Clements
081-394 2626

Directions:

By Car: Exit Junction 9 (M25) and follow signs to Chessington World of Adventures. At the next roundabout, turn right and continue to the junction of Hook Road and Chessington Road.

By BR: Epsom Station (2 miles).

Course Details:

This is a 5,197 yard, eighteen hole course.

The course is set in a designated country park with natural water hazards. The long par 5, 7th hole measuring 560 yards is followed by a 200 yard par 3 with carry over water making a difficult finish to the front nine holes.

Shop Facilities:

The shop offers a range of golf equipment, accessories and designer wear. Clubs can be hired at £3.50 per half set.

Tuition Details:

There is a 26 bay floodlit driving range, together with bunker, putting and fairway area. Video analysis is available.

Individual lessons cost £11.00 per 1/2 hour. A beginners class (Group tuition) costs £55.00 for a series of classes. Contact the Pro shop for details.

Clubhouse Facilities:

Changing facilities including showers are available.

There is a bar, restaurant and function room providing daily catering.

Visitor Restrictions and How to Book:

A handicap certificate is not required.

Bookings are required for the weekend. Telephone bookings are accepted and payment made to the Pro shop.

Societies are welcome. A range of packages are on offer. Contact Ann Lewis on 081-393 8400.

Visitor Playing Costs:

Weekdays / Weekends:

9 holes: £6.00 / NA

18 holes: £11.00 / £13.00

Hurtmore Golf Club

Hurtmore Road
Hurtmore
Godalming
Surrey GU7 2RN

Secretary:
Tony White
0483-426492

Professional:
Maxine Burton
0483-424440

Directions:
By Car: The course is located approximately 6 miles south of Guildford on the A3 at Norney.

Course Details:
This is a 5156 yard, eighteen hole parkland course.

Designed by Peter Alliss and Clive Clark and set in undulating parkland, the course has 7 large water features as well as 92 bunkers. Perhaps the toughest hole on the course is the 3rd which requires a 240 yard drive to the corner of a dog-leg avoiding bunkers on the right and water on the left before facing the second shot to the green.

Shop Facilities:
The shop stocks a range of golf equipment and accessories.

Tuition Details:
Lessons are available from the PGA qualified professional at £12.50 per 1/2 hour. Contact Maxine Burton for details on 0483-424440.

Clubhouse Facilities:
There are full changing facilities in the modern clubhouse, including showers.

A bar and restaurant, which are open all day, provide a range of catering services.

There are disabled facilities in the clubhouse.

Visitor Restrictions and How to Book:
There are no restrictions on visitors, except the normal dress code.

Book by telephone on 0483-426492.

Societies are welcome and must book at least 6 days before playing. Book via the Clubhouse on 0483-424440.

Visitor Playing Costs:
Weekday / Weekend: (18 holes)

Adults - £12.00 / £15.00

OAP / Juniors - £8.00 / £12.00

Day Ticket - £20.00 / £25.00

Kingswood Golf Club

Sandy Lane
Kingsworth
Tadworth
Surrey KT20 6NE

Secretary:

Miss Lynn Thompson
0737-832188

Professional:

Mr. Martin Platts
0737-832334

Directions:

By Car: Exit Junction 8 (M25). The course is 4 miles away on the A217 (Brighton Road).

By BR: Kingswood Station.

Course Details:

This is a 6,513 yard eighteen hole parkland course.

The first five holes are a demanding start to the round, particularly the par 4, 2nd hole. Most club players would also be well satisfied with pars at the 8th and 16th holes, both being challenging par 4's.

Shop Facilities:

The shop, part of the Doug McClelland chain of golf stores, stocks a wide range of golf equipment and accessories.

Clubs are available for hire at £25.

Tuition Details:

The practice facilities include a practice chipping area, putting green and ball dispensing machine. Video analysis is available.

Lessons cost £14/£16 per 30 minutes with the Assistant/Director of Golf.

Clubhouse Facilities:

Full changing facilities, including showers are available.

The clubhouse, with views of the South Downs, provides extensive catering services, including a full a la carte menu. A jacket and tie is required after 6.00pm and on Sunday lunchtimes.

Banqueting facilities are available for up to 140 people.

Visitor Restrictions:

Visitors are welcome, but are not permitted before 1.00pm at weekends.

Bookings are accepted up to 24 hours in advance by telephoning 0737-832188.

Societies are welcomed and a brochure is available outlining the packages available. Contact the Secretary for details.

Visitor Playing Costs:

Weekday / Weekends (after 1.00pm)

£30.00 / £42.00

Laleham Golf Club

Laleham Reach
Mixnams Lane
Chertsey
Surrey KT16 8RP

Secretary:

Rob Fry
0932-564211

Professional:

Hogan Stott
0932-562877

Directions:

By Car: Take the Chertsey exit (M25) and follow signs to Thorpe Park. The entrance to the course is opposite Thorpe Park main entrance.

Course Details:

This is a 6,044 yard eighteen hole course.

An easy walking flat course, it has many bunkers and water hazards, notably on the 9th, 14th and 18th holes.

The course is used for Surrey Golf Union finals and PGA events.

Shop Facilities:

The shop stocks a range of golf equipment, accessories and designer wear.

Tuition Details:

There is a large practice ground and the coaching team is headed by Hogan Stott who has represented Great Britain and Ireland in the P.G.A. Cup team against the USA.

Lessons are available for £12 per 30 mins. Book via the Pro shop.

Clubhouse Facilities:

Full changing facilities are available.

The clubhouse has a bar and restaurant which provide a range of catering services including lunch and dinner.

Visitor Restrictions and How to Book:

Visitors are welcome during the week, but must accompany a member at the weekend.

To book a tee during the week, telephone the Pro shop.

Societies are welcome during weekdays.

Society prices start at £21 for a Society package and full details, including a pack, menus and price list can be obtained from the Secretary's office.

Visitor Playing Costs:

Weekdays Only:

18 holes - £16.50

Day - £25.00

The Leatherhead Golf Club

Kingston Road
Leatherhead
Surrey KT22 0EE

Secretary:

Louise Laithwaite
0372-843966

Professional:

Richard Hurst
0372-843956

Directions:

By Car: Exit Junction 9 (M25). The club is located on the A243 Kingston Road. From the A3, leave at Hook and take the Chessington Road towards the M25.

Course Details:

This is an eighteen hole, parkland course.

Dominated by mature oaks, where accuracy is as important as length, perhaps the three most challenging holes are the 1st, 3rd and 12th.

On the first, many fall short on their second shot. On the 3rd, to hit the green the drive must be played to the right and short of an oak dominating the centre of the fairway. The par 3, 12th hole requires an accurate drive over a ravine to avoid trouble.

Shop Facilities:

The shop stocks a range of golf equipment and accessories. Golf clubs are available for hire at £15 per set.

Tuition Details:

Lessons cost from £10 per half hour. Video analysis is available. Book by telephone on 0372-843956.

Clubhouse Facilities:

The clubhouse provides full changing facilities.

There is a lounge bar, restaurant and cafe/brasserie which provides catering from dawn to dusk.

Visitor Restrictions and How to Book:

Visitors are welcome. A handicap certificate is preferred, but not essential. Weekend mornings and Thursday mornings however are reserved for members. Visitors can book up to 10 days in advance via the Pro shop.

Societies may book up to a year in advance and a maximum of 100 players can be catered for. Contact the Manager for details.

Visitor Playing Costs:

Weekdays / Weekends (PM only)

18 holes: £25.00 / £35.00

Day: £35.00

Lingfield Park Golf Club

Racecourse Road
Lingfield
Surrey RH7 6PQ

Secretary:

Ms Greer Milne
0342-834602

Professional:

Mr. C.K. Morley
0342-832659

Directions:

By Car: Exit Junction 6 (M25) and follow the signs to the racecourse. The course is next to the racecourse.

By BR: Lingfield Station.

Course Details:

This is a 6,500 yard eighteen hole, parkland course.

The course features several water hazards.

Shop Facilities:

The shop stocks a wide range of golf equipment and accessories. Clubs are available for hire at £10 per day.

Tuition Details:

There is a driving range attached to the course, together with a practice ground and bunkers. Video analysis is also available.

Lessons are available from £15 per 30 minutes. Contact the Pro shop for details of tuition.

Clubhouse Facilities:

Changing facilities, including showers, are available in the clubhouse.

Bar snacks are available from the lounge bar. There is also a Spike bar. Breakfast and lunch is available for members. Breakfast, lunch and dinner is available to Societies, by arrangement.

Visitor Restrictions and How to Book:

Visitors are welcome during the week but are not permitted at weekends, unless accompanying a member.

A range of options are available for Societies and these can be tailored to meet individual needs. Contact the Clubhouse office on 0342-834602 to discuss requirements.

Visitor Playing Costs:

Weekday Only:

18 holes - £25.00

Day - £35.00

Pachesham Golf Centre

Oaklawn Road
Leatherhead
Surrey KT22 0BT

Secretary:

Phil Taylor
0372-843453

Professional:

Phil Taylor
0372-843453

Directions:

By Car: Exit Junction 9 (M25) and take the A244 to Oxshott. After half a mile, turn left into Oaklawn Road.

Course Details:

This is a short 1,752 yard 9 hole public parkland course.

At present, the holes alternate between par 3's and par 4's. Plans have been approved to extend the 9 hole course to 3000 yards by May 1995.

Shop Facilities:

The shop stocks a range of golf equipment and accessories. Clubs are available for hire at £5 per set.

Tuition Details:

A 33 bay floodlit driving range is attached to the course. There is also a practice chipping area and bunker. Coaching is available from the resident professionals from £12.50 per 1/2 hour.

Clubhouse Facilities:

Changing facilities, including showers are available.

There is a fully licensed bar and restaurant. A full menu and daily specials are provided.

Visitor Restrictions and How to Book:

A handicap certificate is not required. Visitors can book up to two days in advance on 0372-843453.

Pay in the Pro shop.

Societies are welcomed and can be booked well in advance on receipt of a deposit.

Visitor Playing Costs:

Weekday / Weekend:

9 holes: £6.50 / £11.00

18 holes: £7.50 / £12.50

Juniors: Half Price

Purley Downs Golf Club

106 Purley Downs Road
South Croydon
Surrey CR2 0RB

Secretary:
Peter C Gallienne
081-657 8347

Professional:
Graham Wilson
081-651 0819

Directions:
By Car: 3 miles south of Croydon on the A23. Fork left into the Purley Downs Road.

Course Details:
This is an eighteen hole downland course.

The Club celebrated its centenary year in 1994. This tree-lined course has recently modernised several of its bunkers. The 1st hole is a 160 yard, par 3 offering an immediate challenge for accurate play.

Shop Facilities:
The shop stocks a range of golf equipment, accessories and designer clothing.

Tuition Details:
Practice facilities are available. Lessons are available at £10 per 30 minutes with the Assistant Pro and £12.50 with the Head Pro. Contact Graham Wilson for details.

Clubhouse Facilities:
The clubhouse provides a range of catering facilities through the lounge bar and dining room.

There is also a members only Snooker room.

Visitor Restrictions and How to Book:
A handicap certificate is required. Visitors are not permitted at weekends, unless accompanying a member as a guest. Visitors should book through the Pro shop.

Societies are welcome and should contact the Secretary for details.

Visitor Playing Costs:
Weekday Only:

Day: £30.00

Puttenham Golf Club

Puttenham Heath Road
Puttenham
Nr Guildford
Surrey GU3 1AL

Secretary:

Gary Simmons
0483-810498

Professional:

Gary Simmons
0483-810277

Directions:

By Car: The Club lies off the Hogs Back Road, near Guildford. Off the A31, take the turning sign-posted to Puttenham (B3000).

Course Details:

This is a 6214 yard, eighteen hole heathland course.

The course is mainly attractive heathland with some tight fairways in places. Off the competitive tees, it has 3 par 3's, 2 par 5's and one water hole.

Shop Facilities:

The shop stocks a range of golf equipment and accessories.

Tuition Details:

There is a practice area which includes a bunker. Lessons are available at £10 per half hour. Telephone 0483-810277 for details.

Clubhouse Facilities:

The clubhouse provides full changing facilities, including showers.

There is a fully licensed bar, lounge and dining room. Refreshments are served every day except Sundays. Refreshments range from light snacks to full meals. A jacket and tie is required in the Clubhouse after 6.00pm.

Golfing attire can be worn in the nineteenth bar.

Visitor Restrictions and How to Book:

A handicap certificate is not required.

Visitors are welcome, but are not permitted to play at weekends unless accompanying a member. Green fee bookings are only available subject to 24 hours notice. Pay via the Pro shop.

Society packages are available, although it is normally necessary to book well in advance.

Visitor Playing Costs:

Weekdays Only

18 holes - £21.00

Day - £27.00

Pyrford Golf Club 1993

Warren Lane
Pyrford
Surrey GU22 8XR

Secretary:
Mr. David Renton
0483-723555

Professional:
Mr. Jeremy Bennett
0483-751070

Directions:
By Car: Take the A3 to Portsmouth. From Ripley centre, turn right at the Town and Country Cars Garage. After 2 miles, turn right onto Warren Lane. The course is 1.5 miles on the right.

Course Details:
This is a par 72, 6230 yard, eighteen hole course.

Water plays a part on every hole (there are over 23 acres of lakes on the course). The par 5, 9th hole at 595 yards tests the longest hitters with a dog-leg requiring length and accuracy to make par.

Shop Facilities:
The shop stocks a range of golf equipment and accessories. Sets of clubs can be hired at £5 per round.

Tuition Details:
A driving range is attached to the course. Lessons cost £12 per 40 minutes with an assistant and £20 per 30 minutes with the PGA qualified professional. Contact Jeremy Bennett in the Pro shop for details.

Clubhouse Facilities:
Mens and Ladies changing rooms are available.

There is a main bar, spike bar and a la carte restaurant providing daily catering from 7.00am - 11.00pm.

Visitor Restrictions and How to Book:
Visitors are welcome on weekdays, but must accompany a member on weekends.

Computerised bookings are taken on the telephone and members are given priority. Contact the Pro shop on 0483-751070.

Societies should contact the Secretary for details.

Visitor Playing Costs:
Weekday / Weekend:

£35.00 / £50.00

Reigate Heath Golf Club

Flanchford Road
Reigate
Surrey RH2 8QR

Secretary:

R.J Perkins
0737-226793

Professional:

George Gow
0737-243077

Directions:

By Car: The course is located 1 mile west of Reigate.

Course Details:

This is a 5,658 yard eighteen hole, heathland course playing nine holes from two different tee positions.

The course has plenty of gorse, pine trees, silver birch and heather to contend with. Peter Alliss selected three holes from the course for his BBC series, 'A Round with Alliss'.

Established in 1895, the course celebrates its centenary in 1995.

Shop Facilities:

There is a small golf shop which offers a few basic items to players. There is a club repair service.

Tuition Details:

There is a practice ground on the course and lessons are available for groups or individuals.

Contact George Gow on 0737-243077 for details.

Clubhouse Facilities:

There are changing facilities available. A range of catering is available daily from the Club bar and dining room (with seating for 44).

Visitor Restrictions and How to Book:

Visitors are welcome during the week, but must accompany a member at the weekend.

Though a handicap certificate is not essential, visitors are expected to have golfing ability.

Visitors should book either through the Secretary or Club Steward on 0737-242610.

Societies are welcome on Wednesdays or Thursdays (max. 36 players). Contact the Secretary for details of requirements.

Visitor Playing Costs:

Weekday:

18 holes - £20.00

Day - £28.00

Royal Mid-Surrey Golf Club

Old Deer Park
Richmond
Surrey TW9 2SB

Secretary:

Mr. M.S.R Lunt
0181-940 1894

Professional:

Mr. D Talbot
0181-940 0459

Directions:

By Car: The course is located near the Richmond roundabout on the A316.

By BR / LUG: Richmond Station.

Course Details:

There are two parkland courses at Royal Mid-Surrey.

The Outer course is a 6,052 yard, eighteen hole parkland course. This fairly flat course is framed by Kew Gardens, Syon Park, the River Thames and Old Deer Park. The Inner course is a 5,544 yard, eighteen hole parkland course. Largely set within the bounds of the Outer course, the Inner threads its way around the Georgian Observatory.

Shop Facilities:

The shop offers a range of golf equipment, accessories and designer wear. Clubs can be hired for £7.50 per round.

Tuition Details:

There is both a practice ground and indoor nets for coaching purposes. Tuition costs from £13 per half hour. Contact the Pro shop for details.

Clubhouse Facilities:

There are mens and ladies changing rooms.

There is a mens bar, dining room, buttery and a mixed lounge. The buttery serves snacks through the day. The dining room offers an a la carte menu. Jacket and tie must be worn.

Visitor Restrictions and How to Book:

Visitors must be members of a recognised Club and must have a handicap certificate.

Visitors are not permitted at weekends or bank holidays, unless accompanying a member. It is necessary to telephone the Office on 0181-940 1894 before wishing to play.

Societies are welcome and should contact the Deputy Secretary for details.

Visitor Playing Costs:

Weekday Only:

Per Round or Day: £45.00

Rusper Golf Club

Rusper Road
Newdigate
Surrey RH5 5BX

Secretary:

Mr. G. Hems
0293-871456

Professional:

Karl Spurrier
0293-871871

Directions:

By Car: Take the A24 Dorking to Horsham road to the Beare Green roundabout. Follow the signpost to Newdigate. In the village follow the signpost to Rusper. The course is approximately 1 mile on the right.

Course Details:

This is a pay and play 6,069 yard, eighteen hole course, playing nine holes twice from different tee, and to different pin positions.

The 3rd, 5th and 6th holes all offer drives cut through trees along narrow fairways to well guarded greens. Accuracy, together with some length are required on these holes.

Shop Facilities:

The shop stocks a range of golf equipment and accessories. Clubs are available for hire at £4.50 for nine holes and £7.50 for eighteen holes.

Tuition Details:

There is a twelve bay covered driving range with various targets. Lessons are available from Karl Spurrier, the resident Pro at £15 for 45 minutes.

Book on 0293-871871.

Clubhouse Facilities:

There is a temporary clubhouse with adequate changing facilities. Bar snacks are available. There is also a pool table.

Visitor Restrictions and How to Book:

There are no visitor restrictions. It is possible to book up to 48 hours in advance by telephoning 0293-871871. Normal dress restrictions apply.

Society bookings are welcomed for groups of up to 50 players. A range of packages are available to meet individual requirements.

Visitor Playing Costs:

Weekdays / Weekends:

9 holes: £7.00 / £8.50

18 holes: £11.50 / £15.50

There are reductions available for juniors.

Selsdon Park Golf & CC

Addington Road
Sanderstead
South Croydon
Surrey CR2 8YA

Professional:

Tom O'Keefe
081-6578811

Directions:

By Car: Exit Junction 6 (M25). Follow the A22 to Whyteleafe. Take the B270 toward Warlington. Take the first left to Sanderstead and turn left onto B269. Take the third exit right from first roundabout towards Selsdon on A2022.

Course Details:

This is a 6407 yard, eighteen hole parkland course.

Set within the 200 acre Selsdon Park Estate, the course was designed by J.H.Taylor in 1929. Holes named 'Ash Tree', 'Cedars' and 'Weymouth Pine' give some idea of the established trees that line the fairways of this course which has been a venue for a number of professional tournaments.

Shop Facilities:

The shop is stocked with a range of golf equipment and accessories. Club hire is available at £11.50 per round.

Tuition Details:

The Bob Torrance Golf Academy is based at Selsdon Park and Sam Torrance is the Touring Professional. Lessons cost £15 per 30 minutes. Video analysis is available.

Clubhouse Facilities:

At present, the facilities normally associated with a Clubhouse are provided by the Hotel. Changing facilities are at the west end of the hotel.

A temporary Clubhouse-style facility may be provided if a proposal to launch a Golf and Country Club proceeds, together with necessary planning permissions.

Visitor Restrictions and How to Book:

A handicap certificate is not required. Bookings are taken up to one week in advance. Telephone 081-657 8811 Ext. 671 for reservations.

A range of five packages are available for Societies from £31. There must be a minimum of 10 players in the group.

Visitor Playing Costs:

18 holes:

Weekday - £20.00

Weekend - £30.00

Silvermere Golf Club

Redhill Road
Cobham
Surrey KT11 1EF

Secretary:

Mrs. Pauline Devereux
0932-866007

Professional:

Mr. Doug McClelland
0932-876275

Directions:

By Car: The course is located half a mile from Junction 10 (M25) on the A3. Turn onto the A245 to Byfleet. Redhill Road is 1/2 mile down on the left.

Course Details:

This is a 6,300 yard eighteen hole parkland course.

Designed in 1975 by Neil Coles and Brian Huggett, with more recent improvements, it is noted for its tough four finishing holes. A new 18th hole, due to be opened in 1995 requires a straight drive followed by a second over water to a newly constructed island green.

Shop Facilities:

There is a large shop stocking a wide range of golf equipment, accessories and designer wear.

Tuition Details:

Tuition is available at £12 per half hour for individuals and £25 for 4 one hour group lessons.

Clubhouse Facilities:

There is a brand new clubhouse overlooking the Silvermere Lake.

There is a bar providing a snack and hot food service through the day. The main function room has a seating capacity of up to 120 people.

Visitor Restrictions and How to Book:

Visitors are welcome but are not permitted to play before 12.00noon on weekends.

Telephone bookings are taken up to 7 days in advance on 0932-867275.

Societies are welcome. Details of packages and special offers can be obtained from Pauline Devereux.

Visitor Playing Costs:

Weekday / Weekend (after 12.00noon):

£16.50 / £22.00

Summertime twilight golf tickets from £6.50

Tandridge Golf Club

Oxted
Surrey RH8 9NQ

Secretary:

A.S Furnival
0883-712274

Professional:

Allan Farquhar
0883-713701

Directions:

By Car: Exit Junction 6 (M25). The club is located off the A25 between Redhill and Westerham, just outside Oxted.

Course Details:

This is a 5,854 yard, eighteen hole, wooded, parkland course.

Opened in 1925, the course consists of two nine hole loops which both start and end at the clubhouse. The first nine are fairly gentle, whilst the last nine are more undulating. The 14th hole is probably the most scenic on the course.

Shop Facilities:

The shop stocks a range of golf equipment and accessories. Club hire is available.

Tuition Details:

There are two practice grounds at the course and lessons are available from the resident Pro at £12/£15 per 30/40 minutes. Contact Allan Farquhar for details.

Clubhouse Facilities:

Changing facilities are available.

There is a restaurant and gallery buffet bar providing catering services throughout the day.

Visitor Restrictions and How to Book:

A handicap certificate is required and bookings must be made by prior arrangement. Casual visitors should book through the Pro shop.

Visitors are permitted to play on Mondays, Wednesdays and Thursdays only.

Societies should book through the Secretary's office. Groups of 20-30 can play on Mondays, whilst groups of up to 40 can play on Wednesdays and Thursdays.

Visitor Player Costs

18 holes - £31.00

Day - £40.00

Thames Ditton & Esher Golf Club

Portsmouth Road
Esher
Surrey KT10 9AL

Secretary:

D.I. Kaye
081-398 1551

Professional:

R. Hutton
081-398 1551

Directions:

By Car: The course is by the Marquis of Granby public house at the 'Scilly Isles' roundabout on the A3.

By BR: Esher Station.

Course Details:

This is an eighteen hole heathland course, playing nine holes twice from different tee positions.

The course is flat, well wooded and typical of a common heathland course.

Shop Facilities:

There is a modest selection of golf equipment and accessories.

Tuition Details:

There is no practice ground at the course, though lessons are available from the Pro shop. Lessons cost £8 per 30 minutes,

Contact the Pro shop to book.

Clubhouse Facilities:

Changing facilities, including showers are available.

There is a fully licensed bar. Food is available by prior arrangement.

Visitor Restrictions and How to Book:

No handicap certificate is required. Normal dress restrictions apply. Visitors are not permitted to play before 12.30pm on Sundays. Contact the Pro shop by telephone on 081-398 1551 to book a tee.

Societies up to 25 players can be accommodated. Contact the Secretary with requirements.

Visitor Playing Costs:

Weekday / Weekend (after 12.30pm on Sundays):

18 holes - £10.00 / £12.00

Walton Heath Golf Club

Tadworth
Surrey KT20 7TP

Secretary:

Gp Capt. G.R. James
0737-812380

Professional:

Ken McPherson
0737-812152

Directions:

By Car: The course is located on the B2032. Exit Junction 8 (M25) and follow the A217 north.

Course Details:

There are two eighteen hole courses at Walton Heath.

They are the 6801 yard Old course and the 6609 yard New course. Both are heathland courses with heather, pine and silver birch. The Old course has a challenging finish with several testing closing holes.

Shop Facilities:

The shop stocks a range of golf equipment, accessories and designer wear. Club hire is available.

Tuition Details:

There is a large practice area. Lessons cost £15/£17.50 for 45 minutes with the Assistant/Head Professional. Contact the shop on 0737-812152 for details.

Clubhouse Facilities:

Full changing facilities are available.

The clubhouse has two bars, a dining room and lounge providing a range of catering. A jacket and tie should be worn in public rooms.

Visitor Restrictions and How to Book:

Visitors are welcome on weekdays, but must accompany a member at weekends and on bank holidays.

A current handicap certificate is required and visitors should be members of a recognised golf club. Visitors should book in advance by telephone or letter of introduction.

Societies are welcome on weekdays by prior arrangement and should contact the Secretary for details.

Visitor Playing Costs:

Weekday Only:

£57.00 before 11.30am

£47.00 after 11.30am

Wentworth Club Limited.

Wentworth Drive
Virginia Water
Surrey GU25 4LS

General Manager:

Keith Williams
01344-842201

Professional:

Bernard Gallacher
01344-843353

Directions:

By Car: 21 miles south-west of London, just off the A30 at junction with A329 to Ascot. The M25 and M3 are 3 miles away.

Course Details:

There are three eighteen hole courses and one nine hole course at Wentworth. The West Course is 6,945 yards, S.S.S. 74. The East Course is 6,176 yards, S.S.S 70. The Edinburgh Course is 6,979 yards, S.S.S. 73. The Executive course is nine holes.

The courses are essentially Surrey heathland with a selection of pine, oak and birch trees. The West course has been made famous by the televising of the World Match Play in October and the PGA Championship in May.

Shop Facilities:

Bernard Gallacher's Pro shop stocks a range of golf equipment and accessories. The Wentworth shop offers an exclusive collection of accessories and mementos reflecting the Club's history, philosophy and lifestyle.

Tuition Details:

Tuition is only available to members and guests from the professional staff.

Clubhouse Facilities:

There is a spiked golfers' complex, bar, Club lounge, Dining room offering brasserie and formal dining throughout the day, plus private meeting and function rooms.

Visitor Restrictions and How To Book:

Visitors are welcome on weekdays only. A handicap certificate is required. Men (20) and Ladies (30). Bookings and payment should be made through the Club reception on 01344-842201.

Societies are welcome. Contact the Society Co-ordinator for details.

Visitor Playing Costs:

Weekdays Only: (per round)(1994 fees)

West Course: £90.00

East Course: £70.00

Edinburgh Course: £70.00

West Hill Golf Club (1959) Ltd.

Bagshot Road
Brookwood
Surrey GU24 0BH

Secretary:

M.C Swatton
0483-474365

Professional:

J.A Clements
0483-473172

Directions:

By Car: The course is located 5 miles west of Woking on the A322.

Course Details:

This is a 6,368 yard eighteen hole wooded heathland course.

There are several challenging par 3's on the course. The par 4, 18th hole provides a fine finish to the round.

Shop Facilities:

The shop is well stocked with golf equipment and accessories. Clubs are available for hire at £15 per round or £20 per day.

Tuition Details:

There is a practice ground within the confines of the course. Lessons are available at £15 per hour with the Assistant and £20 with the Head Pro.

Contact the Pro shop to book.

Clubhouse Facilities:

Changing facilities, including showers are available.

Catering is provided in the cafeteria and dining room. A jacket and tie are required in the mixed lounge and dining room.

There is a half way hut on the course available for refeshments.

Visitor Restrictions and How to Book:

Visitors are welcome on weekdays on the production of a handicap certificate. Book by telephone through the Secretary's office and pay in the Pro shop.

Societies are welcome on weekdays, bar Wednesday. Packages range from £29.00 to £61.00. Contact the Secretary for details.

Visitor Playing Costs:

Weekdays Only:

18 holes - £32.00

Day - £42.00

Windlesham Golf Club

Grove End
Bagshot
Surrey GU19 5HY

Secretary:

Philip Watts
0276-452220

Professional:

Alan Barber / Kim Short
0276-472323

Directions:

By Car: Exit Junction 3 (M3). Take the A322 towards Bracknell and then the A30 to Sunningdale. Turn right at the mini roundabout. The entrance is 200 yards on the left.

Course Details:

This is a 6,515 yard, par 71 parkland course.

The course has a mixture of mature trees and natural lakes. The 1st hole poses an immediate challenge with a second shot 200 yard carry over 'Lady Meades' boating lake to the green. The 12th hole requires a shot towards a raised green in front of the Clubhouse.

Shop Facilities:

The shop stocks a wide range of golf equipment and accessories.

Tuition Details:

There is a Teaching Centre and practice ground with grass seeded bays available. Whilst the practice ground is 300 yards in length, there is also a short game practice area. Lessons are available at £18 for 30 minutes. Video analysis is available at the same price.

Contact the Centre on 0276-472323 for details.

Clubhouse Facilities:

Full changing facilities, including showers are available.

Catering is available in the bar and restaurant. There are two function rooms catering for 30/80 people. There is also a spike bar.

Visitor Restrictions and How to Book:

After April 1995, a current handicap certificate will be required. Visitors must telephone to confirm availability. Telephone the Reception on 0276-452220 for enquiries.

Societies are welcome mid-week only and should contact the Reception for details.

Visitor Playing Costs:

Weekdays / Weekends:

£30.00 / £40.00

Woodcote Park Golf Club

Meadow Hill
Bridle Way
Coulsdon
Surrey CR3 2QQ

Secretary:

T. J Fenson
081-668 2788

Professional:

D. Hudspith
081-668 1843

Directions:

By Car: The course is located on the B2030 south of Croydon.

Course Details:

This is a 6,669 yard, eighteen hole parkland course, offering a comfortable round of golf.

Shop Facilities:

The shop stocks a wide range of golf equipment and accessories. Clubs are not available for hire.

Tuition Details:

There is a good practice ground on the course. Lessons are available from the professional at £15 for 45 minutes. Contact the Pro shop on 081-668 1843 to book.

Clubhouse Facilities:

Changing facilities are available. Catering is available seven days a week. There is a lounge bar and large dining room.

There is also a Spike bar.

Visitor Restrictions and How to Book:

A handicap certificate is required. Visitors are welcome to play on weekdays, but must be accompanied by a member at weekends.

Tuesday am is Ladies day.

Casual players should book though the Pro shop.

Societies are welcome (min. 20 players). Contact the Secretary for details of the packages available for Society Days.

Visitor Playing Costs:

Weekdays Only:

18 holes - £25.00

Day - £35.00

GOLF IN HERTFORDSHIRE

Hertfordshire is blessed with a great number of good courses. The majority are found towards the southern end of the county, though the north and west have their fair share of excellent fairways.

Ashridge Golf Club and **Berkhamsted Golf Club,** both on the Chiltern fringe are a delightful combination of heathland and parkland. For those attracted to sand, Berkhamsted has the notable feature of a complete absence of bunkers.

Further south, courses become more parkland in nature. Harpenden is the home to two: **Harpenden Golf Club** and **Harpenden Common Golf Club**. Around Hatfield and Hertford there are several good courses including **Brickendon Grange Golf Club** at Brickendon and **Brookmans Park Golf Club** near Hatfield.

Two courses attached to hotels around Ware require mention. The 9 hole course at the **Briggens House Hotel** and the eighteen hole course at **Hanbury Manor.** The course at Hanbury Manor carefully blends both a downland and a parkland terrain, the design making good use of its natural surroundings.

A View of the 12th Green at Bishops Stortford Golf Club

The greatest concentration of courses in Hertfordshire are found just north of London.

Potters Bar Golf Club in Potters Bar, **Arkley Golf Club, Old Fold Manor Golf Club,** and **Hadley Wood Golf Club**, all in Barnet, are all long-established clubs offering testing rounds of parkland golf. **Moor Park,** near Rickmansworth offers classic parkland golf on its High and its West courses.

For players looking for courses with few restrictions, yet offering competitive and challenging golf, Bushey has two excellent courses; **Bushey Golf and Country Club** and **Bushey Hall Golf Club.**

For relative newcomers to the game, Hertforshire offers several good public and 'pay and play' facilities. **Batchwood Golf Centre** in St. Albans is a well-run municipal eighteen hole course providing a good round of golf. The **Little Hay Golf Complex** near Hemel Hempstead and the **Oxhey Park Golf Course** near Watford both operate on a no restriction basis.

Elstree Golf Club

Bushey Golf and Country Club

134

Aldenham Golf and Country Club
Church Lane
Aldenham
Watford
Hertfordshire WD2 8AL

Mrs Stephanie Taylor
0923-853929

Arkley Golf Club
Rowley Green Road
Barnet
Hertfordshire EN5 3HL

Mr GD Taylor
081-449 0394

Ashridge Golf Club
Little Gadesden
Berkhamsted
Hertfordshire HP4 1LY

Mrs MA West
0442-842244

Batchwood Golf Centre
Batchwood Drive
St. Albans
Hertfordshire AL3 5XA

John Collantine
0727-844250

Berkhamsted Golf Club
The Common
Berkhamsted
Hertfordshire HP4 2QB

Mr Colin Hextall
0442-865832

Bishop's Stortford Golf Club
Dunmow Road
Bishop's Stortford
Hertfordshire CM23 5HP

Mr Brian Hunt
0279-654715

Boxmoor Golf Club
18 Box Lane
Hemel Hempstead
Hertfordshire

Mr Colin Whitney
0442-242434

Brickendon Grange Golf Club
Brickendon
Nr Hertford
Hertfordshire SG13 8PD

Mr Colin Macdonald
0992-511258

Briggens House Hotel Golf Club
Briggens Park
Stanstead Road
Stanstead Abbotts
Hertfordshire SG12 8LD

Mr P Warwick
0279-793742

Brockett Hall Golf Club
Brockett Hall
Welwyn
Hertfordshire AL8 7XG

Miss K Hills
0707-390055

Brookmans Park Golf Club
Brookmans Park
Hatfield
Hertfordshire AL9 7AT

Mr Peter Gill
0707-652487

COURSES IN HERTFORDSHIRE

Bushey Golf and Country Club
High Street
Bushey
Hertfordshire WD2 1BJ

Mr A Barton
081-950 2283

Bushey Hall Golf Club
Bushey Hall Drive
Bushey
Hertfordshire WD2 2EP

Mr Julian Smith
0923-222253

Chadwell Springs Golf Club
Hertford Road
Ware
Hertfordshire SG12 9LE

Mr Raymond White
0920-461447

Cheshunt Golf Club
Park Lane
Cheshunt
Hertfordshire EN7 6QD

Mr C Newton
0992-624009

Chorleywood Golf Club
Common Road
Chorleywood
Hertfordshire WD3 5LN

Mr RM Leonard
0923-282009

Danesbury Park Golf Club
Codicote Road
Welwyn
Hertfordshire AL6 9SD

Mr D Snowdon
0438-840100

Dyrham Park CC
Galley Lane
Barnet
Hertfordshire EN5 4RA

Mr DU Prentice
081-440 3361

East Herts Golf Club
Hamels Park
Buntingford
Hertfordshire SG9 9NA

The Secretary
0920-821978

Elstree Golf Club
Watling Street
Elstree
Hertfordshire WD6 3AA

Mrs C Brown
081-953 6115

The Chesfield Downs Family Golf Centre
Jack's Hill
Graveley
Hertfordshire SG4 7EQ

Ms Jane Fernley
0462-482929

Great Hadham Golf Club
Great Hadham Road
Much Hadham
Hertfordshire SG10 6JE

Mrs J Ovendon
0279-843558

Hadley Wood Golf Club
Beech Hill
Barnet
Hertfordshire EN4 0JJ

Mr Peter Bryan
081-449 4328

Hanbury Manor Golf Club
Thundridge
Ware
Hertfordshire SG12 0SD

Mr D McClaren
0920-487722

Harpenden Golf Club
Hammonds End
Redbourn Lane
Harpenden
Hertfordshire AL5 2AX

Mr JR Newton
0582-712580

Harpenden Common Golf Club
East Common
Harpenden
Hertfordshire AL5 1BL

Mr Robin Parry
0582-715959

Hartsbourne Golf and CC
Hartsbourne Avenue
Bushey Heath
Hertfordshire WD2 1JW

Mr DJ Woodman
081-950 1133

Hatfield London Country Club
Bedwell Park
Essendon
Hatfield

Hertfordshire AL9 6JA

Mrs Christina Jolly
01707-642624

The Hertfordshire Golf Club
White Stubbs Lane
Broxbourne
Hertfordshire EN10 7PY

Kingsway Golf Centre
Cambridge Road
Melbourn
Royston
Hertfordshire SG8 6EY

Mrs AJ Tinston
0763-262727

Knebworth Golf Club
Deards End Lane
Knebworth
Hertfordshire SG3 6NL

Mr Mike Parsons
0438-814681

Laing Sports Club
Rowley Lane
Arkley
Barnet
Hertfordshire

081-441 6051

Letchworth Golf Club
Letchworth
Hertfordshire SG6 3NQ

Mr AR Bailey
0462-683203

Little Hay Golf Complex
Box Lane
Bovingdon

Hemel Hempstead
Hertfordshire HP3 0DQ

Mr D Johnson
0442-833798

Manor of Groves Golf and Country Club
High Wych
Sawbridgeworth
Hertfordshire CM21 0LA

Mr Kevin Moss
0279-722333

Mid-Herts Golf Club
Lamer Lane
Gustard Wood
Wheathampstead
Hertfordshire AL4 8RS

Mr RJH Jourdan
0582-832242

Mill Green Golf Club
Gypsy Lane
Welwyn Garden City
Hertfordshire AL7 4TY

Mr Jonathon Tubb
0707-276900

Moor Park Golf Club
Rickmansworth
Hertfordshire WD3 1QN

Mr JA Davies
0923-773146

Old Fold Manor Golf Club
Hadley Green
Barnet
Hertfordshire EN5 4QN

Mr AW Dickens
081-440 9185

Oxhey Park Golf Course
Prestwick Road
South Oxhey
Watford
Hertfordshire WD1 4ED

Mr TR Warner
0923-248312

Panshanger Golf Club
Old Herns Lane
Welwyn Garden City
Hertfordshire AL7 2ED

Mrs Sheila Ryan
0707-332837

Porters Park Golf Club
Shenley Hill
Radlett
Hertfordshire WD7 7AZ

Mr JH Roberts
0923-854127

Potters Bar Golf Club
Darkes Lane
Potters Bar
Hertfordshire EN6 1DF

Mr Arthur St. John Williams
0707-652020

Redbourn Golf Club Ltd.
Kingsbourne Green Lane
Redbourn
St Albans
Hertfordshire AL3 7QA

Mr Chris Gyford
0582-793493

Rickmansworth Golf Club
Moor Lane
Rickmansworth
Hertfordshire WD3 1QL

Mr Jim Devan
0923-775278

Royston Golf Club
Baldock Road
Royston
Hertfordshire SG8 5BG

Mr David Mear
0763-242696

Shendish Manor Golf Centre
Shendish Manor
London Road, Apsley
Hemel Hempstead HP3 0AA
Hertfordshire

0442-251806

Stevenage Golf Club
Ashton Lane
Stevenage
Hertfordshire SG2 7EL

Mr John Ryder
0438-880322

Stocks Hotel Country Club
Stocks Road
Aldbury
Tring
Hertfordshire HP23 5RX

Ms Hilary Schneiders
0442-851341

Tudor Park Sports Ground
Clifford Road
East Barnet
Hertfordshire

Miss Alison Keifer
081-449 0282

Verulam Golf Club
London Road
St. Albans
Hertfordshire AL1 1JC

Mr C Smith
0727-853327

Welwyn Garden City Golf Club
Mannicotts
High Oaks Road
Welwyn Garden City
Hertfordshire AL8 7BP

Mr Michael Flint
0707-325243

West Herts Golf Club
Cassiobury Park
Watford
Hertfordshire WD1 7SL

Mr CM Brown
0923-236484

Whipsnade Park Golf Club
Studham Lane
Dagnall
Hertfordshire HP4 1RH

Mr D Whalley
0442-842330

Whitehill Golf Club
Dane End
Ware
Hertfordshire SG12 0JS

Mr A Smith
0920-438495

Arkley Golf Club

*Rowley Green Road
Barnet
Hertfordshire EN5 3HL*

Secretary:

G.D Taylor
081-449 0394

Professional:

Mark Squire
081-440 8473

Directions:

By Car: From Stirling Corner on the A1, take the A411 towards Barnet. Turn left into Rowley Lane after passing the Gate pub, then right into Rowley Green Road. The club is on the left.

Course Details:

This is an established undulating, parkland nine hole course with eighteen tees.

The course is fairly tight with many oaks and birches lining the fairways. The 3rd, par 4, 383 yard hole, is probably the prettiest, whilst the 4th, also a par 4 is the most difficult. Drive right and you will be blocked out by a hedge of hawthorn and aspen.

Shop Facilities:

The shop stocks a range of golf equipment and accessories.

Tuition Details:

There is a practice ground and bunker area. Lessons are available at £10 per hour. Group coaching of 6 to 8 persons is available at £20 per hour.

Contact the Pro shop to book.

Clubhouse Facilities:

Changing facilities, including showers are available.

Bar snacks and dining room facilities are available. Smart casual wear is required in the bar and lounge. Jacket, collar and tie are required in the dining room, which can accommodate up to 60 people. Catering is limited on Mondays.

Visitor Restrictions and How to Book:

A handicap certificate is required. Visitors are not permitted to play at weekends, unless accompanying a member. Visitors should book through the Pro shop.

Ladies Day is on Tuesday am.

Societies are welcome and should book through the Secretary on weekday mornings. Packages start at £22.00, including 3 course dinner.

Visitors Playing Costs:

£15.00 per day/ round.

Batchwood Golf Centre

Batchwood Drive
St. Albans
Hertfordshire AL3 5XA

Secretary:

John Collantine
0727-844250

Professional:

Jimmy Thompson
0727-852101

Directions:

By Car: From St. Albans City centre, take Verulam Road from the High Street. Turn right into Batchwood Drive, The course is on the left.

Course Details:

This is an eighteen hole parkland course.

Part of the Batchwood Municipal Leisure complex, the course, established in 1935 offers a challenge to both beginners and established players.

Shop Facilities:

The shop stocks a full range of golf equipment and accessories. Clubs are available to hire at £5 per round.

Tuition Details:

Lessons are available and should be booked through the Pro shop. Lessons cost from £15/£23 for 45 minutes with the Assistant/Head Pro.

Clubhouse Facilities:

There is a large on-site complex which provides a range of catering and sports facilities. There are both indoor and outdoor tennis Courts, a gymnasium club and squash courts.

A bar and restaurant provide a range of catering.

Visitor Restrictions and How to Book:

There are no restrictions.

Because of demand you may be expected to make up a 4-ball group. A telephone booking card is available for £31.50 which enables you to book by telephone up to eight days in advance. Otherwise book in person via the Reception or by telephone on day of play on 0727-844250.

Golf days are available. Contact Gill Milne for details.

Season Tickets are available.

Visitor Playing Costs:

Weekdays - £7.75

Weekends - £10.50

Berkhamsted Golf Club

The Common
Berkhamsted
Hertfordshire HP4 2QB

Secretary:
Colin Hextall
0442-865832

Professional:
Basil Proudfoot
0442-865851

Directions:
By Car: Take the A41 from Hemel Hempstead to the Aylesbury / Berkhamsted turn-off. In Berkhamsted, turn right by the church into Ravens Lane. The club is 500 yards on left at top of the road.

Course Details:
This is an eighteen hole, par 71, heathland course.

Its most outstanding feature is the total absence of bunkers. Tight fairways and the presence of large numbers of trees do not however make this a suitable course for novices.

Shop Facilities:
The shop stocks a full range of golf equipment and accessories.

Tuition Details:
There is a practice ground and fee paying visitors may use the practice ground. Lessons cost £15 for 40 minutes. Contact Basil Proudfoot for details.

Clubhouse Facilities:
Full changing facilities are available.

Bar and catering facilities are available in the bar and restaurant. Jacket, collar and tie are required in the main lounge and restaurant after 6.00pm.

Visitor Restrictions and How to Book:
A handicap certificate is required. Visitors are not permitted to play before 11.30am on weekends. Book through the Pro Shop.

Societies are welcome. Telephone or write with requirements to Colin Hextall on 0442-865832

Visitor Playing Cost:
Weekday /Weekend (after 11.30am)

18 holes - £20.00 / £30 (winter), £35 (summer)

All Day (weekdays) - £30 (winter), £35 (summer)

Bishop's Stortford Golf Club

Dunmow Road
Bishop's Stortford
Hertfordshire CM23 5HP

Secretary:

Mr. B. Hunt
0279-654715

Professional:

Vince Duncan
0279-651324

Directions:

By Car: From Junction 8 (M11), take the A120 (West). Leave the adjacent island onto the B1250 for Bishops Stortford. The Club entrance is 3/4 of a mile on the left.

Course Details:

This is a 6256 yard, par 71, parkland course.

Shop Facilities:

The shop stocks a wide range of golf equipment, accessories and designer wear.

Tuition Details:

There is a practice ground and there are also indoor coaching facilities. Lessons are available at £12 for 30 minutes. Video analysis is available at £20 for 45 minutes. Contact the Pro shop to book.

Clubhouse Facilities:

Full changing facilities are available in the clubhouse.

A bar and restaurant providing a range of catering facilities are available for both lunch and dinner. Teas are also available. A large terrace overlooks the eighteenth green.

Visitor Restrictions and How to Book:

A handicap certificate is required. Visitors are welcome on weekdays, but must accompany a member at weekends. Book through the Pro shop for available tee-times.

Ladies Day is on Tuesday.

Societies are welcomed on Mondays, Wednesdays, Thursdays and Fridays (min. 15 and max. 40). Prices range from £32.00 to £47.00. Breakfasts can be arranged. Full details are available from the Secretary.

Visitor Playing Costs:

Weekdays:

£21.00 per day

Brickendon Grange Golf Club

*Brickendon
Nr Hertford
Hertfordshire SG13 8PD*

Secretary:

C.T. Macdonald
0992-511258

Profesional:

J. Hamilton
0992-511218

Directions:

By Car: Bayford, the closest village to the course, is three miles south of Hertford off the B158.

By BR: Bayford Station.

Course Details:

This is a 6044 yard, eighteen hole parkland course.

Holes such as the par 5, 13th hole 'Langwhang' and the par 4, 17th 'Ace of Hearts', which requires an accurate approach shot to an elevated green, offer a good golfing challenge.

Shop Facilities:

The shop stocks a good range of golf equipment and accessories.

Tuition Details:

Lessons are available at £12.50 for 30 minutes and £17.50 for 45 minutes. Video analysis is available at £25 per hour.

Contact the Pro shop with requirements.

Clubhouse Facilities:

There are Mens and Ladies changing rooms.

There is a bar, dining room and TV lounge in the clubhouse which provide daily catering.

Visitor Restrictions and How to Book:

A handicap certificate is required. Visitors are welcome on weekdays, except Wednesday am which is Ladies Day.

Visitors must accompany a member as a guest at weekends.

Visitors should book via the Pro shop, whilst Societies should make arrangements through the Secretary.

Visitor Playing Costs:

Weekdays Only:

18 holes - £24.00

Day - £30.00

Brookmans Park Golf Club

Brookmans Park
Hatfield
Hertfordshire AL9 7AT

Secretary:

Peter A Gill
0707-652487

Professional:

Ian Jelley
0707-652468

Directions:

By Car: 3 miles south of Hatfield, off the A1000. Alternatively turn off Junction 24 (M25) and through Potters Bar on to the A1000.

By BR: Brookmans Park Station is one mile away.

Course Details:

This is an eighteen hole, par 71, parkland course.

The course has two lakes which come into play. There is an abundance of wildlife on the course including squirrels, muntjacs, Canada geese and moorhens.

Shop Facilities:

The shop is well stocked with golf equipment and accessories.

Tuition Details:

There is a small practice ground. Lessons are available at £7/£9 for 30 minutes from the Assistant/Head Pro and £13/£17.50 for 1 hour. Contact the Pro shop for details.

Clubhouse Facilities:

Full changing facilities are available, including showers.

Catering services are provided by a lounge bar, dining room and men's stud bar. Smart casual wear is allowed in the clubhouse, though jackets are required in the dining room and after 6.30pm in the lounge.

Visitor Restrictions and How to Book:

A handicap certificate is required.

At weekends, visitors are not permitted unless accompanied by a member and should hold a current handicap certificate of 18 or better. Book through the Pro shop or the Secretary's office.

Societies are welcome. Contact Mrs. R. Vincent in the Secretary's office for details.

Visitor Playing Costs:

Weekday:

18 holes - £27.00

Day - £32.00

Bushey Golf and Country Club

High Street
Bushey
Hertfordshire WD2 1BJ

Manager:

Mr A. Barton
081- 950 2283

Professional:

Mike Lovegrove
081-950 2283

Directions:

By Car: The course is off the main high street in Bushey village.

Course Details:

This is a nine hole parkland course, playing as a 5744 yard, eighteen hole course.

Playing from the first tee up a hill with the driving range to the right, the course is set on a slope overlooking the village. The varied holes provide a test for most levels of golfer.

Shop Details:

The shop is part of the Nevada Bob golf chain and stocks a wide range of golf equipment and accessories.

Tuition Details:

There is a two tier driving range on site. Golf lessons are offered by the resident PGA qualified professionals at £10 per 1/2 hour. Contact the shop to book.

Clubhouse Facilities:

The clubhouse provides daily catering through a ground floor bar and lounge. There is a further lounge upstairs which opens onto a balcony overlooking the course.

Other on-site facilities include changing rooms, squash courts and a fully equipped gymnasium.

Visitor Restrictions and How to Book:

Visitors are not permitted to play on Wednesdays.

On other weekdays, visitors are welcome between 9.30 am and 4.30pm. At weekends, visitors can only play after 2.30pm. Book and pay in the shop.

Societies should contact the Clubhouse for details of packages available.

Visitor Playing Costs:

9 holes - £6.00

18 holes - £8.00

Bushey Hall Golf Club

Bushey Hall Drive
Bushey
Hertfordshire WD2 2EP

General Manager:

Mr Julian Smith
0923-222253

Professional:

Mr. K. Wickham
0923-225802

Direction:

By Car: Exit Junction 5 (M1) and take the A41 South to next roundabout (200yds). Take the right turning to Hartspring Road. The course is located about 1/2 a mile away, close to a small roundabout.

Course Details:

This is an eighteen hole, 6099 yard, par 71, tree-lined and established parkland course.

The course offers an interesting test of golf to club golfers. It has recently become a 'pay as you play' course having celebrated its centenary in 1991 as a private members Club. The 9th and 10th holes offer a good par 3 back-to-back challenge.

Shop Facilities:

The shop is stocked with a good range of golf equipment and accessories. Club hire is available at £5.00 per round.

Tuition Details:

There are practice nets, a practice bunker and putting green. Lessons cost £10/£12 for 30 minutes from the Assistant/Head Pro.

Clubhouse Facilities:

Full changing facilities are available, including showers.

There are two bars and a restaurant providing a range of catering facilities throughout the day. There is also a snooker room and sun room.

Visitor Restrictions and How to Book:

There are no visitor restrictions.

All tee-times have to be pre-booked via the Pro shop. Telephone the shop on 0923-225802.

Societies are welcome on weekdays. There should be a minimum of 12 players in the group. Contact the Pro shop for details.

Visitor Playing Costs:

Weekday / Weekend:

Adults: £11.00 / £15.00

The Chesfield Downs Family Golf Centre

Jack's Hill
Graveley
Hertfordshire SG4 7EQ

Secretary:

Jane Fernley
0462-482929

Professional:

Jane Fernley/David Boot
0462-482929

Directions:

By Car: Exit Junction 23 (M25) onto the A1(M). Exit Junction 8 or 9 off the A1(M) onto the B197 through Graveley.

Course Details:

There are two courses at Chesfield Downs.

The Chesfield Downs is an eighteen hole, 6,709 yard, par 71, chalk downland course. The par 3, 3rd hole requires a drive over a lake, whilst the dog-leg right 11th hole requires a good tee shot to bring the green into play with the second shot. The Lannock Links is a 9 hole, par 3 course and is ideal for beginners and those testing their short game.

Shop Facilities:

The large shop stocks a wide range of golf equipment, accessories and designer wear. Sets of clubs are available for hire at £4.50/£7.50 for a half set/full set.

Tuition Details:

There is a 25 bay floodlit driving range attached to the course. Lessons cost from £12 for 30 minutes. A 9 hole playing lesson costs £24.

Clubhouse Facilities:

Full changing facilities are available in the refurbished changing rooms. The clubhouse provides a wide range of catering services in its coffee lounge, function room and Chesfield's Restaurant and Bar.

Visitor Restrictions and How to Book:

There are no visitor restrictions.

Tee times for Chesfield Downs can be booked up to 6 days in advance of play. Players may be asked to make up a 3/4 ball match. Payment must be made at the time of booking. The Lannock Links does not have a booking system.

Societies are welcome. Contact Katie Oldham, Society Administrator for details of packages available.

Visitor Playing Costs:

Chesfield Downs: Weekday/Weekend

18 holes - £12.50 / £17.75

9 holes - £9.00 / £12.00

East Herts Golf Club

Hamels Park
Buntingford
Hertfordshire SG9 9NA

Secretary:

The Secretary
0920-821978

Professional:

Jim Hamilton
0920-821922

Directions:

By Car: The course is 1/4 mile north of Puckeridge on the Western side of the A10.

Course Details:

This is an eighteen hole, 6455 yard, parkland course.

Mature trees line most fairways requiring accuracy on all holes. Length from the tee is a must on the 3rd, 8th and 16th holes.

Shop Facilities:

The shop stocks a good range of golf equipment, accessories and designer wear.

Tuition Details:

The practice ground is available to members and fee-paying players. Lessons cost £10 for 30 minutes and £18 for an hour. Contact the Pro shop with your requirements.

Clubhouse Facilities:

The clubhouse provides a range of bar and restaurant facilities.

Jacket, collar and tie are required in the dining room in the evenings. Otherwise smart casual wear is permitted in the lounge until 7.00pm.

Visitor Restrictions and How to Book:

A handicap certificate is required and visitors are not permitted to play at weekends or on bank holidays, unless accompanying a member.

Book for weekday play through the Pro shop either by telephone or in person.

Societies are welcome. Larger groups play on Mondays and Fridays. Groups of up to 35 are welcome on Tuesdays and up to 25 on Wednesday pm and Thursdays.

Details and booking forms are available from the Secretary's office.

Visitor Playing Costs:

Weekday Only:

18 holes - £23.00

Day - £30.00

Great Hadham Golf Club

Great Hadham Road
Much Hadham
Hertfordshire SG10 6JE

Secretary:

J. Ovenden
0279-843558

Professional:

K. Lunt
0279-843888

Directions:

By Car: Exit Junction 8 (M11) and follow directions to Bishops Stortford. Turn off the A120 onto the B1004 at the Tesco's roundabout to Much Hadham. The course is approximately a mile on the right after crossing 3 roundabouts.

By BR: Stansted Station.

Course Details:

This is an eighteen hole, par 72, parkland course.

Set in 250 acres of parkland and open for just over a year, the 11th hole has established itself as a testing par 5, with a narrow fairway and blind shot to the green. The course itself is however designed with some wide fairways to suit all standards of golfer.

Shop Facilities:

The shop stocks a range of golf equipment, accessories and designer wear. Club hire is available.

Tuition Details:

There is a covered driving range attached to the course, together with three par 3 practice holes next to the first tee. Lessons are available from £11 for 30 minutes. Contact the Pro shop to book.

Clubhouse Facilities:

Full changing facilities, including showers are available.

The bar and restaurant provide a range of catering. The clubhouse stages regular social events with its portable stage and dance floor.

Visitor Restrictions and How to Book:

Visitors must have a minimum handicap of men (24) and ladies (36). Weekend play is restricted to tee times after 11.30am. Computerised bookings are taken. Book via the Club Secretary on 0279-843558.

Societies are welcome. Contact Mrs. Ovenden for details.

Visitor Playing Costs:

Weekday/Weekend (after 11.30am):

£15.00 / £22.00

Hadley Wood Golf Club

Beech Hill
Barnet
Hertfordshire EN4 OJJ

Secretary:

Peter Bryan
081-449 4328

Professional:

Peter Jones
081-449 3285

Directions:

By Car: Exit Junction 24 (M25) and take the A111 towards Cockfosters. After 1 mile, take the third turning on the right (Beech Hill).

Course Details:

This is a 6236 yard, eighteen hole parkland course.

Designed by Dr. Alistair Mackenzie of Augusta fame, the course provides golfers of all standards an interesting test of golf. There are two lakes on the course of which one comes to prominence on the short par 3, 10th hole which requires a shot over the lake to the green with the Georgian Clubhouse in the background.

Shop Facilities:

The shop is well stocked with golf equipment, accessories and designer wear. Club hire is available at £7.50.

Tuition Details:

A large practice ground together with two warm-up nets and a chipping green are adjacent to the first tee. Some covered practice bays are anticipated for the 1995 season. Lessons are available at £15/£22.50 for 40 minutes from the Assistant/Head Pro.

Clubhouse Facilities:

Full changing facilities, including showers are available. A wide range of catering services are available during the day.

Visitor Restrictions and How to Book:

Visitors are welcome on weekdays, except Tuesday am which is reserved for ladies. Visitors are also permitted on most Sundays between 12.00 noon and 1.00pm. Contact the Pro shop to book.

Societies are welcome on weekdays, except for Wednesdays. Contact the Secretary for a brochure and details of Society packages.

Visitor Playing Costs:

18 holes: £30.00

Per Day: £40.00

After 4.00pm: £22.00

Sundays (12.00 - 1.00pm): £35.00

Hanbury Manor
Golf and Country Club

Thundridge
Near Ware
Hertfordshire SG12 0SD

Professional:

Mr P. Blaze
0920-487722

Directions:

Located on the A10, take the A1170 from Ware to Thundridge.

Course Details:

This is an eighteen hole, 6622 yard downland and parkland course.

Designed by Jack Nicklaus 11 of Golden Bear Design Associates and updating an original design by Harry Vardon, this is a course of two halves.

The first nine are played on a downland terrain with lakes coming into play on three holes. The second green is well protected by a lake to the front. The second nine play in a more established parkland environment with water again coming into play, together with good views of the main Manor.

Shop Facilities:

The shop stocks a range of golf equipment and accessories.

Tuition Details:

There is a practice area to the front left of the Manor. Lessons are available from the Pro staff. Contact the shop for details.

Clubhouse Facilities:

There are full changing facilities available.

The clubhouse is based on the Manor house facilities. There are three restaurants and bars. Albert Roux supervises the catering.

There is an on-site Health Club providing swimming, sauna, massage, squash, gymnasium and other facilities.

There is a halfway house offering refreshments at the 10th tee.

Visitor Restrictions and How to Book:

Visitors must either be guests of a member or a hotel resident.

A handicap certificate is required, together with membership of a recognised golf club. Book and pay in the Pro shop.

Visitors must display their tag when playing.

Visitor Playing Costs:

Hotel guest: £40.00

Harpenden Golf Club

Hammonds End
Redbourn Lane
Harpenden
Hertfordshire AL5 2AX

Secretary:

Mr. J.R Newton
0582-712580

Professional:

Mr. D. Smith
0582-712580

Directions:

By Car: Exit Junction 9 (M1). Follow the A5183 towards St. Albans. At the roundabout, turn left onto the B487 towards Harpenden. The club entrance is 1 mile on the right.

Course Details:

This is a par 70, eighteen hole parkland course.

There are two loops of twelve holes and six holes separated by a narrow country lane. The round commences with 3 tough opening holes with an excellent finishing hole driving across a valley, up to a plateau setting up a good second shot to a well-guarded green.

Shop Facilities:

The shop stocks a wide range of golf equipment and accessories. Club hire is available for £5 a set.

Tuition Details:

There is a practice ground including chipping hole, bunkers and putting area. Lessons with the Pro cost £10 for 30 minutes.

Clubhouse Facilities:

The Club celebrated its centenary in 1994.

There are full changing facilities, including showers.

A range of catering services are available in the Clubhouse. Collar and tie must be worn after 7.00pm in the lounge.

Visitor Restrictions and How to Book:

Visitors must have a handicap certificate. Visitors are not permitted at weekends or on bank holidays, unless playing with a member. Thursday am is Ladies day. Book by telephone or in writing through the General Office or Pro shop.

Societies are welcome with a range of packages, including special winter discounts available. Contact the General office for details.

Visitor Playing Costs:

18 holes: £20.00

Day: £30.00

Hatfield London Country Club

Bedwell Park
Essendon
Hatfield
Hertfordshire AL9 6JA

Secretary:

Mrs. C. Jolly
01707-642624

Professional:

Mr. N. Greer
01707-642624

Directions:

By Car: From London, exit Junction 24 (M25) and follow the A1000, towards Potters Bar. At the first traffic lights, turn right onto the A1000 signed to Hatfield. After 2 miles turn right onto the B158 signposted to Essendon.

Course Details:

This is a 6385 yard, eighteen hole parkland course.

Set in undulating Hertfordshire countryside, there are several water hazards on different holes. Large greens are a feature of the course.

Shop Facilities:

The shop is well stocked with golf equipment and accessories. Club hire is available from £12 a set.

Tuition Details:

There is a large practice ground. Lessons are available from the Pro and should be booked in advance.

Clubhouse Facilities:

The clubhouse offers full changing facilities, including showers.

A range of catering services are available from the restaurant, lounge and bar. There is however only a limited service on Mondays.

In addition to the course, tennis courts are also available for hire.

Visitor Restrictions and How to Book:

There are no restrictions on visitors.

Advance booking is however essential. Visitors should book through the Reception by telephone or in person.

Societies are welcome and details of special packages are available through the Reception.

Visitor Playing Costs:

Weekdays / Weekends:

£16.00 / £25.00 (before 8.30am)

Weekends : £32.00 (after 8.30am)

There are a range of special offers, plus reduced rates for twilight rounds.

Little Hay Golf Complex

Box Lane
Bovingdon
Hemel Hempstead
Hertfordshire HP3 0DQ

Professionals:

David Johnson / Steven Proudfoot
0442-833798

Directions:

By Car: The course is off the A41 on the B4505 Hemel Hempstead/Chesham road.

Course Details:

This is a 6311 yard, eighteen hole parkland course.

The course operates on a pay and play basis. There is an additional 9 hole pitch and putt course attached to the course.

Shop Facilities:

The large discount shop stocks a wide range of golf equipment and accessories. Club hire is available at £5 for 1/2 set.

Tuition Details:

There is a 23 bay floodlit driving range attached to the course. There is also an eighteen hole putting green. Lessons are available from the Pro at £13.95 for 30 minutes.

Contact the Pro shop for details and to book.

Clubhouse Facilities:

Full changing facilities are available.

The clubhouse has two bars and a lounge which provide all-day catering.

Visitor Restrictions:

There are no restrictions.

This is a pay and play course. There is a Complex card available which enables users to book by telephone. Otherwise book in person at the shop.

Societies should contact the shop for details of packages available.

Visitor Playing Costs:

Weekday - £7.50

Weekend - £11.25

Mid-Herts Golf Club

Lamer Lane
Gustard Wood
Wheathampstead
Hertfordshire AL4 8RS

Secretary:

R.J.H Jourdan
0582-832242

Professional:

N. Brown
0582-832788

Directions:

By Car: The course is situated 6 miles north of St. Albans on the B651.

Course Details:

This is an eighteen hole parkland course.

This is quite a tight course, playing 6060 yards off the back tees. The 5th hole is a challenging par 3 hole. Indeed the outcome from the par 3's on this course tend to have a major impact on the card.

Shop Facilities:

The shop stocks a good range of golf equipment and accessories.

Tuition Details:

There is a practice ground and coaching is available. Lessons cost £14/£20 for 45 minutes with the Assistant/Head Pro. Contact the Pro shop to book on 0582-832788.

Clubhouse Facilities:

The clubhouse offers full changing facilities, including showers.

A range of catering services are available from the restaurant and bar.

Visitor Restrictions and How to Book:

Visitors are not permitted to play on weekends or bank holidays, unless accompanying a member as a guest.

In addition, visitors are not permitted to play on Tuesday and Wednesday pm.

Societies are welcome on Thursdays and Fridays. Contact the Secretary for details.

Visitor Playing Costs:

Weekdays Only:

18 holes - £21.00

Day - £31.00

Old Fold Manor Golf Club

Hadley Green
Barnet
Hertfordshire EN5 4QN

Secretary:
A.W Dickens
081-440 9185

Professional:
Daniel Fitzimmons
081-440 7488

Directions:
By Car: In Old Fold Lane off the A1000 between Potters Bar and Barnet, the course is opposite the Old Windmill public house.

Course Details:
This is a 6,245 yard, eighteen hole heathland course.

The 11th hole at 431 yards is a dog-leg right with a lake to the right of the fairway. The concluding two holes at 422 yards and 425 yards provide a strong finish. There is a moat across the front of the 18th green, making the second shot very testing.

Shop Facilities:
The shop stocks a wide range of golf equipment and accessories. Club hire is available at £5 per set.

Tuition Details:
A practice ground is available. Lessons cost from £15 for 45 minutes. Video analysis is also available.

Clubhouse Facilities:
The changing facilities, which include showers, are available on non-public play days (all days bar Monday and Wednesday).

Catering is available all day, either in a modern cafeteria or in the main Clubhouse.

Visitor Restrictions and How to Book:
There are no restrictions on the two public play days which are Monday and Wednesday, bar normal dress code.

A handicap certificate is required on all other days. Weekend play is limited to tee-times after 3.00pm for visitors. Visitors should book through the Pro shop.

Societies are welcomed. Contact the Manager with requirements.

Visitor Playing Costs:
Mondays / Wednesdays: £10.00 per round

Other Weekdays: £20.00 per round (£27 per day)

Weekends (after 3.00pm): £25.00 per round

Oxhey Park Golf Course

Prestwick Road
South Oxhey
Watford
Hertfordshire WD1 4ED

Secretary:

Mr. T.R. Warner
0923-210118

Professional:

Gary Pooley
0923-248312

Course Details:

This is a short 9 hole course with an eighteen hole length of 3274 yards.

Despite its length, this is definitely not a pitch and putt course. The many trees make this a testing challenge to the short game. It has an eighteen hole par of 58.

Shop Facilities:

The shop stocks a full range of golf clubs and accessories. Clubs can be hired at £2.50 for a half set.

Tuition Details:

A driving range is attached to the course and two bays and a bunker are allocated for teaching.

Lessons are available at £10 for 30 minutes. Contact the Pro shop with requirements and to book.

Clubhouse Facilities:

Food is available all day in the lounge and dining area.

There are TV's and a pool table available.

Visitor Restrictions and How to Book:

There are no visitor restrictions.

To book, telephone 0923-248312. Societies are welcome. Telephone the Secretary or Pro shop for details and bookings.

Visitor Playing Costs:

Weekdays (9 holes / 18 holes):

£6.00 / £8.00

Weekends:

£8.00 / £10.00

Concessions are available to OAP's, Juniors, Students and UB40's.

Potters Bar Golf Club

Darkes Lane
Potters Bar
Hertfordshire EN6 1DF

Secretary:

Arthur St. John Williams
0707-652020

Professional:

Gary Carver
0707-652987

Directions:

By Car: The club is situated 1 mile north of Junction 24 (M25).

By BR: Potters Bar Station is 1/2 a mile from the course. (Kings Cross: 18 mins)

Course Details:

This is an undulating, eighteen hole, parkland course.

Water comes into play on 15 holes. The par 3, 11th is surely one of the most challenging around. The abundance of trees on the course make accuracy as important as length.

Shop Facilities:

The shop stocks a wide range of golf equipment, accessories and designer wear.

Limited club hire is available.

Tuition Details:

There is a small practice and coaching ground. Lessons are available from the Pro shop. Contact Gary Carver for details.

Clubhouse Facilities:

Extensive changing facilities exist, including showers and a valeting service.

A restaurant and bar provide daily catering. A collar and tie must be worn in public rooms after 6.00pm. Golf clothing is not permitted in the public rooms.

Visitor Restrictions and How to Book:

A handicap certificate is required. Visitors are not permitted to play at weekends, unless accompanying a member or on Wednesday before 12.30pm. (Ladies Day). Visitors should book in person via the Pro shop.

Societies are welcome on Mondays, Tuesdays and Fridays. Details of packages available can be obtained from the Secretary.

Visitor Playing Costs:

Weekdays:

18 holes: £15.00

Day: £25.00

After 4.00pm: £7.50

Redbourn Golf Club Ltd.

Kingsbourne Green Lane
Redbourn
St. Albans
Hertfordshire AL3 7QA

Secretary:

Chris Gyford
0582-793493

Professional:

Dale Brightman
0582-793493

Directions:

By Car: Exit Junction 9 (M1). Take the Redbourn By-Pass to Luton Lane and then on to Kingsbourne Green Lane.

By BR: Harpenden Station.

Course Details:

There are two course at Redbourn: the eighteen hole Ver parkland course and the nine hole, par 3 Kingsbourne course.

Water runs through five holes on the Ver course. The par 3, 7th hole, plays over two streams onto an elevated green. The 585 yard, 18th hole is a par 5, with an approach to a well-guarded green.

Shop Facilities:

The shop stocks a wide range of golf equipment, accessories and designer wear.

Tuition Details:

There is a 20 bay, floodlit driving range attached to the course. Coaching is available from the two resident professionals. Special lesson vouchers are available. Contact the Pro for details.

Clubhouse Facilities:

Full changing facilities, including showers are available.

Catering is available from 7.30 am and throughout the day. In addition to the main bar, members' lounge and restaurant, there is a Spike bar.

Visitor Restrictions and How to Book:

A handicap certificate is not required. Visitors are welcome on weekdays and after 3.00pm on Saturdays and Sundays. Bookings are taken in the Pro shop from 7.30am during the week and from 7.00am at weekends. Bookings can be made three days in advance and payment is not required until the day of play. Telephone bookings are taken.

Societies are welcome (minimum of 12 players). Telephone Alan Knott on 0583-793493 for further details.

Visitor Playing Costs:

Weekday / Weekend:

Ver Course - £14.00 / £18.00

Redbourn (9 holes):from £4.20

Royston Golf Club

Baldock Road
Royston
Hertfordshire SG8 5BG

Secretary:

Mr. David H. Mear
0763-242696

Professional:

Mark Hatcher
0763-243476

Directions:

By Car: After leaving Baldock on the A505, the course is on the right hand side at the top of the hill before entering Royston.

Course Details:

This is an eighteen hole undulating heathland course of 6032 yards.

The par 3, 10th hole, is the only par 3 on the course where you actually see your ball finish on the green.

Shop Facilities:

The shop is well stocked with golf equipment and accessories.

Tuition Details:

Coaching is available from Mark Hatcher, the resident PGA professional both individually or in group lessons. Individual lessons cost £11 for 30 minutes. Contact Mark to book on 0763-243476.

Clubhouse Facilities:

There are full changing facilities, including showers.

There is a lounge bar, the 19th bar, restaurant and snooker room. Bar snacks are available during the day. Jacket and tie must be worn after 8.00pm.

Visitor Restrictions and How to Book:

Visitors are welcome during the week but must accompany a member at weekends.

Green fees and bookings are taken in the Pro shop.

Society bookings are welcome on weekdays. Bookings are taken through the Secretary's office. A standard package of 36 holes and a full days catering costs £31.50.

Visitor Playing Costs:

Weekdays Only:

£20.00

Shendish Manor Golf Centre

Shendish Manor
London Road, Apsley
Hemel Hempstead
Hertfordshire HP3 0AA

Golf Shop:

0442-251806

Directions:

By Car: Exit Junction 20 (M25). The course is located off the A4251, past Kings Langley.

Course Details:

This is a pay and play, mature 9 hole course.

It is shortly to be expanded into an eighteen hole course.

Shop Facilities:

The shop stocks a selection of golf equipment and accessories.

Clubhouse Facilities:

The clubhouse has the Sportsmans Bar, restaurant and private dining rooms, which provide a range of catering services.

Visitor Restrictions and How to Book:

There are no visitor restrictions. Telephone bookings are taken on 0442-251806 and payment is made at the shop.

Societies are welcome. Contact the Golf shop with requirements. Telephone 0442-251806 to book.

Visitor Playing Costs:

Weekdays / Weekends (18 holes):

£10.00 / £14.00

Whipsnade Park Golf Club

Studham Lane
Dagnall
Hertfordshire HP4 1RH

Secretary:

Derek Whalley
0442-842330

Professional:

Mike Lewendon
0442-842310

Directions:

By Car: Off the A414 Hemel Hempstead to Leighton Buzzard road, turn right at Dagnall. After 400 yards, follow the signpost to Studham. The course is on the left at the top of the hill.

Course Details:

This is an eighteen hole parkland course of 6,552 yards.

The first 4 holes are played alongside Whipsnade Zoo. The 1st hole plays over a pond, with the zoo out of bounds on the left.

Try and avoid the ostriches!

Shop Facilities:

The shop is well stocked with golf equipment and accessories. Electric buggies and golf carts are available.

Tuition Details:

There is a large practice ground. Lessons cost £10 for 30 minutes from the Pro. Contact Mike Lewendon for details.

Clubhouse Facilities:

There is a range of catering available from the restaurant and lounge bars. There is also a stud bar. Food is available every day from the restaurant, except Mondays.

A jacket and tie are required in the lounge bar and restaurant after 6.00pm.

Visitor Restrictions and How to Book:

Visitors are not permitted at weekends. A handicap certificate is not required.

Book through the Professional either in person or by phone on 0442-842310.

Societies are welcome. Full or half day packages can be arranged. For example, coffee, golf, lunch, golf and 4-course dinner costs £48.00. Details and booking forms are available from the Secretary's office.

Visitor Playing Costs:

Weekday:

18 holes: £21.00

Day: £31.00

Whitehill Golf Club

Dane End
Ware
Hertfordshire SG12 0JS

Secretary:

Mr. A.K Smith
0920-438495

Professional:

Mr. D. Ling
0920-438495

Directions:

By Car: Turn west off the A10 at the Happy Eater at High Cross. The course is two miles on the left.

Course Details:

This is a 6311 yard, eighteen hole parkland course.

Opened in 1990 and developed into an eighteen hole course in 1991, this course has a number of interesting holes.

The short par 4 has a green protected by a pond, ditch and deep rough. Further water poses problems on the 16th with the danger on the left to which the fairway slopes.

Shop Facilities:

The shop stocks a range of golf equipment and accessories.

Tuition Details:

There is a 25 bay floodlit covered range, together with an outdoor range and practice bunker. Lessons cost £10 for 30 minutes and £20 for one hour. Video analysis is available at the same price.

Contact the Pro shop to book.

Clubhouse Facilities:

Full changing facilities are offered.

The clubhouse has a bar and restaurant which provide daily catering, together with a snooker room.

Visitor Restrictions and How to Book:

A handicap certificate is required or visitors must be prepared to take a competence test.

Book via the Pro shop on 0920-438702 and pay on arrival. Visitors should arrive at least 15 minutes before tee-off time.

Societies are welcome and packages start at £18 per head. Contact the Secretary for details.

Visitor Playing Costs:

Weekdays / Weekends:

£15.00 / £18.00

9 holes (restricted):

£7.50 / £9.00

GOLF IN ESSEX

In recent years, Essex has seen an enormous expansion in the range of its golf facilities. As trends go, this one looks set to run and run as more developments are being planned to meet the growing demand for the the game.

Essex has a mixture of inland and seaside links-style courses. Of the latter, **Frinton Golf Club** epitomises the challenge posed on links courses by variable wind and weather. Amongst other courses which come into this category are **Burnham-on-Crouch Golf Club, Castle Point Golf Course** on Canvey Island and **Clacton-on-Sea Golf Club.**

Inland, many of the new courses provide both good design and a testing game. Often they form part of larger leisure complexes. **Earls Colne Golf and Country Club** near Colchester has a challenging eighteen hole course and provides a range of non-golfing leisure facilities. **Stapleford Abbotts Golf Club** has not one, but three golf courses. Other Clubs which offer more than one course include **Three Rivers Golf and Country Club, Channels Golf Club,** both near Chelmsford and **Gosfield Lake Golf Club**, near Halstead.

For those seeking to play on courses where there are only limited visitor restrictions, **Birch Grove Golf Club** near Colchester, **Castle Point Golf Course** on Canvey Island, **Loughton Golf Club** at Loughton, **the Risebridge Golf Centre,** near Romford and **Towerlands Golf Club,** at Braintree all provide good facilities.

Forrester Park Golf Club

165

Abridge Golf & CC
Epping Lane
Stapleford Tawney
Abridge
Essex RM4 1ST

Mr PG Pelling
0708-688396

Ballards Gore Golf Club
Gore Road
Canedon
Rochford
Essex SS4 2DA

Mr N Patient
0702-258917

Basildon Golf Club
Clay Hill Lane
Basildon
Essex

Mr A Burch
0268-533297

The Burstead Golf Club
Tythe Common Road
Little Burstead
Billericay
Essex CM12 9SS

Mr LJ Mence
0277-631171

Belfairs Golf Club
Eastwood Road North
Leigh-on-Sea
Essex SS9 4LR

Mr Jim Pacey
0702-526911

Belhus Park Municipal Golf Club
Belhus Park
South Ockendon
Essex RM15 4QR

Mr D Faust
0708-852248

Bentley Golf & Country Club
Ongar Road
Brentford
Essex CM15 9SS

Mr JA Vivers
0277-373179

Benton Hall Golf Club
Wickham Hill
Witham
Essex CM8 3LH

Mr RA Newman
0376-502454

Birch Grove Golf Club
Layer Road
Colchester
Essex CO2 0HS

Mrs M Marston
0206-734276

Boyce Hill Golf Club
Vicarage Hill
Benfleet
Essex SS7 1PD

Mr JE Atkins
0268-793625

Braintree Golf Club
Kings Lane
Stisted
Braintree
Essex CM7 8DA

COURSES IN ESSEX

Mr M.N.D Robinson
0376-346079

Braxted Park Golf Club
Braxted Park
Witham
Essex CM8 3EN

Mrs Amanda Fitzpatrick
0621-892305

Bunsay Downs Golf Club
Little Baddow Road
Woodham Walter
nr Malden
Essex CM9 6RW

Mr M Durham
0245-222648

Burnham-on-Crouch Golf Club
Burnham on Crouch
Essex CM0 8PQ

Mr WF Miller
0621-782282

Canons Brook Golf Club
Elizabeth Way
Harlow
Essex CM19 5BE

Mr Reid
0279-421482

Castle Point Golf Course
Somnes Avenue
Canvey Island
Essex SS8 9FG

Mr Doug Humphris
0268-510830

Channels Golf Club
Belsteads Farm Lane
Little Waltham
Chelmsford
Essex CM3 3PT

Mr AM Squire
0245-440005

Chelmsford Golf Club
Widford Road
Chelmsford
Essex CM2 9AP

Mr Andrew Johnson
0245-256483

Clacton-on-Sea Golf Club
West Road
Clacton-on-Sea
Essex CO15 1AJ

Mr HF Lucas
0255-421919

Chigwell Golf Club
High Road
Chigwell
Essex IG7 5BH

Mr M Farnsworth
081-500 2059

Chingford Golf Club
158 Station Road
Chingford
Essex E4

Mr Brian Sinden
081-529 2107

Colchester Golf Club
Braiswick
Colchester

Essex CO4 5AU

Mrs J Boorman
0206-853396

Colne Valley Golf Club
Station Road
Earls Colne
Colchester
Essex CO6 2LT

Miss L Spall
0787-224343

Crondon Park
Stock Road
Stock
Essex CM4 9DP

Mr John Lewis
0277-841115

Earls Colne Golf & Country Club
Earls Colne
Colchester
Essex CO6 2NS

Malcolm Hobbs
0787-224466

Fairlop Waters Golf Club
Forest Road
Barkingside
Ilford
Essex IG6 3JA

Mr Tony Bowers
081-500 9911

Forrester Park Golf Club
Beckingham Road
Great Totham
Maldon
Essex CM9 8EA

Mr TR Forrester-Muir
0621-891406

Frinton Golf Club
1 The Esplanade
Frinton-on-Sea
Essex CO13 9EP

Lt Col RW Attrill
0255-674618

Gosfield Lake Golf Club
The Manor House
Gosfield
Halstead
Essex CO9 1SE

Mr A O'Shea
0787-474747

Hainault Forest Golf Club
Chigwell Row
Hainault Forest
Essex

Mr DK Cope
081-500 0385

Hanover Golf & CC
Hullbridge Road
Rayleigh
Essex SS69 9QS

Mr Gordon Harrold
0702-230033

Hartswood Golf Club
King George's Playing Fields
Brentwood
Essex CM14 5AE

Mr A Jevans
0277-218850

COURSES IN ESSEX

Harwich & Dovercourt Golf Club
Station Road
Parkeston
Harwich
Essex CO12 4NZ

Mr BQ Dunham
0255-503616

Nazeing Golf Club
Middle Street
Nazeing
Essex EN9 2LW

Mr J Speller
0992-893798

High Beech Golf Club
Wellington Hill
Loughton
Essex IG10 4AH

Mr Clark Baker
081-508 7323

Ilford Golf Club
291 Wanstead Park Road
Ilford
Essex IG1 3TR

Mr Peter Newson
081-554 2930

Langdon Hills Golf Club
Lower Dunton Road
Bulpham
Essex RM14 3TY

Mrs C Hammond
0268-548061

Loughton Golf Club
Clays Lane
Debden Green

Loughton
Essex IG10 2RZ

Mr Alan Day
081-502 2923

Maldon Golf Club
Beeleigh
Langford
Maldon
Essex CM9 6LL

Mr GR Bezant
0621-853212

Maylands Golf & CC Ltd
Colchester Road
Harold Park
Romford
Essex RM3 0AZ

Mrs C Brand
0708-373080

North Weald Par 3 Golf Course
Epping Road (B181)
North Weald
Essex CM16 6AJ

Mr Clark Baker
0992-524142

Orsett Golf Club
Brentwood Road
Orsett
Essex RM16 3DS

The Secretary
0375-891352

Quietwaters Golf Club
Colchester Road
Tolleshunt Knights
nr Maldon

Essex CM9 8HX

Mr PD Keeble
0621-860410

Risebridge Golf Centre
Risebridge Chase
Romford
Essex RM1 4DG

Rochford Hundred Golf Club
Rochford
Essex

Mr AH Bondfield
0702-544302

Romford Golf Club
Heath Drive
Gidea Park
Romford
Essex RM2 5QB

Mr BE Fox
0708-740007

Saffron Walden Golf Club
Windmill Hill
Saffron Walden
Essex CB10 1BX

Mr David Smith
0799-522786

Stapleford Abbotts Golf Club
Horseman's Side
Tysea Hill
Stapleford Abbotts
Essex RM4 1JU

Mr K Fletcher
0708-381108

Stock Brook Manor Golf Club
Queen's Park Avenue
Stock
Billericay
Essex CM12 0SP

Mr K Roe
0277-653616

Stoke-by-Nayland Golf Club
Keepers Lane
Leavenheath
Colchester
Essex CO6 4PZ

Mr Jonathon Losmak
0206-262836

Stonyhill Golf Club
Brentwood Road
Herongate
Brentwood
Essex CM13 3LW

Mr Andrew Redman
0277-812033

Southend-on-Sea Golf Club
Eastwood Road North
Eastwood
Essex

Mr P Metcalfe
0702-524836

Theydon Bois Golf Club
Theydon Bois
Epping
Essex CM16 4EH

Mr DT Jones
0992-813054

Thorndon Park Golf Club
Ingrave

Brentwood CM13 3RH
Essex

Mr JE Leggitt
0277-810345

Thorpe Hall Golf Club
Thorpe Hall Avenue
Thorpe Bay
Essex SS1 3AT

Three Rivers Golf & Country Club
Stow Road
Purleigh
Nr Chelmsford
Essex CM3 6RR

Mr Graham Packer
0621-828631

Toot Hill Golf Club
School Road
Toot Hill
Ongar
Essex CM5 9PU

Mrs C Cameron
0277-365523

Top Meadow Golf Club
Fen Lane
North Ockendon
Essex RM14 3PR

Mr G Bourton
0708-852239

Towerlands Golf Club
Panfield Road
Braintree
Essex CM7 5BJ

Mr K Cooper
0376-326802

Upminster Golf Club
114 Hall Lane
Upminster
Essex RM14 1AU

Mr K Moyse
0708-222788

Warley Park Golf Club
Magpie Lane
Little Warley
Brentwood
Essex CM13 3DX

Mr K Regan
0277-224891

Warren Golf Club
Woodham Walter
Maldon
Essex CM9 6RW

Mr Mark Durham
0245-223258

Weald Hall Golf Club
Rayley Lane
North Weald
Essex CM16 6AR

West Essex Golf Club
Bury Road
Stewardstonebury
Chingford E4 7QL
Essex

Mr PH Galley MBE
081-529 7558

Woodford Golf Club
2 Sunset Avenue
Woodford Green
Essex IG8 0ST

Mr GJ Cousins
081-504 3330

Basildon Golf Club

Clay Hill Lane
Basildon
Essex

Secretary:

Mr A Burch
0268-533297

Professional:

Mr W Paterson
0268-533532

Directions:

By Car: South of Basildon, take the A176 off the A13 to the Kingswood roundabout. Follow the signs to Kingswood. Clay Hill Lane is the second on the right.

By BR: Basildon Station.

Course Details:

This is an eighteen hole, 6153 yard, eighteen hole parkland course.

The par 4, 13th hole features a double dog-leg whilst the 442 yard, 16th hole has a narrow tree lined fairway requiring a straight drive for safety.

Shop Facilities:

The shop stocks the usual range of golf equipment and accessories.

Tuition Details:

There is a large practice area. Lessons are available at £12 per 1/2 hour from the Pro staff. Video analysis is available by arrangement.

Clubhouse Facilities:

Changing facilities, including showers are available.

Full catering services ranging from light snacks to full meals are available in the bar and restaurant.

Visitor Restrictions and How to Book:

This is a public course and there are no visitor restrictions.

There is a booking system available for weekends. Otherwise book in the Pro shop.

Societies should contact the Secretary for details of available packages.

Visitor Playing Costs:

Weekday / Weekend:

£8.70 / £14.50

Bentley Golf & Country Club

Ongar Road
Brentford
Essex CM15 9SS

Secretary:

Mr. J. Vivers
0277-373179

Professional:

Nick Garrett
0277-372933

Directions:

By Car: Situated on the A128 mid-way between Brentwood and Ongar. From Brentwood, the club is approximately 3 miles on the right off the A128.

Course Details:

This is an eighteen hole, 6,382 yard parkland course.

The course is gently undulating with some interesting par 3's, particularly the 2nd and 8th holes. There are also some water features. The last three holes offer different golfing challenges to all levels of player.

Shop Facilities:

The shop is well stocked with golf equipment and accessories.

Tuition Details:

There is a large practice area, together with nets and practice bunker. Lessons are available at £12.50 for 40 minutes.

Video analysis is available at £25 for 40 minutes.

Clubhouse Facilities:

The Clubhouse provides a range of catering. Breakfast is available from 9.00am -10.00am weekdays, lunch is available from 11.00am-3.00pm and evening meals are by arrangement only.

Tea, coffee and soft drinks are available from the bar which is open all day.

Visitor Restrictions and How to Book:

Visitors are welcome on weekdays after 8.00am (Wednesdays after 11.00am). Handicap certificates may be required.

Visitors should book in person and pay at the Pro shop. Advance bookings will only be taken for groups of 20 or more.

Societies (groups of over 20) are welcome on weekdays. Prices and details of packages are available from the Secretary's office.

Visitor Playing Costs:

Weekdays Only:

18 holes: £21.00

Day: £27.00

Birch Grove Golf Club

Layer Road
Colchester
Essex CO2 0HS

Secretary:

Mrs. M Marston
0206-734276

Directions:

By Car: Take the B1026. The course is located 2 miles south of Colchester town.

Course Details:

This is a 2019 yard, 9 hole parkland course.

Though short, the course remains challenging.

Shop Facilities:

The shop stocks a range of golf equipment and accessories.

Tuition Details:

There is a practice net and green for chipping, though no coaching is currently available.

Clubhouse Facilities:

There are changing facilities.

Bar snacks are available in the bar area and more extensive catering is available, including 4 course dinners for parties, by arrangement. Jeans are not allowed in the Clubhouse or on the course.

Visitor Restrictions and How to Book:

Handicap certificates are not required. There is a Ladies competition on Wednesday mornings and a Mens competition on Sundays.

Visitors are not permitted before 1.00pm on Sundays.

Societies are welcomed, by prior arrangement. Contact Mrs Marston with requirements.

Visitor Playing Costs:

Weekdays / Sundays:

(18 holes)

£10.00 / £12.00

(9 holes)

£7.00 / £8.00

Braintree Golf Club

Kings Lane
Stisted
Braintree
Essex CM7 8DA

Secretary:

M. N. D Robinson
0376-346079

Professional:

A. K. Parcell
0376-343465

Directions:

By Car: 1st turn north, off the A120 east of Braintree by-pass.

Course Details:

This is an eighteen hole, 6199 yard parkland course.

Set in a peaceful river valley each hole has its own name (The 'Cedars', 'Chestnuts' etc.). Ponds are found on the 11th, 14th, 17th and 18th holes. The river runs behind the 12th and 14th holes.

Shop Facilities:

The shop stocks a comprehensive range of golf equipment and accessories.

Tuition Details:

There are three practice areas, including an eleven acre site.

Lessons are available from the Head Professional at £18 and the Assistant at £14. Contact the Pro shop for details.

Clubhouse Facilities:

The Clubhouse provides a full range of catering facilities. Catering for groups of up to 100 is available. A jacket and tie is to be worn for dinner. Smart casual wear at other times.

Visitor Restrictions and How to Book:

Visitors are welcome during weekdays and a handicap certificate is required on Fridays.

Ladies competition day is Tuesday, but the afternoon is usually less busy.

There are no tee reservations for visitors but the professional will advise on availability.

Societies are welcome on Mondays, Wednesdays and Thursdays. Contact the Secretary for details of packages and free places.

Visitor Playing Costs:

Weekdays Only:

Per Day - £25.00

18 holes after 2.00pm - £18.00

Burnham-on-Crouch Golf Club

Burnham on Crouch
Essex CM0 8PQ

Secretary:

W.F. Miller
0621-782282

Professional:

S. Parkin
0621-782282

Directions:

By Car: Take the main road from Maldon to Burnham-on-Crouch. The course is approximately 1 mile from the town.

Course Details:

This is a par 70, 5056 yard, eighteen hole course.

The course runs along the River Crouch with particularly fine views of the river along the back nine holes. This is a new, well-planted course.

Shop Facilities:

The shop is small with limited though essential stock.

Tuition Details:

There is a practice ground and lessons are available at £7.20 for 30 minutes. Video analysis is also available with the Pro by prior arrangement. Contact the Pro shop to book.

Clubhouse Facilities:

The Clubhouse has recently been extensively refurbished.

There are changing facilities, including showers.

Bar food and snacks are available every day, except Mondays.

Visitor Restrictions and How to Book:

A handicap certificate is required. There are some restricted tee times and visitors are advised to contact the Secretary's office before arrival.

Ladies Day is on Thursday.

Societes are welcome on Tuesdays and Fridays. A range of Society packages are available from approximately £35 including golf, coffee, lunch and dinner. Contact the Secretary's office for details.

Visitor Players Costs:

Per day: £20

Castle Point Golf Course

Somnes Avenue
Canvey Island
Essex SS8 9FG

Management:

Doug Humphris/Bill Sharp
0268-510830

Professional:

John Hudson
0268-511758

Directions:

By Road: Take the A13 to Saddler's Farm roundabout. Follow the sign to Canvey Island. The course is located in the centre of the Island, opposite the Waterside Farm Leisure complex.

By BR: Benfleet Station (on the Fenchurch Line).

Course Details:

This is a par 71, eighteen hole links style course.

Wind and water both feature on the course. The senior professional is the only PGA professional to score two consecutive holes in one in competition.

Shop Facilities:

The large shop stocks a wide range of golf equipment and accessories. A full club repair service is available.

Tuition Details:

A 17 bay floodlit driving range is attached to the course.

Tuition is available from the PGA professionals at approximately £12.50 per 30 mins. Video analysis is also available by prior arrangement.

Clubhouse Facilities:

Changing facilities include showers.

Catering and bar facilities are available. Dress is smart casual. Children under 14 are not allowed in the bar.

Visitor Restrictions and How to Book:

Handicap certificates are not required. Booking is recommended at weekends, via the Professional shop. There is a Veterans competition most Wednesday mornings.

Societies are welcomed and a range of packages are available. Contact the Manager for details.

Visitor Playing Costs:

Weekdays / Weekends:

£7.95 / £11.95

Special rates are available for juniors and seniors.

Channels Golf Club

Belsteads Farm Lane
Little Waltham
Chelmsford
Essex CM3 3PT

Secretary:

A.M. Squire
0245-440005

Professional:

I.B. Sinclair
0245-441056

Directions:

By Car: The course is 2 miles north east of Chelmsford on the A130.

Course Details:

There are two courses:

The Channels course is a par 71, eighteen hole course created around restored gravel workings. It is undulated with plenty of water and wildlife. The par 3, 17th hole has water all the way.

The Belsteads course is a nine hole course ideal for beginners or those wanting a short game.

Shop Facilities:

The shop stocks a full range of golf equipment and accessories.

Tuition Details:

A 20 bay floodlit driving range (open until 10.00pm) is attached to the course. Lessons cost £15 for 45 minutes. Contact the Pro shop to book.

Clubhouse Facilities:

The 13th century Clubhouse provides a full range of catering facilities from snacks to a la carte. Smart casual wear is required.

Visitor Restrictions and How to Book:

On Channels, visitors are not permitted to play at weekends unless accompanied by a member. Belsteads is available all week, including weekends.

Book through the Starter during the week (Charlie O'Brien: 0245-443311) and the Professional shop during weekends.

Societies are welcome. Contact the Secretary with your requirements and for the details of packages available.

Visitor Playing Costs:

18 Holes - £15.00

Day - £28.00

Chelmsford Golf Club

Widford Road
Chelmsford
Essex CM2 9AP

Secretary:

Andrew Johnson
0245-256483

Professional:

Dennis Bailey
0245-257079

Directions:

By Car: The course is reached from the old A12 through Chelmsford. Turn off at Widford.

Course Details:

This is a 5,944 yard, eighteen hole parkland course.

Set between Wood Street and Widford Hill, the course makes use of Thrift Woods which run across the course.

Shop Facilities:

The shop is well stocked with golf equipment, accessories and designer wear.

Tuition Details:

The practice ground is small which limits the use of longer clubs. A single bay indoor facility is available in inclement weather. Lessons are available at £16 for 45 minutes. Contact the Pro shop to book.

Clubhouse Facilities:

Full changing facilities are available, together with showers.

The bar is located in the upstairs lounge overlooking the 18th green. A range of catering services are provided. Players can make use of the balcony in golf wear. Otherwise the dress code is smart casual.

Visitor Restrictions and How to Book:

A handicap certificate is required. Visitors are welcome on weekdays, but are not permitted to play at weekends.

Tuesday is Ladies Day and carries tee restrictions. Start off times from the 1st and 10th tees are clearly defined. Visitors should book through the Pro shop.

Societies are welcome. Contact the Secretary for details of the packages and options available.

Visitor Playing Costs:

Weekdays:

18 holes - £23.00

Day - £34.00

Clacton-on-Sea Golf Club

West Road
Clacton-on-Sea
Essex CO15 1AJ

Secretary:

H.F. Lucas
0255-421919

Professional:

S. Levermore
0255-426304

Directions:

By Car: The course is located on the seafront, opposite the airfield.

Course Details:

This is a 6,494 yard, eighteen hole parkland course by the sea.

The wind plays a major factor, as does water which features on 16 holes. The round is not too strenuous, though watch out for the par 3, 17th hole with its shot over a pond to the green. 10,000 trees have been planted on the course.

Shop Facilities:

The shop stocks a range of golf equipment and accessories.

Tuition Details:

There is a practice ground and lessons are available from the resident Pro at £15 per hour. Video analysis is available at the same price.

Contact the Pro shop to book.

Clubhouse Facilities:

There is a bar and restaurant that provide daily catering. Up to 130 can be catered for at dinner functions.

Visitor Restrictions and How to Book:

A current handicap certificate is required. Visitors should book either through the Pro shop or through the Secretary's office.

Societies are welcome. They should contact the Secretary's office for details of the packages and options available.

Visitor Playing Costs:

Weekday / Weekends:

£20.00 / £30.00

Colne Valley Golf Club

Station Road
Earls Colne
Colchester
Essex CO6 2LT

Secretary:

Lynda Spall
0787-224343

Professional:

Kimberley Martin
0787-224233

Directions:

By Car: Turn off the A12 onto the A604 to Earls Colne. Drive through the village and Station Road is on the right.

Course Details:

This is a 5838 yard, eighteen hole meadowland course set in 140 acres.

Undulating, the course has challenging holes in the valley, a river to the north of it and lakes and ditches on it. This provides an enjoyable round in very picturesque country.

Shop Facilities:

The shop stocks a wide range of golf equipment and accessories.

Tuition Details:

There is a practice ground with yardage boards. Lessons are available from the Head and Assistant Professionals. For booking availablity and prices, telephone 0787-224233.

Clubhouse Facilities:

Under new ownership since April 1994, there is a now a new clubhouse. It provides changing facilities, locker rooms, a range of catering, a sauna and a snooker room.

Visitor Restrictions and How to Book:

Visitors are welcome on weekdays. At weekends, green fees are not permitted before 10.00am.

Though booking is not essential, visitors are advised to contact the Pro shop by telephone to check that there is no conflicting event on.

Societies are welcome. Telephone 0787-224343 for details.

Visitor Playing Costs:

Weekdays - £12.00

Weekends - £18.00

Earls Colne Golf & Country Club

Earls Colne
Colchester
Essex CO6 2NS

Secretary:

Malcolm Hobbs
0787-224466

Professional:

Owen McKenna
0787-224466

Directions:

By Car: The course is located on the B1024 Earls Colne - Coggeshall road, four miles from the A12, two miles from the A120 (Euro-Route) and one mile from the A604.

Course Details:

There are two courses at Earls Colne. The eighteen hole, 6,491 yard, main course features 14 lakes which offer a challenging, but fair test.

Earls Colne also has the short 9 hole Honeywood course. This provides a challenge to those seeking to improve their short game.

Shop Facilities:

The shop is well stocked with golf equipment, accessories and designer wear. Club hire is available at £7.50.

Tuition Details:

There is a 20 bay floodlit driving range, together with an indoor bunker range, a video teaching studio and a 4 hole teaching course.

Lessons are available from £10 per 1/2 hour. Video analysis is available at £25 per hour. Contact the Pro shop to book.

Clubhouse Facilities:

The Clubhouse being part of a larger complex, includes indoor and outdoor tennis courts, indoor bowls, indoor swimming pool and a gymnasium.

Catering is provided in the coffee lounge, poolside grill, spike bar and Flights restaurant.

Creche facilities are open 6 days a week.

Visitor Restrictions and How to Book:

A handicap certificate is not required. Visitors should book via the Clubhouse.

Societies are welcome and details of the packages available can be obtained from the Clubhouse.

Visitor Playing Costs:

Weekday / Weekend : (18 holes)

£15.00 / £18.00

(9 holes)

£8.00

Forrester Park Golf Club

Beckingham Road
Great Totham
Maldon
Essex CM9 8EA

Secretary:

T.R. Forrester-Muir
0621-891406

Professional:

Gary Pike
0621-893456

Directions:

By Car: 5 miles NE of Maldon on Tiptree Road (B1022). 5 miles from the A12 Rivenhall End turn-off. Follow the sign to Great Braxted and continue for 3 miles. Turn right onto the B1022 for 2 miles.

Course Details:

This is an eighteen hole, par 71, parkland course.

The 8th, 10th and 12th holes require longish lofted approach shots to clear trees guarding the green. The 7th hole is a sharp dog-leg par 5 with a pond requiring a carry in excess of 200 yards to clear.

Shop Facilities:

The shop stocks a full range of golf equipment and accessories.

Tuition Details:

There is a ten acre practice ground available to green fee paying visitors. Lessons are available for £25 per 45-60 minutes with the Head Pro. Video analysis is also available.

Book through the Pro shop.

Clubhouse Facilities:

The clubhouse, a converted 16th century barn provides changing facilities, including showers.

Light snacks are available all day. Lunch is served from 10.30am - 2.00pm. On Sunday a carvery is available which requires pre-booking.

Visitor Restrictions and How to Book:

Visitors are not permitted to play before 12.30pm on Saturdays or Sundays. There are restricted tee times on Tuesday and Wednesday mornings. Contact the Clubhouse to book.

Societies are welcome on Mondays, Thursdays and Fridays all day and on Tuesday, Saturday and Sunday afternoons. Contact the Secretary for details of the options available.

Visitor Playing Costs:

18 holes- £17.00

Day - £22.00

After 4.00pm - £10.00 any day.

Frinton Golf Club

1 The Esplande
Frinton-on-Sea
Essex CO13 9EP

Secretary:

Lt Col R.W. Attrill
0255-674618

Professional:

Peter Taggart
0255-671618

Directions:

By Car: Frinton is based 17 miles east of Colchester and can be reached by the A12, A133 and the B1033.

Course Details:

This is an eighteen hole 6256 yard, par 71, flat seaside links course. Like many links courses, the strength of the wind can be a feature on every hole. Tidal ditches can also make this a challenging course.

There is also a nine hole course open to visitors. This is open 7 days a week from 8.00am and is made up of par 3's and 4's.

Shop Facilities:

The shop offers a full range of golf equipment and accessories. Club hire is available.

Tuition Details:

There is a practice ground, together with indoor and outdoor nets. Lessons are available from the Pro staff at £12.50 for 30 minutes.

Clubhouse Facilities:

Changing facilities including showers are available.

Bar and restaurant facilities provide a range of daily catering services. Jeans, trainers and T-shirts are not allowed.

Visitor Restrictions and How to Book:

A handicap certificate is required on the main course. Visitors are not permitted to play on the main course before 11.00am. Bookings are taken by telephone or in writing to the Secretary.

Societies are welcomed on Wednesdays and Thursdays. Groups of 12 or less are catered for on Fridays. Contact the Secretary for details of the various options available.

Visitor Playing Costs:

Day: (18 holes)

Adults - £22.00

Juniors (under 17) - £11.00

(9 holes)

£7.50

Gosfield Lake Golf Club

The Manor House
Gosfield
Halstead
Essex C09 1SE

Secretary:

Tony O'Shea
0787-474747

Professional:

Richard Wheeler
0787-474488

Directions:

By Car: Off the A1017 north of Braintree, the course lies just north of Gosfield Lake.

Course Details:

There are two courses:

The Lakes Course is an eighteen hole, 6707 yard parkland course. The 3rd hole, called 'Lake Lookout', is one of several where water plays a part.

The Meadows course is a 4180 yard, nine hole course double-teed to eighteen holes and is ideal for beginners. The courses were constructed in 1988.

Shop Facilities:

The shop stocks the usual range of golf equipment, accessories and designer wear.

Tuition Details:

Lessons cost £10/£13.50 for a 30 minute lesson with an Assistant /Head Pro. A 9-hole playing lesson costs £10/£20 respectively.

Clubhouse Facilities:

Changing facilities are available including showers and free use of a sauna.

The modern Clubhouse provides a range of catering facilities in the Club, Sir Henry Cotton and Tournament lounges.

Visitor Restrictions and How to Book:

A handicap certificate is required for the Lakes course but not Meadows. Book via the Professional shop which is open from 8.00am -7.00pm.

Visitors are not permitted to play on Saturdays or Sundays before 12.00 noon.

Societies are welcome. Contact the Manager with requirements.

Visitor Playing Costs:

Lakes Course:

Weekday / Weekend (after 12.00 noon)

£25.00 per day / £25 per round

Meadows Course:

£10 per day / £10 per round

Ilford Golf Club

291 Wanstead Park Road
Ilford
Essex IG1 3TR

Secretary:

P.H Newson
081-554 2930

Professional:

S. Dowsett
081-554 0094

Directions:

By Car: Take the A406 to the junction of the A12. Take the first turn off the A12 into the Drive. Wanstead Park Road is the 5th turning on the right.

Courses Details:

This is a flat 5308 yard, eighteen hole, parkland course.

The dominating feature of the course is the River Roding which together with the Aldersbrook Stream feature on ten holes.

Shop Facilities:

The shop stocks a range of golf equipment, accessories and designer wear.

Tuition Details:

Lessons are available at £11 for 30 minutes. Video analysis is available at £25 for one hour.

Contact the Pro shop to book.

Clubhouse Facilities:

Changing facilities are available.

The clubhouse provides daily catering facilities through its bar and restaurant.

Visitor Restrictions and How to Book:

This is a pay and play course. Telephone bookings are not taken, but visitors can telephone the Pro shop from 8.00am for details of timings and availability for the day.

Visitors can play between 10.30am - 12.30pm on Saturdays and after 3.30pm on Sundays.

Societies are welcomed on Mondays, Wednesdays and Fridays. Contact the Secretary for details.

Visitor Playing Costs:

Weekday / Weekend (per round):

£13.50 / £16.00

Loughton Golf Club

Clays Lane
Debden Green
Loughton
Essex IG10 2RZ

Secretary:

Alan Day
081-502 2923

Professional:

Stuart Layton
081-502 2923

Directions:

By Car: The course is located north of Loughton on the edge of Epping Forest.

Course Details:

This is a nine hole hilly parkland course.

It is wooded and operates on a pay and play basis. It is a testing round, particularly for the short game with 4 par 3's and 5 par 4's.

Shop Facilities:

The shop stocks a range of golf equipment and accessories.

Tuition Details:

There is a practice area and lessons are available from Stuart Layton, the PGA professional at £10 per half hour. Telephone 081-502 2923 to book.

Clubhouse Facilities:

There are no changing rooms or showers at the present time.

The Clubhouse has a fully licensed bar which provides a range of light snacks.

Visitor Restrictions and How to Book:

There are no visitor restrictions, bar normal dress code. It is recommended that visitors telephone to book.

Weekend bookings are taken from the previous Thursday.

Societies are welcome. Contact the Pro shop for details.

Visitor Playing Costs:

Weekday / Weekend:

9 holes: £5.00 / £6.00

18 holes: £8.00 / £10.00

Maldon Golf Club

Beeleigh
Langford Maldon
Essex CM9 6LL

Secretary:

G.R Bezant
0621-853212

Directions:

By Car: Take the B1019 Maldon to Hatfield Peverel road. Turn off this road where signposted by the Essex Waterworks at Langford.

Course Details:

This is a nine hole meadowland course with eighteen different tee positions.

The course lies between the Chelmer/Blackwater Navigation canal and the tidal reaches of the River Chelmer.

Fairways are tight with small well-guarded greens. The par 4, 10th hole, usually into a prevailing wind and the par 3, 14th hole are particularly testing holes.

Shop Facilities:

The members shop provides a limited range of items including gloves, balls, tees, waterproofs and shoes.

Tuition Details:

There is a practice net on the course.

Clubhouse Facilities:

Changing facilities, including showers are available.

The Clubhouse offers a full catering service which includes a Stud bar and bar/restaurant. Smart casual wear is required, but jacket and tie must be worn when dining in the evening.

Visitor Restrictions and How to Book:

A handicap certificate is required. Visitors are not permitted to play at weekends or bank holidays. During the week, visitors must tee off before 2.00pm.

Tuesday morning is Ladies day and Wednesday morning is Veterans day.

Telephone bookings are not taken. Telephone however to check availability. Book via the Clubhouse.

Societies (up to 24) are welcomed on Mondays and Thursdays. Contact the Secretary for details.

Visitor Playing Costs:

Weekday Only:

£15.00 (per round)

£20.00 (per day)

Maylands Golf & Country Club Limited Ltd

Colchester Road
Harold Park
Romford
Essex RM3 0AZ

Secretary:

Mrs. C. Brand
0708-373080

Professional:

Mr John Hopkin
0708-346466

Directions:

By Car: Situated on the A12. Take Junction 28 off the M25.

By BR: Harold Wood station is one and a half miles from the Club.

Course Details:

This is a 6172 yard, eighteen hole undulating, parkland course.

Once part of the Ingrebourne Estate, there are a number of challenging holes on this course, established 60 years ago. The 7th hole, known locally as 'Bomb Alley' offers no option but a straight shot to stay out of trouble.

Shop Facilities:

The shop, located in the converted dairy of Maylands farm, stocks a wide range of golf equipment, accessories and designer wear.

Tuition Details:

There is a large practice area and coaching is available for individuals and groups. Lessons start at £10 for 30 minutes. Book through the Pro shop.

Clubhouse Facilities:

The Clubhouse provides a range of catering facilities. There is a stud bar, bar and restaurant. Snacks are available through the day. Jackets and tie are required in the main bar after 7.00pm.

Visitor Restrictions and How to Book:

A handicap certificate or membership of another recognised Club is required.

Visitors are not permitted at weekends or bank holidays, unless accompanying a member. Book through the Pro shop.

Societies are welcome on Mondays, Wednesdays and Fridays from April - October.

Contact the Secretary on weekdays before 1.00pm for details.

Visitor Playing Costs:

Weekday Only:

18 holes - £20.00

Day - £30.00

Orsett Golf Club

Brentwood Road
Orsett
Essex RM16 3DS

Secretary:

The Secretary
0375-891352

Professional:

Mr. Robert Newberry
0375-891797

Directions:

By Car: From the roundabout at the junction of the A13 and the A128, take the road south towards Chadwell St. Mary.

Course Details:

This is a 6121 yard, eighteen hole parkland / heathland course.

A regional qualifying course for the British Open, the course has good drainage making it an excellent winter course.

Shop Facilities:

The shop stocks a full range of golf equipment, accessories and designer wear.

Tuition Details:

There is a practice field, together with a pitching and chipping green. Lessons cost £15 for 30 minutes and video analysis is available at £25 an hour.

Contact the Pro shop to book.

Clubhouse Facilities:

There are full changing facilities in the Clubhouse.

There is a bar, restaurant and tee bar providing a range of catering. Strict dress rules apply. Jackets, collars and ties are required in the restaurant after 10.30am.

Visitors Restrictions and How to Book:

A handicap certificate and membership of a Club (with proof) is required. Visitors are welcome on weekdays but are not permitted to play at weekends, unless playing with a member. Bookings can be made either through the Secretary's office or the Pro shop.

Societies are welcome on Mondays, Tuesdays and Wednesdays. Contact the Secretary for details.

Visitor Playing Costs:

£30.00 per day/ round

£20.00 after 1.00pm

Risebridge Golf Centre

Risebridge Chase
Romford
Essex RM1 4DG

Secretary:

Paul Jennings
0708-741429

Directions:

By Car: Take the A12 to Gallows Corner. Follow Strait Road until you reach Lower Bedfords Road. Turn left after 1/2 mile to Risebridge Chase.

Course Details:

There are two courses at the Risebridge Golf Centre.

There is an eighteen hole, 6,200 yard parkland course.

There is also a short par 3, nine hole course which is ideal for beginners.

Shop Facilities:

The shop stocks a wide range of equipment, accessories and designer wear. Club hire is available for £4.50.

The shop and the professional staff specialise in beginners.

Tuition Details:

A 20 bay driving range is attached to the course and a range of lessons are available seven days per week. Lessons cost £12 for 30 minutes.

Contact the Pro shop for details and to book.

Clubhouse Facilities:

There is an on course cafe and bar. The bar is only open for limited hours.

Visitor Restrictions and How to Book:

There are no restrictions and a handicap certificate is not required. Book by telephone or in person at the Pro shop.

Societies are welcome. Contact the Professional for details of the options available.

Visitor Playing Costs:

Weekday / Weekend

(18 holes)

£8.90 / £10.80

Saffron Walden Golf Club

Windmill Hill
Saffron Walden
Essex CB10 1BX

General Manager:

David Smith
0799-522786

Professional:

Philip Davis
0799-527728

Directions:

By Car: Exit M11 at Junction 9 (to Stumps Cross). Proceed south to Saffron Walden on the B184. The course is on the right just before you enter the town.

Course Details:

This is a 6371 yard, eighteen hole undulating parkland course.

Situated by Audley End Mansion and with trees planted by 'Capability' Brown and the adjacent Spring Wood, there are many game birds around, particularly on the 4th and 5th. The 2nd and 18th holes give excellent views of St. Mary's Church in Saffron Walden.

Shop Facilities:

The shops stocks a full range of golf equipment, accessories and designer wear. Club hire costs £10.

Tuition Details:

There is a practice ground, practice net and chipping area. Lessons are available at £10 for 30 minutes. Video analysis costs £25 per hour.

Contact the Pro shop to book.

Clubhouse Facilities:

There are full changing facilities in the Clubhouse.

A range of catering services are available in the bar and dining area. Smart casual dress is required during the day. A jacket, collar and tie is required in the main lounge and dining area after 7.00pm. Smart casual dress is permitted in the small bar at any time.

Visitor Restrictions and How to Book:

A handicap certificate is required. Advanced bookings are not essential, but visitors are recommended to contact the Pro shop first to ensure there are no conflicting events.

Societies are welcome. Contact the General Manager, David Smith for details.

Visitor Playing Costs:

Day: £28.00

Stapleford Abbotts Golf Club

Horseman's Side
Tysea Hill
Stapleford Abbotts
Essex RM4 1JU

Secretary:

Keith Fletcher
0708-381108

Professional:

Dominic Eagle
0708-381278

Directions:

By Car: Exit Junction 28 (M25). The course is located 2 miles from Romford on the B1175.

Course Details:

There are three courses at Stapleford Abbotts.

They are the eighteen hole, 5457 yard, Priors course, where water hazards are significant on the 1st, 11th and 14th holes.

The longer eighteen hole Abbotts course at 6,129 yards provides a good test of golf whilst the short par 3, nine hole Friars course compliments the short game. All are in a parkland setting.

Shop Facilities:

The shop is well stocked with golf equipment, accessories and designer wear.

Tuition Details:

There are two practice fields, together with the short Friars course. Lessons are available at £10 for 30 minutes, whilst video analysis is available at £20 per hour.

Clubhouse Facilities:

There is a large mens changing room which includes a sauna and multi-gym for golf players' use.

All day catering is available from the stud bar, tea room and large function room.

Visitor Restrictions and How to Book:

Visitors are welcome on weekdays, but must accompany a member at week-ends.

During the week, visitors may play on the Priors course. Telephone 0277-373344.

Societies are welcome to play on the Abbotts course. Details of the packages and options available can be obtained from the Secretary.

Visitor Playing Costs:

Priors Course (Weekday only)

£15.00

Stoke-by-Nayland Golf Club

Keepers Lane
Leavenheath
Colchester
Essex CO6 4PZ

Secretary:

Jonathan Loshak
0206-262836

Professional:

Kevin Lovelock
0206-262769

Directions:

By Car: Come off Junction 28 (M25) and take the A12 to Colchester. Approximately 8 miles from Colchester on the A134 Sudbury road, follow the signpost to the B1068 and Club entrance.

Course Details:

There are two eighteen hole, par 72, parkland courses, set in 'Constable' style country.

Water hazards are a major feature on both courses. Both 18th holes are par 3's, which require a shot over a reservoir to the green.

Shop Facilities:

The recently enlarged golf shop stocks a full range of golf equipment and accessories.

Tuition Details:

There is an open practice area, together with a new 20 bay covered driving range. Lessons cost £12.50 for 30 minutes. Video analysis is available at £25 per hour.

Clubhouse Facilities:

The refurbished clubhouse includes full changing facilities, a spike bar and coffee shop, together with lounge, dining room and squash court. Breakfasts are available from 8.00am.

A 17th century thatched cottage with 4 beds is available for golfing breaks.

Visitor Restrictions and How to Book:

A handicap certificate is required for weekend play. Members competitions have priority on Saturday and Sunday.

Ladies Day is on Thursday am and Veterans Day is on Monday am.

Societies are welcome. Contact Joy Howard, the Clubhouse Manager, for details of the Society packages available. A £50 deposit is required with confirmed bookings.

Visitor Playing Costs:

Weekday / Weekend:

(18 holes)

£24.00 / £28.00

Theydon Bois Golf Club

Theydon Bois
Epping
Essex CM16 4EH

Secretary:

D.T Jones
0992-813054

Professional:

R. Hall
0992-812460

Directions:

By Car: Exit Junction 26 (M25). Follow the signs to Loughton. At the roundabout, follow the sign to Theydon Bois. Take the first road on the left.

Course Details:

This is a 5,251 yard eighteen hole course.

Though not long by some of today's standards, the course, set in the mature woodland of Epping Forest, presents a challenge to all categories of golfer.

The par 4, 441 yard, 4th hole is a particularly testing hole. The last six holes provide a good finish to the round.

Shop Facilities:

The shop stocks a full range of golfing equipment and accessories.

Tuition Details:

There is a practice ground large enough to cater for long irons, short irons and putting. Lessons cost £12.50 for 30 minutes, whilst video analysis is available at £26 for the same period.

Contact the Pro shop for further details and booking.

Clubhouse Facilities:

There are full changing facilities, including showers.

The clubhouse has a fully licensed bar and provides a range of catering.

Visitor Restrictions and How to Book:

Visitors are welcome on weekdays and after 2.00pm at weekends. Visitors are recommended to contact the Pro shop by telephone to check availability. Tees can be booked through the Pro shop on 0992-812460.

Societies are welcome. For details of available packages and options, contact the Secretary on 0992-813054.

Visitor Playing Costs:

18 holes - £23.00

Three Rivers Golf & Country Club

Stow Road
Purleigh
Nr Chelmsford
Essex CM3 6RR

Golf Director:

Graham Packer
0621-828631

Directions:

By Car: From Junction 29 (M25) it takes approx. 30 minutes by road. From the A127 to Wickford, take the B1010 to Stow Marie (Stow Road).

By BR: Wickford Station.

Course Details:

There are two courses at Three Rivers. The eighteen hole, 6,500 yard, par 72, Kings course was completed in 1974. It is set in 265 acres of mature parkland and overlooks the valley to the three rivers that give the Club its name: the Crouch, the Blackwater and the Roach.

The adjacent Queens course is a nine hole 'par 3' course aimed at beginners and those seeking an opportunity to improve their short game.

Shop Facilities:

The shop is said to be the largest on-course shop in the country stocking a wide range of golf equipment, acces-

sories and designer wear.

Tuition Details:

Lessons cost £10 per 30 minutes. The Club has its own Video Swing and Computer Club Fitting Analysis Centre. Contact the Pro shop for details.

Clubhouse Facilities:

The clubhouse offers a range of sports facilities including tennis, squash, snooker, a swimming pool and a men's sauna.

Bars, restaurants and 'suites', provide a la carte to basket meals 7 days a week.

Visitor Restrictions and How to Book:

A handicap certificate is preferred for the Kings course, but need not be shown. No such restriction applies to the Queens course.

Visitors are welcome on both courses seven days a week. Book and pay at the Pro shop.

Visitor Playing Costs:

Weekday / Weekend:

Kings:

18 holes - £19.00 / £25.00

Day - £22.00 / £28.00

Queens:

9 holes - £7.50 / £8.50

Toot Hill Golf Club

School Road
Toot Hill
Ongar
Essex CM5 9PU

Secretary:

C. Cameron
0277-365523

Professional:

G. Bacon
0277-365747

Directons:

By Car: The course is located on the A414 between Epping and Ongar.

Course Details:

This is an eighteen hole, undulating, 5749 yard, parkland course.

There are three lakes on the course with water hazards on the 9th and 12th holes. Several holes offer particular challenges on this testing course.

Shop Facilities:

The shop stocks a range of golf equipment, accessories and designer wear.

Tuition Details:

A practice range is available and lessons can be arranged with the Pro shop for £15 for 30 minutes. Video analysis is available at £25 per hour.

Clubhouse Facilities:

There is a bar and dining area. Hot food is served between 9.00am and 2.30pm. Sandwiches are available all day. Smart casual wear is required in the clubhouse.

Visitor Restrictions and How to Book:

A handicap certificate is required. Visitors are welcome during the week, but must accompany a member at weekends. Book through the Pro shop.

Societies are welcome. Society days are Tuesday and Thursday. A range of options from £33.00, including 3 course dinner are available. Contact the Secretary for details.

Visitor Playing Costs:

Weekdays:

18 holes - £25.00

Day - £35.00

Towerlands Golf Club

Panfield Road
Braintree
Essex CM7 5BJ

Secretary:

K. Cooper
0376-326802

Professional:

R. Taylor
0376-347951

Directions:

By Car: The course is located on the B1053 north of Braintree.

Course Details:

This is a nine hole parkland course, with an eighteen hole length of 5406 yards.

The course is gently undulating. The 1st hole is probably the most difficult being very tight. There are a couple of small ponds/lakes on the course.

Shop Facilities:

The shop stocks a range of golf equipment and accessories. Club hire is available at £4.

Tuition Details:

There is a practice range, practice nets and practice holes. Lessons from the resident Pro cost £9 for 45 minutes and video analysis is also available. Contact the Pro shop for details.

Clubhouse Facilities:

The clubhouse offers full changing facilities, including showers.

A fully licensed bar and restaurant provide daily catering.

Other on-site activities include equestrian facilities, squash courts, indoor bowls and a full sports hall.

Visitor Restrictions and How to Book:

Visitors are welcome, but are not permitted to play before 1.00pm at weekends.

Thursday is Ladies day.

Visitors should book through the golf shop on 0376-347951.

Society packages are available. Contact the Clubhouse on 0376-326802 for details.

Visitor Playing Costs:

Weekdays / Weekends:

9 holes - £7.00 (weekdays only)

18 holes - £9.00 / £12.50

Warley Park Golf Club

Magpie Lane
Little Warley
Brentwood
Essex CM13 3DX

Secretary:

Keith Regan
0277-224891

Professional:

Pat O'Connor
0277-212552

Directions:

By Car: Exit Junction 29 (M25). Take the A127 to Southend. After 1 mile, turn left by the Esso garage into Little Warley Hall Lane. Turn left at the 'T' junction. The course is approximately 400 yards on the left.

Course Details:

This is a 27 hole parkland course featuring several lakes and ditches.

The 27th, 198 yard, par 3 hole plays from a raised tee to an elevated green over a lake. Bobby Locke put 3 balls into the woods on the 24th hole, where a narrow entrance to the green and woods on the right both pose problems.

Shop Facilities:

The shop stocks a full range of golf equipment, accessories and designer wear. Club hire is available at £5.

Tuition Details:

There is a large practice area and lessons are available at £20 per hour. Video analysis is available at £25 for one hour.

Clubhouse Facilities:

Full changing facilities, including showers are available.

The Spike bar, with an outside patio, is open all day for drinks and light snacks. The lounge restaurant provides an a la carte menu if required.

Visitor Restrictions and How to Book:

A handicap certificate is required. Visitors are not permitted at weekends unless accompanying a member.

Visitors are welcome during the week and can book via the Pro shop up to 24 hours in advance. Pay in the Pro shop.

Societies are welcome during the week. Packages and prices are available on application to the Secretary.

Visitor Playing Costs:

Weekdays:

18 holes - £24.00

36 holes - £36.00

Woodford Golf Club

2 Sunset Avenue
Woodford Green
Essex IG8 0ST

Secretary:

G. J. Cousins
081-504 3330

Professional:

Ashley Johns
081-504 4254

Directions:

By Car: 2 miles off the M11 and 4 miles off the M25, the course lies directly behind Woodford Police Station.

By LUG: Woodford Underground Station.

Course Details:

This is a 5466 yard, eighteen hole, course set in a forest.

Playing nine holes twice, the greens have a reputation for being fast. The par 3, 9th hole, plays over a pond and over the rest of the course, accuracy rather than length is essential to set up a good score.

Shop Facilities:

The shop stocks a full range of golf equipment and accessories.

Tuition Details:

There is no practice ground, though coaching is available from qualified P.G.A. staff. Lessons cost £12.50 for 30 minutes.

Clubhouse Facilities:

Full changing facilities, including showers are available.

Players are asked to change out of golfing attire before entering the clubhouse. There is a dining room and bar. A range of catering is provided, though this is restricted on Mondays.

Visitor Restrictions and How to Book:

Visitors are not permitted to play on Tuesday am, Saturday or Sunday morning.

Due to forestry regulations, either a RED top or RED trousers must be worn on the course.

Book and pay in the Pro shop.

Societies are welcome. Details of packages available can be obtained from the Secretary's office.

Visitor Playing Costs:

Weekday: £15.00

After 2.00pm: £10.00

Junior: £6.00

GOLF IN BERKSHIRE (part)
& BUCKINGHAMSHIRE (part)

In all the discussions about the definition 'Around London' , the inclusion of these two counties gave rise to the greatest debate. Since both county borders end a good deal away from London, it was decided to apply some editorial discretion. The result is contained in the following pages.

Berkshire boasts several fine heathland courses, but by no means are all Berkshire's courses played on this terrain. Perhaps the most famous is **The Berkshire.** Set in that famous corner of Berkshire adjoining the borders of Surrey, it matches the best that heathland golf can offer.

Closer to Reading and the River Thames reside a number of courses which are more parkland in character. The Blue **Mountain Golf Centre** near Bracknell, **Calcot Park Golf Club** near Reading and **Temple Golf Club** near Maidenhead are all worth a visit.

Sonning Golf Club is essentially parkland, though has a heathland feel. **Sand Martins Golf Club** near Wokingham has a similarly mixed feel with the old sand

Hazlemere Golf Club

The Berkshire

Beaconsfield Golf Club

workings on the inward nine, giving the course a links feel. And not a seagull in sight!

Lavender Park Golf Centre in Ascot is a short 'pay and play' course with few restrictions. It will suit those new to the game.

Buckinghamshire finds that many of its finest courses are located in the south. Of all the natural terrains in this area, possibly it is the Chilterns that give several of the courses their particular character. Certainly **Chartridge Park Golf Club** near Chesham, **Chiltern Forest Golf Club** near Aylesbury, **Little Chalfont Golf Club,** in Little Chalfont and **Weston Turville Golf and Squash Club** would fall into this category.

Players looking for a game on courses with few restrictions should note **Aylesbury Golf Centre, Little Chalfont Golf Club** and finally **Wycombe Heights Golf Centre** which has an eighteen hole par 3 course, in addition to a full length eighteen hole parkland course.

part Berkshire

Bearwood Golf Club
Mole Road
Sindlesham
Berkshire RG11 5DB

Mr Howard Barker
0734-760060

The Berkshire Golf Club
Swinley Road
Ascot
Berkshire SL5 8AY

Maj P.D Clarke
0344-21496

Birds Hill Golf Club
Drift Road
Hawthorn Hill
Nr. Maidenhead
Berkshire SL6 3ST

Mr Nick Brown
0628-771030

Blue Mountain Golf Centre
Wood Lane
Binfield
Bracknell
Berkshire RG12 5EY

Mr NCF Dainton
0344-300200

Castle Royle Golf Club
Knowl Hill
Reading
Berkshire RG10 9XA

Miss Lisa Marie Smith
0628-829252

Datchet Golf Club
Buccleuch Road
Datchett
Slough
Berkshire SL3 9BP

Mrs A. Perkins
0753-543887

Downshire Golf Club
Easthampstead Park
Wokingham
Berkshire RG11 3DH

Mr P. Watson
0344-302030

East Berkshire Golf Club
Ravenswood Avenue
Crowthorne
Berkshire RG11 6BD

Mr W.H Short
0344-772041

Hennerton Golf Club
Crazies Hill Road
Wargrave
Berkshire RG10 8LT

Mr PJ Hearn
0734-401000

Hurst Golf Club
Sandford Lane
Hurst
Berkshire RG10 0SQ

Mr A.G Poncia
0734-344355

Lavender Park Golf Centre
Swinley Road
Ascot
Berkshire SL5 1BD

COURSES IN BERKS / BUCKS

David Johnson
0344-884074

Maidenhead Golf Club
Shoppenhangers Road
Maidenhead
Berkshire SL6 2PZ

Mr I.G Lindsay
0628-24693

Mill Ride Golf Club
Mill Ride Estate
Mill Ride
North Ascot
Berkshire SL5 8LT

Mr C.R Freemantle
0344-886777

Royal Ascot Golf Club
Winkfield Road
Ascot
Berkshire SL5 7LJ

Mr D.D Simmonds
0344-25175

Sandmartins Golf Club
Finchhampstead Road
Wokingham
Berkshire RG11 3RG

Mr P. Watkin
0734-792711

Sonning Golf Club
Duffield Road
Sonning-on-Thames
Berkshire RG4 0GJ

Mr P.F Williams
0734-693332

Stokes Poges Golf Club
North Drive
Park Road
Stoke Poges
Slough
Berkshire SL2 4PG

Mr R.C Pickering
0753-526385

Swinley Forest Golf Club
Coronation Road
South Ascot
Berkshire SL5 9LE

Mr I.L Pearce
0344-20197

Temple Golf Club
Henley Road
Hurley
Maidenhead
Berkshire SL6 5LH

Lt Col JCF Hunt
0628-824794

Wexham Park Golf Club
Wexham Street
Wexham
Slough
Berkshire SL3 6ND

Mr P.J Gale
0753-663271

Winter Hill Golf Club
Grange Lane
Cookham
Maidenhead
Berkshire SL6 9RP

Mr G.B Charters-Rowe
0628-527613

part Buckinghamshire

Aylesbury Golf Centre
Hulcott Lane
Bierton
Aylesbury
Buckinghamshire HP22 5GA

Mr Kevin Partington
0296-393644

Beaconsfield Golf Club
Seer Green
Beaconsfield
Buckinghamshire HP9 2UR

Mr PI Anderson
0494-676545

Buckinghamshire Golf Club
Denham Court
Denham Court Drive
Denham
Buckinghamshire UB9 5BG

Mr Kevin Munt
0895-835777

Burnham Beeches Golf Club
Green Lane
Burnham
Buckinghamshire SL1 8EG

Mr A.L Buckner
0628-661448

Calcot Park Golf Club
Bath Road
Calcot
Reading
RG3 5RN

Mr AL Bray
0734-427124

Chalfont Park Golf Club
Three Households
Chalfont St. Giles
Buckinghamshire HP8 4LW

Mr Grant Harvey
0494-871277

Chartridge Park Golf Club
Chartridge
Chesham
Buckinghamshire HP5 2TF

Mrs A Gibbins
0494-791772

Chesham and Ley Hill Golf Club
Ley Hill
Chesham
Buckinghamshire HP5 1UZ

Mr John Taylor
0494-784541

Chiltern Forest Golf Club
Ashton Hill
Halton
Aylesbury
Buckinghamshire HP22 5NQ

Mr L.E.A. Clark
0296-631267

Denham Golf Club
Tilehouse Lane
Denham
Buckinghamshire UB9 5DE

Wg Cdr Graham
0895-832022

COURSES IN BERKS / BUCKS

Ellesborough Golf Club
Butlers Cross
Aylesbury
Buckinghamshire HP17 0TZ

Mr K.M Flint
0296-622114

Farnham Park Golf Club
Park Road
Stokes Poges
Buckinghamshire SL2 4PS

Mrs M. Brooker
0753-647065

Flackwell Heath Golf Club
Treadaway Road
Flackwell Heath
Buckinghamshire HP10 9PE

Mr P Jeans
0628-520929

Gerrards Cross Golf Club
Chalfont Park
Gerrards Cross
Buckinghamshire SL9 0QA

Mr P.H Fisher
0753-883263

Harewood Downs Golf Club
Cokes Lane
Chalfont St Giles
Buckinghamshire HP8 4TA

Mr M.R. Cannon
0494-762184

Harleyford Golf Club
Henley Road
Marlow
Buckinghamshire

Mr B.S.Folley
0628-471361

Hazlemere Golf and Country Club
Penn Road
Hazlemere
High Wycombe
Buckinghamshire HP15 7LR

Mrs D Hudson
0494-714722

Iver Golf Club
Hollow Hill Lane
Langley Park Road
Iver
Buckinghamshire SL0 0JJ

Miss Jerry Teschner
0753-655615

Lambourne Golf Club
Dropmore Road
Burnham South
Buckinghamshire SL1 8NF

Mr Colin Lumley
0628-666755

Little Chalfont Golf Club
Lodge Lane
Little Chalfont
Buckinghamshire HP8 4AJ

Mr Michael Dunne
0494-764877

Princes Risborough Golf Club
Lee Road
Saunderton Lee
Princes Risborough
Buckinghamshire HP27 9NX

Mr J.F Tubb
0844-346989

Thorney Park Golf Club
Thorney Mill Lane
Iver
Buckinghamshire SL0 9AL

Mr G Stevens
0895-422095

Weston Turville Golf and Squash Club
New Road
Weston Turville
Aylesbury
Buckinghamshire HP22 5QT

Mr Barry Hill
0296-24084

Whiteleaf Golf Club
The Clubhouse
Whiteleaf
Aylesbury
Buckinghamshire

Mrs B.A Parsley
0844-274058

Wycombe Heights Golf Centre
Rayners Avenue
Loudwater
High Wycombe
Buckinghamshire HP10 9SW

Mr Peter Talbot
0494-813185

Bearwood Golf Club

Mole Road
Sindlesham
Berkshire RG11 5DB

Secretary:
Howard M Barker
0734-760060

Professional:
Mark Griffiths
0734-760156

Directions:
By Car: The course is located on the B3030 between Winnersh and Arborfield.

Course Details:
This is a nine hole parkland course.

The 6th, 7th and 8th holes have a 40 acre lake as a back-drop. The lake comes into play on the 7th hole and although a short par 4, it poses a real test.

Shop Facilities:
The shop stocks a range of golf equipment and accessories. Club hire is not available.

Tuition Details:
There is a 9 hole pitch and putt course, together with practice ground. Lessons are available at £10/£16 for 30 minutes from the Assistant/ Head Pro.

Clubhouse Facilities:
There is a lounge bar and dining room that seats 20. Catering is limited on Mondays.

Visitor Restrictions and How to Book:
A handicap certificate is required and visitors are not permitted to play at weekends, unless accompanying a member.

Small societies are accepted on Thursdays. Contact the Manager, Barry Tustin, on 0734-760643 to discuss requirements, prices etc.

Visitor Playing Costs:
Weekdays Only:

9 holes - £8.00

18 holes - £15.00

Day - £20.00

The Berkshire Golf Club

Swinley Road
Ascot
Berkshire SL5 8AY

Secretary:
P.D Clarke
01344-21496

Professional:
P. Anderson
01344-22351

Directions:
By Car: The course is located on the A332 between Ascot and Bagshot.

Course Details:
There are two courses at the Berkshire.

The Red course is a 6139 yard, eighteen hole course.

The Blue course is a 6022 yard, eighteen hole course.

Designed in 1928 by Herbert Fowler, both courses are heathland with an abundance of both fir trees and silver birch. The Berkshire has hosted several important amateur tournaments.

Shop Facilities:
The shop stocks a range of golf equipment, accessories and designer wear.

Tuition Details:
There is a large practice ground and lessons are available from the resident PGA qualified professional staff. Contact the Pro shop on 01344-22351 for details.

Clubhouse Facilities:
Full changing facilities, including showers, are available.

The large clubhouse offers fine views of the course. There are lounges, bars, a snack bar and a dining room which provide a range of catering daily.

Visitor Restrictions and How to Book:
A handicap certificate is required. Visitors are only permitted to play on weekdays. It is only possible to book through the Secretary. Telephone enquiries and bookings can be made on 01344-21496.

Societies are welcome to apply to the Secretary's office for details.

Visitor Playing Costs:
Weekdays only: (1994 rates)

18 holes - £50.00

Day - £65.00

Blue Mountain Golf Centre

Wood Lane
Binfield
Bracknell
Berkshire RG12 5EY

Professional:

Neil C.F Dainton
0344-300200

Directions:

By Car: Exit Junction 10 (M4) for the A329 to Bracknell, then take the first exit (B3408) Wokingham and Binfield and take left exit on the roundabout. One and a half miles to Binfield and the course is signposted on roundabout.

Course Details:

This is an eighteen hole, undulating parkland course.

With large greens and bunkers, lakes are a feature of the course. Indeed, the par 3's are a feature of the course since they all feature water hazards. Putting is very important given the size of some of the greens.

Shop Facilities:

The two storey shop stocks a wide range of golf equipment, accessories and designer wear. Clubs can be hired at £10 per round.

Tuition Details:

There is a 30 bay floodlit driving range and practice putting green. Four registered PGA professionals are available for lessons ranging from £7.50. Contact the Pro shop for details.

Clubhouse Facilities:

The Tournament bar serves a wide range of menus including Sunday lunches. Tables can be booked in advance in the dining room.

There are private function rooms for hire.

Visitor Restrictions and How to Book:

There are no restrictions, except normal dress code.

Visitors must book in person, up to 9 days in advance, at the Pro shop. Telephone bookings are not taken for visitors.

Societies are welcome. A wide range of packages are available. Contact the Pro shop for details.

Visitor Playing Costs:

Weekdays / Weekends:

£14.00 / £18.00

Calcot Park Golf Club

Bath Road
Calcot
Reading
Berkshire RG3 5RN

Secretary:

A L Bray
0734-427124

Professional:

A Mackenzie
0734-427797

Directions:

By Car: Exit Junction 12 (Westbound - M4). Take the A4 towards Reading. Continue through 3 mini roundabouts for approximately 1.5 miles. The club is on the left hand side. There are two entrances, East and West.

Course Details:

This is a 6283 yard, eighteen hole parkland course.

This is an undulating course with an abundance of trees and shrubs. The par 3, 7th hole is played over a lake to the green.

Shop Facilities:

The shop stocks a range of golf equipment and accessories.

Tuition Details:

There are three small practice areas and a putting green. Lessons cost £15 for 30 minutes and £30 per hour. Contact the Pro shop for details on 0734-427797.

Clubhouse Facilities:

Full changing facilities, including showers are available.

The bar is open all day and full catering is provided, although a prior booking is advisable. A jacket and tie are required after 7.00pm.

Visitor Restrictions and How to Book:

Visitors must have either a handicap certificate or a letter of introduction from their golf club. Visitors are welcome on weekdays, but are not permitted to play at weekends, unless accompanying a member. Book in person at the Pro shop.

Societies are welcome (minimum 20) and bookings must be confirmed in writing. Texas Scramble is not allowed under any circumstances.

Visitor Playing Costs:

Weekday Only:

per round or day: £30.00

(After 4.00pm) £20.00 (Summer)

(After midday) £20.00 (Winter)

Datchet Golf Club

Buccleuch Road
Datchet
Berkshire SL3 9BP

Secretary:

Mrs A. Perkins
0753-541872

Professional:

Mr B. Mainwaring
0753-542755

Directions:

By Car: The course is located 2 miles from Slough and Windsor off the B376.

Course Details:

This is a nine hole parkland course with an eighteen hole length of 5978 yards.

This established course celebrated its centenary in 1990.

Shop Facilities:

The shop stocks a range of golf equipment and accessories.

Tuition Details:

There is a large practice ground. Individual and group lessons are available.

Contact the Pro shop on 0753-542755 for details.

Clubhouse Facilities:

There are full changing facilities available.

Catering is provided by a lounge and bar. Though coffee is available all day, more substantial catering is available at lunchtime only.

Visitor Restrictions and How to Book:

A handicap certificate is required. Visitors are welcome on weekdays between 9.00am - 3.00pm.

At weekends, visitors should accompany a member as a guest. To book, contact the Pro shop.

Societies are welcome on Tuesdays only. Contact Mrs Perkins for details on 0753-541872.

Visitor Playing Costs:

Weekdays Only:

18 holes - £16.00

Day - £24.00

Hennerton Golf Club

Crazies Hill Road
Wargrave
Berkshire RG10 8LT

Secretary:

Peter J Hearn/Sylvia Dean
0734-401000

Professional:

William Farrow
0734-404778

Directions:

By Car: Situated between Maidenhead and Reading, the course is two miles from Henley.

Course Details:

This is a 2880 yard, 9 hole parkland course, with an eighteen hole par of 72.

There are several mature copses and two water hazards on the course. The 7th hole plays straight across a valley with good views of the surrounding countryside.

Shop Facilities:

The shop stocks a range of golf equipment and accessories. Clubs can be hired at £4 for 9 clubs and £8 for a full set.

Tuition Details:

There is a seven bay driving range and a practice putting green. Lessons are available at £12/£15 for 30 minutes from the Assistant/Head Pro. There is no extra cost for video analysis.

Clubhouse Facilities:

The timber built clubhouse provides a range of social and leisure amenities.

There is a bar and restaurant facility which can cater for up to 70, together with a spike bar.

Visitor Restrictions and How to Book:

Visitors are welcome and a handicap certificate is not required. Visitors should book via the Pro shop.

Visitors are recommended to contact the Pro shop in advance by telephone to check that there are no competitions etc. on 0734-404778.

Societies are welcome and should contact the Secretary's office on 0734-401000 for details of the Society packages available.

Visitor Playing Costs:

Weekdays / Weekends:

18 holes: £12.00 / £18.00

9 holes: £9.00 / £14.00

Lavender Park Golf Centre

Swinley Road
Ascot
Berkshire SL5 1BD

Secretary:

David Johnson
0344-884074

Professional:

Wayne Owers
0344-886096

Directions:

By Car: Off the Ascot - Bracknell road, turn left into the course opposite the Forresters public house.

Course Details:

This is a nine hole pay and play course. It features eight par 3's and one par 4 hole.

This is a good course for beginners.

Shop Facilities:

The shop stocks a range of golf equipment and accessories. Clubs can be hired at £2.75 for a half set.

Tuition Details:

There is a 30 bay floodlit driving range attached to the course.

Lessons cost £12 for 30 minutes. Contact the Pro shop on 0344-886096 to book.

Clubhouse Facilities:

The clubhouse provides catering all day and has a fully licensed bar. The course is part of a Golf and Snooker centre.

There is a 10 table snooker hall on-site.

Visitor Restrictions and How to Book:

There are no restrictions.

Book at the shop on a first come, first serve basis.

Visitor Playing Costs:

Weekdays - £3.25

Weekends - £4.50

Royal Ascot Golf Club

Winkfield Road
Ascot
Berkshire SL5 7LJ

Secretary:

D D Simmonds
0344-25175

Professional:

Garry Malia
0344-24656

Directions:

By Car: The course is located inside the racecourse on Ascot Heath and off the A329 (Ascot High Street).

Course Details:

This is an eighteen hole heathland course, set on undulating terrain within the confines of the racecourse.

Shop Facilities:

The shop stocks a range of golf equipment and accessories.

Tuition Details:

Practice facilities are available. Lessons cost £12.50 for 30 minutes. Video analysis is available at £25 for one hour. Contact Garry Malia in the Pro shop to book.

Clubhouse Facilities:

The clubhouse is available to members, their guests and booked societies.

Visitor Restrictions and How to Book:

Visitors can only play as guests of members.

Societies are welcome on Wednesdays and Thursdays. Contact the Secretary's office for details of Society packages.

Visitor Playing Costs:

Since visitors can only play as guests of members, prices are only available on application.

Sand Martins Golf Club

Finchampstead Road
Wokingham
Berkshire RG11 3RG

Secretary:

Peter Watkin
0734-792711

Professional:

Andrew Hall
0734-770265

Directions:

By Car: The course is located 1 mile south of Wokingham and 4 miles from Reading. The Club is easily reached from Junction 10 off the M4, or Junction 3 or 4 off the M3.

Course Details:

This is a 6279 yard eighteen hole, parkland course.

Designed on gently undulating land, the outward nine are played on a wooded countryside setting, whilst the inward nine have been built on old sand workings to give a links feel to the course. A lake and smaller ponds add some interesting water hazards to the round.

Shop Facilities:

The shop is well stocked with golf equipment and accessories.

Tuition Details:

There is a practice range, together with a bunker and chipping green. Lessons are available from the Head Pro at £20 for 30 minutes and £27.50 for 45 minutes. Video analysis is inclusive.

Clubhouse Facilities:

The clubhouse provides extensive catering facilities and has a lounge bar, together with a separate Function / Dining room and bar.

There is a halfway house on the course for mid-round refreshments.

Visitor Restrictions and How to Book:

A handicap certificate is not required, though visitors are expected to be bona fide players. Visitors are welcome on weekdays, but must accompany a member at weekends. Book and pay through the Pro shop.

Societies are welcome on weekdays and should contact the Secretary's office for details.

Visitor Playing Costs:

Weekdays Only:

18 holes - £25.00

Day - £40.00

Sonning Golf Club

Duffield Road
Sonning on Thames
Berkshire RG4 0GJ

Secretary:

P.F. Williams
0734-693332

Professional:

R.T. McDougall
0734-692910

Directions:

By Car: The course is on the A4 between Maidenhead and Reading. Take the turning to Woodley (Pound Lane) and then 1st left into Duffield Road.

Course Details:

This is a 6090 yard, eighteen hole course.

Though essentially parkland, it has a heathland feel to it. The course itself stands on higher ground than the village of Sonning and provides fine views of the surrounding countryside.

Shop Facilities:

The shop stocks a wide range of golf equipment and accessories.

Tuition Details:

There is a small practice ground. Lessons are available from the Pro. For details, contact the Pro shop on 0734-692910.

Clubhouse Facilities:

There is a new clubhouse which provides daily catering in the Spike bar and restaurant. A function suite is available for hire.

A jacket and tie must be worn in the restaurant.

Visitor Restrictions and How to Book:

A handicap certificate is required. Visitors are welcome on weekdays, but must accompany a member at weekends.

Telephone the Pro shop to check availability. Tee times are not booked.

Societies are welcome on Wednesdays only. Contact the Secretary for details.

Visitor Playing Costs:

Weekdays Only:

Day - £30.00

After 10.30am - £20 for 18 holes

Temple Golf Club

Henley Road
Hurley
Maidenhead
Berkshire SL6 5LH

Secretary:

John Hunt
0628-824794

Professional:

Alan Dobbins
0628-824254

Directions:

By Car: Exit Junction 4 (M40) or Junction 8/9 (M4) to A404. The course is off the Henley Road (A4130).

Course Details:

This is a 6206 yard eighteen hole parkland course.

Designed in 1908 by Willie Park, the course is surrounded by belts of well established trees and has views of a long stretch of the River Thames. A wildlife habitat, there is an abundance of fauna, orchids, flowers and butterflies.

Shop Facilities:

The shop stocks a range of golf equipment and accessories. Clubs are available for hire at £10 per set.

Tuition Details:

There is an extensive practice ground and lessons are available at £18 for 45 minutes. Video analysis is also available. Contact Alan Dobbins in the Pro shop to book.

Clubhouse Facilities:

There are Gents and Ladies changing facilities.

The clubhouse is open from 8.00am and provides a range of catering throughout the day.

Visitor Restrictions and How to Book:

A handicap certificate or proof of an ability to play are required. Visitors must book by telephone through the Pro shop or the Secretary. Green fees are paid in the Pro shop.

Societies are welcome. Full day society packages are available on all weekdays, bar Thursday. Thursday pm is available for half day meetings.

There are Summer and Winter packages available. Societies should contact the Secretary's office for details.

Visitor Playing Costs:

Weekday / Weekend:

18 holes: £25.00 / On Request

Day: £40.00 / £45.00

Aylesbury Golf Centre

Hulcott Lane
Bierton
Aylesbury HP22 5GA
Buckinghamshire

Secretary:

Kevin Partington
0296-393644

Professional:

Andy Taylor
0296-393644

Directions:

By Car: The course is located 1 mile north of Aylesbury on the A418 towards Leighton Buzzard.

Course Details:

This is a 5,190 yard eighteen hole parkland course, playing nine holes twice.

Though short by many standards, out of bounds come into play on the 1st, 2nd, 6th, 7th and 8th holes. Accuracy is therefore as important as length.

Shop Facilities:

The shop stocks a range of golf equipment and accessories.

Tuition Details:

There is a 30 bay floodlit driving range between the clubhouse and ninth tee.

There are two resident PGA qualified professionals available for lessons at £11 per 30 minutes.

Contact Andy Taylor in the Club shop to book.

Clubhouse Facilities:

There are no changing facilities.

The clubhouse provides a range of catering facilities all week with the exception of Monday lunchtime.

Visitor Restrictions and How to Book:

There are no visitor restrictions.

Visitors should book via the Club shop. Telephone bookings are available.

Societies are welcome. Contact the Secretary for details of the packages available.

Visitor Playing Costs:

Weekday / Weekend:

9 holes: £6.00 / £6.50

18 holes: £9.00 / £10.00

There are no day rates.

Beaconsfield Golf Club

Seer Green
Beaconsfield HP9 2UR
Buckinghamshire

Secretary:

P.I. Anderson
0494-676545

Professional:

M.W. Brothers
0494-676616

Directions:

The course is located at Seer Green off the A355 between Beaconsfield and Amersham.

Course Details:

This is an eighteen hole, parkland course.

The very large greens and 100 bunkers are a feature of the course.

The par 4, 6th hole is possibly the most testing hole on the course requiring both accuracy and length.

Shop Facilities:

The shop stocks a range of golf equipment, accessories and designer wear.

Tuition Details:

There is a large practice ground and lessons are available at £12/£15 for 30 minutes from the Assistant/Head Pro. Contact the Pro shop to book.

Clubhouse Facilities:

The traditional clubhouse has modern facilities.

All day catering is available with both a fully licensed bar and dining room, offering an extensive menu.

Normal dress restrictions apply in both the clubhouse and on the course.

Visitor Restrictions and How to Book:

Visitors are welcome to play on weekdays. At weekends, visitors should accompany a member as a guest. Book via the Pro shop.

Societies are welcome and should contact the Secretary on 0494-676545 for details of the packages available which start at £62 per day.

Visitor Playing Costs:

Weekdays Only:

18 holes - £34.00

Day - £42.00

Buckinghamshire Golf Club

Denham Court Drive
Denham UB9 5BG
Buckinghamshire

Operations Manager:

Kevin Munt
0895-835777

Professional:

John O'Leary
0895-835777

Directions:

By Car: Exit Junction 16B (M25) or Junction 1 (M40). The entrance is off the Denham roundabout on the A40.

Course Details:

This is an eighteen hole, 6880 yard wooded, parkland course.

The feature hole is probably the 7th. The hole plays over a stream and then the River Misbourne. The green is guarded by a lake on the right.

Shop Facilities:

The shop stocks a wide range of golf equipment, accessories and designer wear. Clubs are available to hire at £23.50 per round.

Tuition Details:

There is a 350 metre practice ground. Balls cost £2.00 per basket. Lessons are available from John O'Leary. Contact John on 0895-835777 for details.

Clubhouse Facilities:

The clubhouse is a converted mansion house. The ground floor is spike proof and catering is provided by a brasserie-style bar menu and the Heron Restaurant which offers an a la carte menu.

Visitor Restrictions and How to Book:

Some visitor arrangements can be made on weekdays only. Otherwise visitors must be guests of members.

To book, contact the Reception by telephone. Payment should also be made to the Reception.

Societies are welcome on weekdays. Societies should contact Margaret Yoshikawa or John O'Leary for details.

Visitor Playing Costs:

Weekdays Only:

£47.00 per round.

Chartridge Park Golf Club

*Chartridge
Chesham HP5 2TF
Buckinghamshire*

Secretary:

Mrs. Anita Gibbins
0494-791772

Professional:

Peter Gibbins
0494-791772

Directions:

By Car: The course is 2 miles from the town centre.

By LUG: Chesham Station.

Course Details:

This is a 5244 yard, eighteen hole flat parkland course.

With views across the Chiltern Hills, the course has possibly the most holed - in - one hole in the 15th. On average, it is holed-in-one on ten to twenty occasions a year. Water hazards are found on the 9th and 13th holes.

Shop Facilities:

The shop stocks a full range of golf equipment and accessories. Clubs are available for hire at £5 for half a set.

Tuition Details:

Lessons are available at £10 for 30 minutes and £20 per hour. Contact the Pro shop for details.

Clubhouse Facilities:

There are male and female changing rooms in the modern country house - style clubhouse.

The clubhouse, which provides a range of catering services all day, has facilities available for private hire.

Visitor Restrictions and How to Book:

Visitors are welcome at most times. Telephone bookings are taken through the clubhouse switchboard.

Visitors are advised to ring the Pro shop to check availability.

Societies are welcome 7 days a week. Contact the Secretary for details of the packages available which include coffee, ploughmans lunch, 3 course dinner and 36 holes of golf for £40.

Visitor Playing Costs:

18 holes - £20.00

Chiltern Forest Golf Club

Aston Hill
Halton
Aylesbury HP22 5NQ
Buckinghamshire

Secretary:

L.E.A Clark
0296-631267

Professional:

C Skeet
0296-631817

Directions:

By Car: From London on the A41 (M). Off the A4011 linking Wendover, Tring and Aston Clinton.

Course Details:

This is a 5537 yard, eighteen hole hilly course.

Set in the Chilterns, this is a very scenic course. The fairways are heavily tree-lined and accuracy is essential to achieve a good score.

Shop Facilities:

The shop stocks a range of golf equipment and accessories.

Tuition Details:

There is a limited practice area and lessons are available by appointment with the Pro at £15 for an hour. Contact the Pro shop to book.

Clubhouse Facilities:

The clubhouse has a licensed bar which is open at both lunchtime and in the evening.

Full catering is available, though only by prior arrangement on Tuesdays and Thursdays.

Visitor Restrictions and How to Book:

Visitors are welcome on weekdays only. At weekends, they must accompany a member as a guest.

Ladies day is Monday.

Book at the Pro shop, which is open from 8.00am.

Societies are welcome (minimum of 15) and should contact the Society Organiser, T. Noble, for details of the Society packages available.

Visitor Playing Costs:

Weekdays Only:

Day - £22.00

Societies - £40.00

Harewood Downs Golf Club

Cokes Lane
Chalfont St. Giles
Buckinghamshire
HP8 4TA

Secretary:

M.R Cannon
0494-762184

Professional:

G. Morrie
0494-764102

Directions:

By Car: The course is located 2 miles east of Amersham off the A413.

Course Details:

This is a 5958 yard, eighteen hole parkland course.

Though not particularly long, (there are four par 3's under 150 yards), this is an undulating hilly course which is lined with trees and offers a good test of golf.

Shop Facilities:

The shop stocks a range of golf equipment and accessories. The shop offers full club repair facilities.

Tuition Details:

Lessons are available from the Professional. Contact the Pro shop on 0494-764102 for details.

Clubhouse Facilities:

The clubhouse has a fully licensed bar and restaurant which provide a full daily catering service.

A jacket and tie must be worn in the restaurant in the evening.

Visitor Restrictions and How to Book:

A current handicap certificate is required and visitors must be pre-booked to play.

It is possible to book either through the clubhouse office or Pro shop by telephone.

Societies are welcome on weekdays. Pre-book through the Secretary's office for packages starting at £22 per round or £30 per day.

Visitor Playing Costs:

Weekdays / Weekends:

18 holes - £20.00 / £30.00

Day - £27.00

Hazlemere Golf and Country Club

Penn Road
Hazlemere
High Wycombe HP15 7LR
Buckinghamshire

Secretary:

Mrs. D. Hudson
0494-714722

Professional:

Steve Morvell
0494-718298

Directions:

By Car: The course is 3 miles north of High Wycombe on the B474.

Course Details:

This is a 5652 yard, eighteen hole parkland course.

Set in a scenic location, the course offers a challenge to players of all standards. A tee shot over water is required at the par 3, 3rd hole. Well placed bunkers are to be found along a number of fairways and protecting greens.

Shop Facilities:

The shop stocks a wide range of golf equipment, accessories and designer wear. Club hire is available at £10 per set.

Tuition Details:

There are three practice grounds, nets, a practice bunker and putting green. Lessons are available for £12.50 for 30 minutes and £25 for an hour. Video analysis is available at the same price.

Contact Steve Morvell in the Pro shop to book.

Clubhouse Facilities:

There are Gents and Ladies locker rooms.

Snacks and full bar / restaurant facilities are available daily.

Visitor Restrictions and How to Book:

Handicap certificates are not required. Visitors are welcome at all times, except weekend mornings when Club tournaments may be held. Tees can be booked through the Pro shop.

Societies are welcome and should contact the Secretary's office for details. Other groups should contact the Pro shop.

Visitor Playing Costs:

Weekday / Weekend:

18 holes - £26.00 / £40.00

Day - £35.00

Lambourne Golf Club

Dropmore Road
Burnham SL1 8NF
South Buckinghamshire

Secretary:

Colin Lumley
0628-666755

Professional:

R.A Newman
0628-662936

Directions:

By Car: Exit Junction 2 (M40) and take the A355 towards Slough. After 350 yards, turn right across the dual-carriageway towards Burnham. The course entrance is two and a half miles on the right.

Course Details:

This is a 6,536 yard eighteen hole parkland course.

Set in 180 acres, it has a large number of mature trees, lakes and undulating landscape. The 7th hole is a short par 3, played over a lake to a green protected by bunkers. The 18th hole provides a challenging finish with an accurate drive essential to hit the small green with the second shot.

Shop Facilities:

The shop stocks a range of golf equipment, accessories and designer wear. Clubs are available for hire at £10 per round.

Tuition Details:

There is a practice ground and three assistant PGA professionals provide lessons at £15 per 45 minutes.

Clubhouse Facilities:

The changing rooms include showers, sauna and steam bath.

A bar and restaurant provide all day catering.

A half-way hut is available for food and drinks after nine holes.

Visitor Restrictions and How to Book:

Visitors must have a handicap certificate and can play at weekends during quiet periods. Visitors should book and pay at the Pro shop. Telephone bookings are taken.

Society bookings are not taken at anytime.

Visitor Playing Costs:

Weekday / Weekend:

18 holes - £30.00 / £40.00

Little Chalfont Golf Club

Lodge Lane
Little Chalfont HP8 4AJ
Buckinghamshire

Secretary:

Michael Dunne
0494-764877

Professional:

Michael Dunne
0494-762942

Directions:

By Car: Exit Junction 18 (M25). After 2 miles along the A404 towards Amersham, turn left into Lodge Lane after 'Chenies Garden Centre'.

By BR and LUG: Chalfont and Latimer Station.

Course Details:

This is a nine hole parkland course which plays twice as a 68 par, eighteen hole course.

The course is set in the midst of the Chilterns and provides a range of challenging holes on a gently undulating terrain.

Shop Facilities:

The shop offers a range of golf equipment and accessories. The shop also offers tea, coffee and snacks. Clubs are available for hire at £3 per set.

Tuition Details:

There is a practice area, including practice nets and putting green. Lessons are available at £15 for 45 minutes through pre-booking with the Pro shop.

Clubhouse Facilities:

There are male and female changing rooms.

The clubhouse has a restaurant, bar and pool table and provides a range of catering. The bar opens onto a patio area overlooking the course. A function room is available for hire.

Visitor Restrictions and How to Book:

There are no visitor restrictions, except for the normal dress code. Visitors should book via the Pro shop or Club Secretary.

Societies are welcome and should contact Michael Dunne for details of available packages on 0494-762942.

Visitor Playing Costs:

Weekday / Weekend:

18 holes - £10.00 / £12.00

Weston Turville Golf and Squash Club

*New Road
Weston Turville
Aylesbury HP22 5QT
Buckinghamshire*

Secretary:

Barry Hill
0296-24084

Professional:

Tom Jones
0296-25949

Directions:

By Car: The Club is off the A41 between Aston Clinton and Aylesbury.

Course Details:

This is a par 69, eighteen hole parkland course.

The course has been owned and managed by Master Golfer Ltd, since 1991. Situated at the foot of the Chiltern Hills, the course provides a challenge to the accomplished player, whilst not being too daunting for the higher handicap player.

Shop Facilities:

The shop stocks a wide range of golf equipment and accessories, all carrying the Master Golfer price promise. Clubs are available for hire at £5 per round.

Tuition Details:

Lessons are provided for groups and individuals. Individual lessons cost £15 for 30 minutes. Clinics and video analysis are organised by the professional staff. Contact the Pro shop for details.

Clubhouse Facilities:

The clubhouse has recently been enlarged to provide a more extensive range of facilities. Catering is provided through the day.

Function suites are available for hire.

Visitor Restrictions and How to Book:

There are no visitor restrictions.

To book, telephone 0296-25949 / 24084.

Societies are welcome. Groups of 12 - 60 are catered for. A range of packages are available starting from £12 per head. Contact the Secretary for details.

Visitor Playing Costs:

Monday / Remaining Weekdays / Weekends:

£10.00 / £15.00 / £20.00

There are discounts for juniors and seniors.

Wycombe Heights Golf Centre

Rayners Avenue
Loudwater
High Wycombe HP10 9SW
Buckinghamshire

Secretary:

Peter Talbot
0494-813185

Professional:

David Marsden
0494-812862

Directions:

By Car: Exit Junction 3 (M40). Follow the A40 to High Wycombe for about 3/4 of a mile. Rayners Avenue is on the right.

Course Details:

This is a 6253 yard, eighteen hole parkland course.

(There is also an eighteen hole par 3 course).

The 461 yard, 7th hole requires an accurate drive with three bunkers down the left hand side of the fairway. The 13th hole also poses problems with two bunkers guarding a narrow fairway and a ditch running in front of the green. The finishing hole, at 343 yards, is downhill with longer drivers capable of getting close to the green from the tee.

Shop Facilities:

The shop supplies golf equipment, accessories and refreshments. Clubs are available for hire.

Tuition Details:

There is a 24 bay driving range, plus the par 3 course.

3 PGA qualified professionals provide lessons from £12 per half hour, including video analysis. Contact the Pro shop for details.

Clubhouse Facilities:

Mens and Ladies changing rooms, plus lockers are available.

There is a licensed bar, a family eating area and a function room. Smart casual dress is required.

Visitor Restrictions and How to Book:

There are no visitor restrictions.

Book and pay in the Reception. Telephone bookings are taken.

Societies are welcome and a leaflet giving details of the packages on offer is available from the Reception.

Visitor Playing Costs:

Weekday / Weekend:

Adult: £10.50 / £13.50

Par 3 course: £5.00 / £7.00

READERS' COMMENTS

The publishers of this Guide are anxious that the information provided is as accurate as possible. We do however need to know what you think of the Clubs, courses and driving ranges that have been included in the Guide.

Perhaps your favourite course, Club or driving range has not been featured. If so, please send details for possible inclusion in the next edition. We will acknowledge your assistance in the next Guide, unless you request otherwise.

If you are opening a new golfing facility which you think will interest our readers, please let us know.

REMEMBER: Clubs, courses and driving ranges do not pay to enter this Guide. It is an independent publication which requires the support of its readers to ensure that the information supplied is as relevant and up-to-date as possible.

If you have any comments, criticisms, suggestions, then please write to us. We will attempt to acknowledge all individual letters. Your comments will be read and may be included in the next edition.

Please send your comments to our editorial address:

THE EDITOR
BETULA PUBLISHING
83 MILL LANE
WEST HAMPSTEAD
LONDON NW6 1NB

Editors Note: Readers comments are important. Do let us know your views of the courses and driving ranges covered in this edition. We are also keen to hear your recommendations of courses and driving ranges NOT included in this Guide. Your comments will be considered for future editions.

Introduction to Driving Ranges

Driving ranges offer golfers an excellent opportunity to improve aspects of their game. With over 80 such facilities around London, there is no shortage to tempt the interested player.

Many of these ranges are attached to existing courses. Indeed, a feature of many new golf developments, is the automatic inclusion of a range facility. They give both experienced players the chance to improve elements of their game, whilst they offer new players a chance to learn to play in an environment totally dedicated to developing and improving golfing skills.

The Guide seeks to introduce many of these ranges and their facilities.

The Guide covers the following features of each range:

- Name and address
- The name of the manager and/ or professional
- Details of bays
- Opening times
- Cost of balls
- Cost of tuition (generally speaking, the cost relates to individual tuition. Most driving ranges offer a number of tuition options, including group classes for beginners, juniors, ladies, seniors etc. Details of the range of tuition options available can be obtained from the Range Manager).
- Other facilities (details of the availability of refreshments and other leisure facilities of interest).

Whilst every effort has been taken to ensure the accuracy of the information, certain details may change from time to time.

ESSEX

Belhus Park Leisure Centre
Belhus Park
South Ockendon
Essex RM15 4PX
Telephone: 0708-856297 / 852248
Centre Manager: Gary Weatherley
Professional: Gary Lunn

Directions: Belhus Park is located off the Aveley by-pass and is close to Junction 30/31 (M25).

Bays: 11 floodlit open air covered bays.
Opening Times: 7 days a week.
On weekdays: 9.00am - 10.00pm
Exception: Wednesday (11.30am - 10.00pm).
On weekends: Saturday (9.00am - 6.00pm) and Sunday (8.00am - 8.00pm).

Cost of Balls:
50 balls / £1.00.
100 balls / £1.50.
Cost of Tuition: Contact Gary Lunn on 0708-852248 for details.

Other Facilities: The range is attached to an eighteen hole public course. There is an adjacent Leisure centre with a swimming pool, sauna and sunbeds. An on-site public house has both a restaurant and a cafeteria which provide all-day catering.

Benton Hall Golf Range
Wickham Hill
Witham
Essex CM8 3LH
Telephone: 0376-502454
Range Manager: Peter Holmes

Directions: The range is located outside Witham off the A12.

Bays: 20 floodlit bays.
Opening Times: 7 days a week from 7.30am - 8.30pm.

Cost of Balls:
40 balls / £2.00.
80 balls / £3.50.
Cost of Tuition: Lessons cost £10 for 30 minutes. Six lessons are available for £50.00.

Other Facilities: The range is attached to an eighteen hole golf course. On-site refreshments are available.

Brentwood Park Golf Range
Warley Gap
Brentwood
Essex CM13 3LG
Telephone: 0277-211994
General Manager: Mr. Graham Dove
Professional: Mr. Jason Groat

Directions: Exit Junction 28 (M25). The range is located off the B186.

Bays: 22 floodlit, open-air bays.
Opening Times: 7 days a week from 7.30am - 10.00pm.

Cost of Balls:
Small buckets / £2.
Large buckets / £4.
Discount cards are available.
Cost of Tuition: A trial lesson costs £5.00. Thereafter 30 minute lessons cost £9.50 during daytime and £11 for evenings / weekends. Balls cost extra. There is a 'Kids' morning on Saturdays from 10.30am - 11.45am. This costs £2.50. Balls and club hire are included.

Other Facilities: On-site facilities include a dry ski slope, health club, off-road karting, bars and restaurant. The 'Inn' is open from 7.30am offering refreshments and meals.

Bunsay Downs Indoor Driving Range
Little Baddow Road
Woodham Walter
Essex CM9 6RW
Telephone: 0245-222648
Manager: Mr M. Durham

Bays: 4 indoor bays.
Opening Times: 7 days a week from 7.00am - 9.00pm.

Cost of Balls:
50 balls / £1.50.

Other Facilities: The range is attached to

a nine hole golf course. There is a bar and restaurant which provide catering.

Castle Point Golf Range
Somnes Avenue
Canvey Island
Essex SS8 9FG
Telephone: 0268-511758
Managers: Mr James Sharp / Mr James Hogsden

Directions: The range is located on Canvey Island, opposite the Waterside Farm Leisure complex.

Bays: 17 floodlit bays.
Opening Times: 7 days a week from 7.00am - 9.00pm.

Cost of Balls:
50 balls / £2.00.
100 balls /£3.00.
Tuition Costs: Lessons are available for £12.50 for 30 minutes.

Other Facilities: The range is attached to an eighteen hole course. Refreshments are available from an on-site bar and restaurant.

Chingford Golf Range
Waltham Way
Chingford
Essex E4 8AQ
Telephone: 081-529 2409
Manager: Mr Gordon Goldie

DRIVING RANGES

Bays: 18 floodlit bays.
Opening Times: 7 days a week from 9.30am - 10.00pm.

Cost of Balls:
40 balls / £1.50.
60 balls / £1.95.
100 balls / £2.75.
Tuition Costs: Lessons cost £10 for 30 minutes.

Other Facilities: On-site refreshments are available.

Colchester Golf Range
Old Ipswich Road
Ardleigh
Colchester
Essex CO7 7GR
Telephone: 0206-230974
Owner: Chester Jervis
Professional: Miss Sarah Wilson

Bays: 14 floodlit bays.
Opening Times:
Weekdays: 10.00am - 9.00pm.
Weekends: 10.00am - 5.00pm.

Cost of Balls:
50 balls / £1.75.
Tuition Costs: Lessons are available at £12 for 30 minutes.

Other Facilities: There is a public house on-site. Refreshments are available.

Docklands Golf Range
Brunswick Wharf Road
Leamouth Road
London E14
Telephone: 071-712 9944
Manager: Mr Perry Warnes
Professional: Mr Sean Simpson

Bays: 29 floodlit bays.
Opening Times:
Weekdays: 10.00am - 10.00pm.
Weekends: 9.00am - 9.00pm.

Cost of Balls:
50 balls / £2.00.
Tuition Costs: Lessons cost £15 per 30 minutes. This includes video analysis.

Other Facilities: There is a cafeteria on-site.

Earls Colne Golf and Country Club Ltd
Earls Colne
Colchester
Essex CO6 2NS
Telephone: 0787-224466
Professional: Owen McKenna

Bays: 20 floodlit bays. There is also an indoor bunker range (undercover).
Opening Times:
Weekdays: 9.00am - 10.00pm.
Weekends: 8.00am - 9.00pm.

Cost of Balls:
50 balls / £1.95.

Tuition Costs: Lessons are available at £10 for 30 minutes. A video studio is available for video analysis.

Other Facilities: The range is attached to an eighteen hole course which also has a 4 hole training course. Extensive facilities include tennis, bar, restaurant and poolside grill.

Fairlop Waters Golf Range
Forest Road
Barkingside
Ilford
Essex IG6 3JA
Telephone: 081-500 9911
Golf Professional: Tony Bowers
Teaching Pro: Steve Burridge

Bays: 36 floodlit bays.
Opening Times: 7 days a week from 8.30am - 10.00pm.

Cost of Balls:
80 balls / £2.50.
Tuition Costs: Lessons are available at £12 per 30 minutes.

Other Facilities: The range is attached to an eighteen hole and 9 hole, par 3 course. There are full bar and restaurant facilities.

Hockley Golf Range
Aldermans Hill
Hockley
Southend-on- Sea

Essex
Telephone: 0702-207218
Owner: T.C. Harrold
Professional: T. Blackburn

Bays: 17 indoor and 4 outdoor floodlit bays.

Cost of Balls:
A bucket of balls / £1.80.
Tuition Costs: Contact the Pro shop on 0702-207218 for details.

Other Facilities: There is a Pro shop.

Langdon Hills Driving Range
Lower Dunton Road
Bulphan
Essex RM14 3TY
Telephone: 0268-548444
Manager: Mark Rosser
Professionals: (Head) Andy Labers / Stuart Emery

Bays: 22 floodlit bays.
Opening Times:
Weekdays: 7.00am - 9.00pm.
Weekends: 6.00am - 8.00pm.

Cost of Balls:
32 balls / £1.00.
Tuition Costs: Lessons cost £11 for 30 minutes and £20 for 1 hour.

Other Facilities: The range is attached to an eighteen hole course. Refreshments are available.

DRIVING RANGES

Leigh Golf Driving Range
Leigh Marshes
Leigh-on-Sea
Essex SS9 2EU
Telephone: 0702-710586
Owner: K.B. Martin
Professional: Roger Smith

Directions: 1/2 mile from Leigh-on-Sea Railway Station.

Bays: 18 floodlit bays.
Opening Times: 7 days a week from 10.00am - 9.30pm.

Cost of Balls:
50 balls / £1.70.
100 balls / £3.25.
Tuition Costs: Contact Roger Smith on 0702-710586 for details.

Other Facilities: Refreshments are available throughout the time the range is open.

Mardyke Valley Golf Centre Ltd
South Road
South Ockendon
Essex RM15 6RR
Telephone: 0708-855011
Manager: Inger Perkins
Director of Golf: Jimmy Burns

Directions: Off the A186, 1/2 mile north of A13 (Thurrock).

Bays: There are covered and open driving range bays, plus a range of other practice facilities, including chipping greens, bunkers and 3 golf holes, played as 9.
Opening Times:
Tuesday - Friday: 10.00am - dusk (plus Mondays in the Summer).
Weekends: 9.00am - 6.00pm.

Cost of Balls:
50 balls / £1.00 on weekdays and £1.50 at weekends.
Tuition Costs: Individual lessons cost £15 for 30 minutes and £25 for one hour. Contact Jimmy Burns for details on 0708-855011.

Other Facilities: Refreshments are available.

Tiptree Driving Range
Newbridge Road
Tiptree
Essex CO5 0HS
Telephone: 0621-819374
Manager: Mr Martin Peters

Bays: 14 floodlit bays.
Opening Times:
Weekdays: 10.00am - 9.00pm.
Weekends: 10.00am - 6.00pm.

Cost of Balls:
50 balls / £1.50.

Tuition: Lessons are not available at this range.

Other Facilities: Refreshments are available.

Towerlands Golf Range
Panfield Road
Braintree
Essex CM7 5BJ
Telephone: 0376-347951
Manager: Mr R. Barrell

Directions: The range is located on the B1053 north of Braintree.

Bays: This is a grass driving range.
Opening Times: The range is open daily from 8.00am - 6.00pm.

Cost of Balls:
40 balls / £1.25.
Cost of Tuition: Contact the Pro shop on 0376-347951 for details.

Other Facilities: The range is attached to a nine hole course. There are squash courts, a sports centre and equestrian facilities available. Refreshments are available from both the clubhouse bar and restaurant.

Warren Park Golf Centre
Whalebone Lane North
Chadwell Heath
Essex RM6 6SB
Telephone: 081-597 1120
Director of Golf: Alan Walker

Directions: The range is located on the A12 opposite the Moby Dick Public House.

Bays: 27 floodlit bays.
Opening Times:
Sunday - Friday: 9.00am - 10.00pm.
Saturdays: 9.00am - 9.00pm.

Cost of Balls:
40 balls / £1.40.
80 balls / £2.80.
120 balls / £3.50.
Tuition Costs: Lessons from 7 PGA professionals starts at £10 for 1/2 hour individual tuition.

Other Facilities. There is a golf shop. A function suite is available for hire.

Woodham Mortimer Golf Range
Woodham Mortimer
Maldon
Essex CM9 6SR
Telephone: 024522 2276
Proprietor: Ian Moss
Professional: Steven Parkin

Directions: Just off the A414 (4 minutes from the A12 junction) on the B1010.

Bays: 15 undercover floodlit bays, plus 8 uncovered bays in the summer.

Cost of Balls:
A small bucket / £2.00.
150 balls / £4.50.

Tuition Costs: Contact Steven Parkin on 024522-2276 for details.

Other Facilities: There is a 9 hole pitch and putt course attached to the range. A snack bar and toilets are also available.

Hertfordshire

A1 Golf Driving Range
Rowley Lane
Arkley
Hertfordshire EN5 3HW
Telephone: 081-449 5033
Manager: Bob Townsend
Professional: Nigel Lawrence

Directions: Located on the A1 at the Arkley, Elstree and Borehamwood intersection.

Bays: 45 indoor and 12 outdoor floodlit bays.
Opening Times: 7 days a week from 9.00am - 10.00pm.

Cost of Balls:
50 balls / £2.00.
Cost of Tuition: Contact Nigel Lawrence on 081-449 5033 for details.

Other Facilities: There is a golf shop, drinks, public telephone and toilets on-site.

Bushey Golf Range
High Street
Bushey
Hertfordshire WD2 1BJ
Telephone: 081-950 2283
Manager: Mr A. Barton

Directions: The range is located off the main high street in Bushey.

Bays: 30 floodlit bays on a two-tier range.
Opening Times: 7 days a week from 8.00am - 10.00pm.

Cost of Balls:
60 balls / £2.00.
Cost of Tuition: Lessons are available at £10 for 30 minutes.

Other Facilities: The range is attached to a nine hole golf course. There is a Nevada Bob golf shop. Refreshments, toilets, pool and squash courts are on-site.

Chesfield Downs Golf Range
Jack's Hill
Graveley
Stevenage
Hertfordshire SG4 7EQ
Telephone: 0462-482929
Manager: Paul McCullough
Professional: Beverley Huke

Bays: 25 floodlit bays.
Opening Times: 7 days a week from 7.00am - 10.00pm.

Cost of Balls:
60 balls / £2.00.
Tuition Costs: Lessons are available from £12 - £13.50 for 30 minutes.

Other Facilities: The range is attached to both an eighteen hole and a nine hole course. Refreshments are available from a bar and restaurant in the clubhouse.

Elstree Golf Range
Watling Street
Elstree
Hertfordshire WD6 3AA
Telephone: 081-953 6115
Manager: Ken Ellis
Professionals: Mark Warwick / Mark Wood

Bays: 60 floodlit bays, together with 5 sand bays.
Opening Times: 7 days a week from 7.00am -10.00pm.

Cost of Balls:
60 balls / £2.00.
Cost of Tuition: Lessons are available at £13 for 30 minutes.

Other Facilities: The range is attached to an eighteen hole course. Free coffee and water is available in the range. More substantial refreshments and toilets are available in the clubhouse.

Gosling Golf Range
Stanborough Road
Welwyn Garden City
Hertfordshire AL8 6XE
Telephone: 0707-323443
Manager: Mr Andrew Nicholl
Professionals: Bryan Lewis / Michael Corlass

DRIVING RANGES

Directions: The range is located off the A6129, south of the town centre.

Bays: 22 covered, floodlit bays.
Opening Times:
Monday-Thursday (10.00am - 10.00pm)
Friday (10.00am - 9.00pm)
Weekends (10.00am - 8.00pm).

Cost of Balls:
48 balls / £1.50 (member) and £2.00 (non-member).
Cost of Tuition: Individual lessons are available at £12 for 30 minutes. Video analysis is available at £22 for 45 minutes.

Other Facilities: There is a golf shop, dry ski slope, tennis courts, squash courts and a range of other on-site leisure facilities. Refreshments are available.

Little Hay Golf Range
Box Lane
Bovington
Hemel Hempstead
Hertfordshire HP3 0DQ
Telephone: 0442-833798
Managers: David Johnson / Stephen Proudfoot

Bays: 23 floodlit bays.
Opening Times:
Weekdays: 10.00am - 9.00pm
Weekends: 8.00am - 7.30pm.

Cost of Balls:
40 balls / £1.75.
80 balls / £3.00.
Cost of Tuition: Lessons are available at £13.95 for 30 minutes.

Other Facilities: The range is attached to an eighteen hole course. There are refreshments available, together with a golf shop.

Oxhey Golf Range
Prestwick Road
South Oxhey
Watford
Hertfordshire WD1 4ED
Telephone: 0923-248312
Manager: Terry Warner

Bays: 20 floodlit bays.
Opening Times: The range is open from 7.00am - 10.00pm, except on Tuesdays / Fridays when it opens at 10.00am.

Cost of Balls:
25 balls / £1.00.
55 balls / £2.00.
Cost of Tuition: Lessons are available at £10 for 30 minutes.

Other Facilities: Refreshments and toilets (incl. disabled toilets) are available on-site.

Redbourn Golf Range
Kingsbourne Green Lane
Redbourn

St. Albans
Hertfordshire AL3 7QA
Telephone: 0582-793493
Manager: Chris Gyford
Professional: Dale Brightman

Bays: 20 floodlit bays.
Opening Times: 7 days a week from 8.00am - 9.30pm.

Cost of Balls:
50 balls / £1.75.
Cost of Tuition: Lessons are available at £11.50 / £12.50 for 30 minutes from the Assistant Pro / Head Pro.

Other Facilities: The range is attached to an eighteen hole and a nine hole course. The clubhouse offers a range of catering from bar snacks to full meals.

Shooters Golf Centre

Shooters Way
Berkhamsted
Hertfordshire HP4 3UL
Telephone: 0442-872048
Manager: Mrs Karen Smith
Professional: Mr Richard May

Bays: 25 floodlit bays.

Opening Times: 7 days a week from 9.00am - 9.30pm.

Cost of Balls:
50 balls / £1.50.
100 balls / £3.00.

Costs of Tuition: Lessons are available at £10 for 30 minutes.

Other Facilities: There is a main bar, restaurant and swimming pool (outdoor) on-site.

Stevenage Golf Range

Ashton Lodge
Stevenage
Hertfordshire SG2 7EL
Telephone: 0438-880424
Manager / Professional: Neil Robinson

Bays: 24 floodlit bays
Opening Times: 7 days a week from 8.00am - 10.00pm.

Cost of Balls:
36 balls / £1.00.
Cost of Tuition: Lessons are available at £9 / £11 for 30 minutes from the Assistant Pro / Head Pro.

Other Facilities: Refreshments are available .

Watford Driving Range

Sheepcot Lane
Garston
Watford
Hertfordshire
Telephone: 0923-675560
Manager: Mathew Baker
Professional: David Bailey

Bays: 30 floodlit bays.
Opening Times: 7 days a week from 9.00am -11.00pm.

Cost of Balls:
40 balls / £1.00.
Cost of Tuition: Lessons are available at £12 for 30 minutes.

Other Facilities: There are refreshments available.

Whitehill Golf Centre
Dane End
Ware
Hertfordshire SG12 0JS
Telephone: 0920-438495
Manager: Mr A. Smith
Professional: Mr D. Ling

Bays: 25 floodlit bays
Opening Times: 7 days a week from 7.00am - 9.30pm.

Cost of Balls:
80-90 balls / £2.50.
Tuition Costs: Lessons are available at £11 for 30 minutes and £22 for 1 hour.

Other Facilities: The range is attached to an eighteen hole course. Refreshments are available on-site in the clubhouse.

Kent

Birchwood Park Golf Range
Birchwood Road
Wilmington
Dartford
Kent DA2 7HJ
Telephone: 0322-662038
Manager: Fred Thompson

Bays: 30 covered and 8 outdoor, floodlit bays. There is also an indoor teaching centre, with video analysis.
Opening Times: 7 days a week from 8.00am - 10.00pm.

Cost of balls:
On Monday - Friday (12.30pm - 5.30pm), 85 balls / £2.
At all other times, 51 balls /£2.
Cost of Tuition: Individual lessons are available from £10 per 30 minutes.

Other Facilities: The range is attached to an eighteen and a nine hole course. There is a viewing lounge where light refreshments are available.

Boughton Golf Range
Brickfield Lane
Boughton
Faversham
Kent ME13 9AJ
Telephone: 0227-752277

Manager: Phillip Sparks

Bays: 15 uncovered bays.
Opening Times: The range is open during daylight hours.

Cost of Balls:
36 balls / £1.50.
Cost of Tuition: Contact Phillip Sparks for details of lessons.

Other Facilities: The range is attached to an eighteen hole course. Refreshments are available in the clubhouse.

Chatham Golf Centre
Street End Road
Chatham
Kent ME5 0BG
Telephone: 0634-848907
Manager: R. Burden

Directions: The range is located 5 minutes from Rochester Airport,

Bays: 30 floodlit, covered bays.
Opening Times: 7 days a week from 10.00am - 10.00pm.

Cost of Balls:
65 balls / £2.00.
Cost of Tuition: Lessons are available. Contact Mr Burden for details.

Other Facilities: There is a fully stocked Pro shop and licensed snack bar on-site.

Edenbridge Golf Range
Crouch End House
Edenbridge
Kent TN8 5LQ
Telephone: 0732-865202
Professional: Keith Burkin

Bays: 16 floodlit bays.
Opening Times:
Monday - Thursday: 7.00am - 9.00pm.
Fridays - Saturdays: 7.00am - 8.00pm.
Tuition Costs: Lessons are available at £12 for 30 minutes.

Other Facilities: The range is attached to the Edenbridge Golf and Country Club. Refreshments are available from the clubhouse.

Herne Bay Golf Driving Range
Bullockstone Road
Herne Bay
Kent CT6 7TL
Telephone: 0227-742742
Owners: Mr & Mrs Reeves
Professional: Simon Wood

Directions: From London, turn right at the Greenhill roundabout and turn immediately left. The range is approximately 1/2 a mile on the left.

Bays: 15 floodlit bays
Opening Times: 7 days a week from 9.00am - 10.00pm.

Cost of Balls:
50 balls / £2.00.
100 balls / £3.00.

Tuition Costs: Lessons cost £10 per 30 minutes. Video analysis costs £15 for 1 hour.

Other Facilities: There is a licensed bar and tea and coffee is available.

Hewitts Golf Centre
(Now: Chelsfield Lakes Golf Centre)
Court Road
Orpington
Kent BR6 9BX
Telephone: 0689-896266
Manager: Derek Howe
Head Professional: Nigel Lee / Bill Hodkin

Directions: The A224 (Court Road) is just off Junction 4 of the M25.

Bays: 40 floodlit bays.
Opening Times: 7 days a week from 7.00am - 10.00pm.

Cost of Balls:
40 balls / £1.70 (£2.20 at weekends and after 5.00pm).
80 balls / £3.00 (£3.80 at weekends and after 5.00pm).
Cost of Tuition: Individual lessons cost from £11 for 30 minutes.

Other Facilities: The range is attached to an eighteen hole course and a nine hole, par 3 course. There is a large Pro shop and catering is provided.

JLS Golf Centre
Thong Lane
Gravesend
Kent DA12 4LG
Telephone: 0474-335002
Managers: Anna Radford / Steve Peckham
Professional: Jenny Lee-Smith

Bays: 30 floodlit bays.
Opening Times: 7 days a week from 9.00am - 10.00pm.

Cost of Balls:
70 balls cost / £2.00.
Cost of Tuition: Lessons are available at £15 for 30 minutes.

Other Facilities: Refreshments are available.

Langley Park Driving Range
Sutton Road
Maidstone
Kent ME17 3NQ
Telephone: 0622-863163
Professional: Nick McNally

Bays: 30 floodlit bays.
Opening Times: 7 days a week from 10.00am - 10.00pm.

Cost of Balls: On weekdays, 40 balls / from £1.50. At weekends, 45 balls / £2.00.
Cost of Tuition: Lessons are available from £12 per 30 minutes.

Other Facilities: A bar provides daily refreshments.

The Oast Golf Centre
Church Road
Tonge
Sittingbourne
Kent ME9 9AR
Telephone: 0795-473527
Managing Director: David Chambers
Professional: Gordon Nixon

Directions: The range is 1 mile north of Tonge, off the A2 at the junction between Sittingbourne and Faversham.

Bays: 17 floodlit bays.
Opening Times: 7 days a week from 9.00am - 10.00pm.

Cost of Balls:
30 balls / £1.00.
Club hire / £1.00
Cost of Tuition: Lessons cost £12.50 for 30 minutes with Gordon Nixon.

Other Facilities. The range is attached to a nine hole, par 3 approach course. There is a licensed bar which provides refreshments.

Prince's Golf Range
Prince's Golf Club
Sandwich
Kent CT13 9QB
Telephone: 0304-613797
Professional: Chris Evans

Bays: This is an open air driving range with pitching/chipping areas and a practice bunker / green.

Opening Times: 7 days a week from 7.30am - 6.00pm.

Cost of Balls:
50 balls / £2.00.
100 balls / £3.50.
Cost of Tuition: Lessons cost £9 / £13 for 30 minutes with the Head Assistant / Professional. Video analysis is available.

Other Facilities: The range is attached to Prince's Golf Club. Refreshments are available.

Ruxley Park Golf Centre
Sandy Lane
St. Paul's Cray
Orpington
Kent BR5 3HY
Telephone: 0689-871490
Manager / Professional: Richard Pilbury

Bays: 28 floodlit bays.
Opening Times:
Weekdays: 6.30am - 10.00pm.
Weekends: 6.00am - 10.00pm.

Cost of Balls:
100 balls / £1.70 (weekdays) and £3.50 (weekends). After 5.00pm on weekdays, weekend rates apply.
At weekends, 50 balls / £2.00.
Cost of Tuition: Lessons are available at £10 / £12.50 for 30 minutes from the Assistant Pro / Head Pro.

Other Facilities: The range is attached to an eighteen hole course. Refreshments are available from the clubhouse from 8.00am.

Swanley Golf Centre

Beechenlea Lane
Swanley
Kent BR8 8DR
Telephone: 0322-669201
Manager / Professional: Andy Trainer

Bays: 18 covered floodlit and 12 open air bays.
Opening Times: 7 days a week from 10.00am - 11.00pm (10.30pm on Sundays)

Cost of Balls:
From Monday - Friday (10.00am - 5.00pm), 50 balls / £1.00.
At all other times, 50 balls / £2.00 and 75 balls / £3.00.
Cost of Tuition: Lessons cost £12 for 30 minutes.

Other Facilities: Refreshments are available from the bar / restaurant.

Upchurch River Valley Golf Range

Oak Lane
Upchurch
Sittingbourne
Kent ME9 7AY
Telephone: 0634-379592
Manager / Professional: Martin Daniels

Bays: 16 floodlit bays.

Opening Times:
Weekdays: 7.00am - 9.00pm.
Weekends: 6.00am - 8.00pm.

Cost of Balls:
30 balls / £1.00.
Cost of Tuition: Lessons are available at £9 for 30 minutes.

Other Facilities: The range is attached to an eighteen hole and a nine hole course. Refreshments are available.

Middlesex and London

Airlinks Golf Range
Southall Lane
Hounslow
Middlesex TW5 9PE
Telephone: 081-561 1418

Bays: 36 floodlit bays.
Opening Times: 7 days a week from 10.00am - 10.00pm.

Cost of Balls:
45 balls / £1.10.
104 balls / £2.20.
Cost of Tuition: Lessons are available at £10 for 30 minutes.

Other Facilities: Full catering (pub style).

Ealing Golf Range
Rowdell Road
Northolt
Middlesex UB5 6AG
Telephone: 081-845 4967
Manager: Mike Allen
Professional: David Elliot

Bays: 42 floodlit bays.
Opening Times: 7 days a week from 10.00am - 10.00pm.

Cost of Balls:
50 balls / £2.00.

Cost of Tuition: Lessons are available at £12 for 30 minutes.

Other Facilities: Refreshments are available.

Fairways Golf Driving Range
Walthamstow Avenue
London E4 8TA
Telephone: 081-531 5126

Directions: 200 yards west of the Crooked Billet roundabout on the A406.

Bays: 31 floodlit bays.
Opening Times: 7 days a week from 7.00am - 10.00pm.

Cost of Tuition: Contact the Pro shop on 081-531 5126 for details.

Other Facilities. There is a fully stocked Pro shop and on-site licensed bar.

Hazelwood Golf Centre
Croysdale Avenue
Sunbury-on-Thames
Middlesex TW16 6QU
Telephone: 0932-770932
Centre Manager: Mark Jellicoe

Directions: 1/2 mile from Junction 1 (M3).

Bays: 36 floodlit bays.
Opening Times: 7 days a week from 8.00am - 9.30pm.

Cost of Balls: 48 balls / £2.00.
Costs of Tuition: Lessons are available from the Golf Academy. There is a computerised swing analyser together with a seminar room for video viewing. Lessons range from £9.00 - £16.00 per 30 minutes.

Other Facilities: The range is attached to a nine hole course. The 'Bunkers' theme bar and restaurant offers refreshments including barbecues.

London Golf Centre
Ruislip Road
Northolt
Middlesex UB5 6QZ
Telephone: 081-845 3180
Manager: Jonathon Clifford
Professional: Gary Newall

Bays: 20 floodlit bays.
Opening Times: 7 days a week from 9.00am - 10.00pm.

Cost of Balls:
25-30 balls / £1.00.
70-80 balls / £2.00.
Cost of Tuition: Lessons are available at £13 for 30 minutes.

Other Facilities: The range is attached to a nine hole course. Bars and a restaurant offer all day refreshments.

Lee Valley Leisure Centre
Picketts Lock Lane
Edmonton
London N9 0AS
Telephone: 081-345 6666
Manager / Professional: Andy Hanwell

Bays: 20 covered, floodlit bays.
Opening Times: Weekend (8.00am - 8.30pm). Weekdays (8.00am - 9.30pm)

Cost of Balls:
70 balls / £2.00.
Cost of Tuition: Lessons are available at £12 for 30 minutes.

Other Facilities: Vending machines are available for hot and cold drinks. The Leisure Centre is situated 400 yards away with an eighteen hole course, swimming pool and other leisure and fitness facilities.

Ruislip Golf Centre
Ickenham Road
Ruislip
Middlesex HA4 7DQ
Telephone: 0895-638081
Manager: Mike Menhennett

Directions: 1 mile north of the A40 at the Master Brewer Hotel opposite West Ruislip Tube.

Bays: 40 covered floodlit bays.
Opening Times:
(Summer): 9.00am - 10.00pm

(Winter): 10.00am - 10.00pm

Cost of Balls:
28 balls / £1.00.
56 balls / £2.00.
Cost of Tuition. Contact Mike Menhennett for details.

Other Facilities: The range is attached to an eighteen hole course. Bar and restaurant facilities provide catering. There are pool tables and a snooker room.

Sunbury Driving Range
Charlton Lane
Shepperton
Middlesex TW17 8QA
Telephone: 0932-772898
Manager: Paul Davison
Professional: Alistair Hardaway

Bays: 32 floodlit bays.
Opening Times: 7 days a week from 9.00am - 10.00pm.

Cost of Balls:
60 balls / £2.00.
Cost of Tuition: Lessons are available at £13 for 30 minutes.

Other Facilities: A bar and restaurant provide refreshments.

Trent Park Driving Range
Bromley Road
Southgate

London N14 4UW
Telephone: 081-366 7432
Manager: Jeremy Sturgess
Professional: Tony Sheaff

Bays: 27 floodlit bays. It includes newly built Japanese style bay dividers, outdoor heaters and sound system.
Opening Times: 7 days a week from 8.00am - 10.00pm.

Cost of Balls: 45 balls / £2.50.
Cost of Tuition: Lessons are available at £14 for 30 minutes.

Other Facilities:Refreshments are available.

Twickenham Park Golf Range
Staines Road
Twickenham
Middlesex TW2 5JD
Telephone: 081-783 1698
Manager: Keith Bagley
Professional: Steve Lloyd

Bays: 27 floodlit bays.
Opening Times: 7 days a week from 7.30am - 9.30pm.

Cost of Balls:
65 balls / £2.00.
Cost of Tuition: Lessons cost £13 / £15 for 30 minutes with the Assistant Pro / Head Pro.

Other Facilities: A nine hole course and bar and cafateria are available.

Surrey

Beverley Park Golf Range
Kingston By-Pass
New Malden
Surrey KT3 4PH
Telephone: 081-949 9200
General Manager: Rhett Davies
Head Professional: Jon Woodroffe

Directions: Located on the A3 near Raynes Park.

Bays: 60 floodlit bays at this two-tier facility.
Opening Times:
Weekdays: 8.00am - 10.00pm.
Weekends: 8.00am - 9.00pm.

Cost of Balls:
A bucket of balls / £2.30.
Range cards are available at £20 for 10 buckets.
Cost of Tuition: Lessons are available at £13 for 30 minutes. Video analysis is available at £15. Group lessons cost £65 (8 x 90 minute classes).

Other Facilities: There is a golf shop on-site. Refreshments are available.

Chessington Golf Centre
Garrison Lane
Chessington
Surrey KT9 2LW

Telephone: 081-391 0948
Manager: Tony Maxted
Professionals: Tony Martin / Gratton Smallman

Bays: 18 floodlit bays.
Opening Times:
Weekdays: 8.00am - 10.00pm.
Weekends: 8.00am - 9.00pm.

Cost of Balls:
35 balls / £1.00.
Cost of Tuition: Lessons are available at £10 for 30 minutes.

Other Facilities: Refreshments are available.

Croydon Golf Driving Range
175 Long Lane
Addiscombe
Croydon
Surrey CR0 7TE
Telephone: 081-656 1690
Manager / Professional: Bill Woodman

Direction: The range is located halfway between Beckenham and Croydon on the A222.

Bays: 24 covered floodlit bays.
Opening Times:
Weekdays: 9.00am - 10.00pm.
Weekends: 9.00am - 9.00pm.

Cost of Balls:
40 balls / £2.00.

80 balls / £3.75.
Cost of Tuition: Lessons are available
from 6 resident teaching professionals.
Contact Bill Woodman's Golf Shop on
081-656 1690 for details.

Other Facilities: There is a well-stocked
discount golf shop on-site.

Fairmile Golf Range
Portsmouth Road
Cobham
Surrey
Telephone: 0932-864419
Manager/ Professional: David Hartley

Bays: 24 floodlit bays.
Opening Times: 7 days a week from
10.00am - 10.00pm.

Cost of Balls:
70 balls / £2.00.
100 balls / £2.50.
150 balls /£3.75.
Cost of Tuition: Lessons cost £15 per 30
minutes.

Other Facilities: Refreshments are available.

Foxhills Driving Range
Stonehill Road
Ottersham
Surrey KT16 0EL
Telephone: 0932-872050

*Important Notice: This range is only
available to members and their guests.*

Bays: 12 bays.
Opening Times: 7 days a week from
7.30 am - 10.00pm.

Cost of Balls:
80 balls / £2.50.

Other Facilities: The range is attached to
Foxhills.

Hoebridge Golf Centre
Old Woking
Surrey GU22 8JH
Telephone: 0483-722611
Manager: Mr Heron
Professional: Tim Powell

Bays: 24 floodlit bays.
Opening Times: 7 days a week from
7.00am - 11.00pm.

Cost of Balls:
30 balls / £1.75.
60 balls / £2.75.
90 balls / £3.75.
Cost of Tuition: Contact Tim Powell on
0483-722611 for details.

Other Facilities: Refreshments are available from 7.30am - 10.00pm.

Horton Park Driving Range
Hook Road
Ewell
Surrey KT19 8QG
Telephone: 081-393 8400

Manager: Paul Hart
Professionals: Gary Clements / Jerry Robson

Bays: 26 floodlit bays.
Opening Times: 7 days a week from 8.00am - 10.00pm.

Cost of Balls:
70 balls / £2.00. During 'Happy Hour' (2.00pm - 5.00pm) the cost is £1.50.
Cost of Tuition: Lessons are available at £11 for 30 minutes.

Other Facilities: The range is attached to an eighteen hole course. Refreshments are available from the bar and restaurant in the clubhouse.

Lingfield Park Golf Range
Racecourse Road
Lingfield
Surrey RH7 6PQ
Telephone: 0342-834602
Manager: Ms Greer Milne
Professional: Mr C. Morley

Bays: 14 open air bays.

Cost of Balls:
50 balls / £3.00.
90 balls / £4.00.

Tuition Costs: Lessons cost £15 for 30 minutes. This includes video analysis.

Other Facilities: Refreshments are available.

Oaks Sports Centre
Woodmansterne Road
Carshalton
Surrey SM5 4AN
Telephone: 081-643 8363

Manager: David McNab
Professional: Mike Pilkington

Bays: 16 floodlit bays.
Opening Times: 7 days a week from 9.00am - 10.00pm.

Cost of Balls:
30 balls / £1.00.
Cost of Tuition: Lessons are available at £10 / £15 for 30 minutes with the Asst. Pro / Head Pro.

Other Facilities: An on-site cafe and restaurant provide daily refreshments.

Pachesham Golf Centre
Oaklawn Road
Leatherhead
Surrey KT22 0BT

Telephone: 0372-843453
Manager/ Professional: Phil Taylor

Directions: Exit Junction 9 (M25). Take the A244 to Oxshott. The range is 1/2 a mile on the left.

Bays: 33 floodlit bays.
Opening Times:
Weekdays: 9.00am - 10.00pm.
Weekends: 9.00am - 9.00pm.

Cost of Balls:
25 balls / £1.00.
60 balls / £2.00.
90 balls / £2.75.
Cost of Tuition: Lessons are available from 7 resident professionals. Contact Phil Taylor on 0372-843453 for details.

Other Facilities: The range is attached to a nine hole course. A bar and restaurant, open to the public, offer refreshments.

Pine Ridge Golf Range
Old Bisley Road
Frimley
Surrey GU16 5NX
Telephone: 0276-675444
Manager: Clive Smith
Professionals: Alistair Kelso / Simon Williams

Bays: 36 floodlit bays.
Opening Times: 7 days a week from 8.00am - 10.00pm.

Cost of Balls:
50 - 55 balls / £2.30
Cost of Tuition: Lessons are available at £14 for 30 minutes. 6 x 30 minute lessons cost £75.00.

Other Facilities: The range is attached to an eighteen hole course. The clubhouse offers both bar and restaurant facilities.

Richmond Golf Range
The Athletic Ground
Kew Foot Road
Richmond
Surrey TW9 2SS
Telephone: 081-332 9200
General Manager: David Skinner
Head Professional: Jon Fitzpatrick

Bays: 24 floodlit bays.
Opening Times:
Weekdays: 9.30am - 10.00pm.
Weekends: 9.00am - 9.30pm. The range closes on Saturday afternoons between September and May because of rugby.

Cost of Tuition. Contact David Skinner for details on 081-332 9200.

Other Facilities: There is a golf shop on-site. Club hire is available.

Sandown Golf Centre
More Lane
Esher
Surrey KT10 8AN

DRIVING RANGES

Telephone: 0372-463340
Manager: Peter Barriball
Professional: Neal Bedward

Bays: 36 floodlit bays.
Opening Times: 7 days a week from 10.00am -10.00pm.

Cost of Balls:
70 balls / £2.00.
120 balls / £3.00.

Cost of Tuition: Lessons are available at £14 for 30 minutes. Six lessons are available for the price of five.

Other Facilities: The range is attached to a nine hole course. Refreshments are available from the clubhouse.

Silvermere Driving Range
Redhill Road
Cobham
Surrey KT11 1EF
Telephone: 0932-867275
Manager / Professional:
Doug McClelland

Bays: 32 floodlit bays.
Opening Times:
Weekdays: 8.00am - 9.30pm.
Weekends: 7.00am - 8.00pm.

Cost of Balls:
58 balls / £1.50.
75 balls / £2.50.

There are off-peak discounts.
Cost of Tuition: Lessons cost £12 for 30 minutes. Group lessons cost £25 for 4 x 1 hour classes.

Other Facilities: The range is attached to an eighteen hole course. Refreshments are available on-site.